INTERNATIONAL MONETARY FUND

CW01574902

EXTERNAL SECTOR REPORT

Divergent Recoveries and Global Imbalances

2021

©2021 International Monetary Fund

Cataloging-in-Publication Data
IMF Library

Names: International Monetary Fund, publisher.
Title: External sector report (International Monetary Fund).
Other titles: ESR
Description: Washington, D.C. : International Monetary Fund, 2012- | Annual | Some issues also have thematic titles. | Began in 2012. | Includes bibliographical references.
Identifiers: ISSN 2617-3832 (print) | ISSN 2617-3840 (online)
Subjects: LCSH: Balance of payments—Periodicals. | Debts, External—Periodicals. | Investments, Foreign—Periodicals. | International finance—Periodicals.
Classification: LCC HG3882.I58

ISBN: 978-1-51357-667-1 (Paper)
978-1-51358-754-7 (ePub)
978-1-51358-759-2 (PDF)

The *External Sector Report* (ESR) is a survey by the IMF staff published once a year, in the summer. The ESR is prepared by the IMF staff and has benefited from comments and suggestions by Executive Directors following their discussion of the report on July 16, 2021. The views expressed in this publication are those of the IMF staff and do not necessarily represent the views of the IMF's Executive Directors or their national authorities.

Recommended citation: International Monetary Fund. 2021. *External Sector Report: Divergent Recoveries and Global Imbalances.* Washington, DC, August.

Publication orders may be placed online, by fax, or through the mail:
International Monetary Fund, Publications Services
P.O. Box 92780, Washington, DC 20090, USA
Tel.: (202) 623-7430 Fax: (202) 623-7201
E-mail: publications@imf.org
www.bookstore.imf.org
www.elibrary.imf.org

CONTENTS

Figures

Tables

FURTHER INFORMATION

Corrections and Revisions

The data and analysis appearing in the *External Sector Report* are compiled by IMF staff at the time of publication. Every effort is made to ensure their timeliness, accuracy, and completeness. When errors are discovered, corrections and revisions are incorporated into the digital editions available from the IMF website and on the IMF eLibrary. All substantive changes are listed in the online table of contents.

Print and Digital Editions

Print

Print copies of this *External Sector Report* can be ordered from the IMF Bookstore at imfbk.st/29844

Digital

Multiple digital editions of the *External Sector Report*, including ePub, enhanced PDF, Mobi, and HTML, are available on the IMF eLibrary at www.elibrary.imf.org/ESR21

Download a free PDF of the report and data sets for each of the charts therein from the IMF website at www.imf.org/publications/ESR or scan the QR code below to access the *External Sector Report* web page directly:

SCAN ME

Copyright and Reuse

Information on the terms and conditions for reusing the contents of this publication are at www.imf.org/external/terms.htm

PREFACE

Produced since 2012, the IMF's annual *External Sector Report* analyzes global external developments and provides multilaterally consistent assessments of external positions, including current accounts, real exchange rates, external balance sheets, capital flows, and international reserves, of the world's largest economies, representing over 90 percent of global GDP. Chapter 1 discusses the evolution of global external positions in 2020, external developments throughout the COVID-19 crisis, and policy priorities for reducing excess imbalances over the medium term. Chapter 2 analyzes how the unprecedented fiscal support provided in response to the COVID-19 crisis has affected external positions at the individual and global level. It also focuses on how withdrawal of such support will impact external positions in the medium term. Chapter 3, "Individual Economy Assessments," provides details on the different aspects of the overall external assessment and associated policy recommendations for 30 economies. This year's report and associated external assessments are based on the latest vintage of the External Balance Assessment (EBA) methodology and on data and IMF staff projections as of June 30, 2021.

Together with the *World Economic Outlook* and Article IV consultations, this report is part of a continuous effort to assess and address the possible effects of spillovers from members' policies on global stability and to monitor the stability of members' external positions in a comprehensive manner.

This report was prepared under the overall guidance of Gita Gopinath, IMF Economic Counsellor and Director of Research, and under the direction of the External Sector Coordinating Group—comprising staff from the IMF's area departments (African Department, Asia and Pacific Department, European Department, Middle East and Central Asia Department, and Western Hemisphere Department) as well as the Fiscal Affairs Department; the Statistics Department; the Strategy, Policy, and Review Department; the Monetary and Capital Markets Department; and the Research Department—namely, Ali Al-Eyd, Fadhila Alfaraj, Vivek B. Arora, Serkan Arslanalp, Tim Callen, Nigel Chalk, Ana Lucia Coronel, Alfredo Cuevas, Jörg Decressin, Chris Erceg, Raphael Espinoza, Gaston Gelos, Sonali Jain-Chandra, Venkateswarlu Josyula, Martin Kaufman, Vitaliy Kramarenko, Daniel Leigh (Chair), Paulo Mauro, Paulo A. Medas, Srobona Mitra, Jonathan D. Ostry, Catherine Pattillo, Ratna Sahay, Carlos Sánchez-Muñoz, Alfred Schipke, Niamh Sheridan, Piyaporn Sodsriwiboon, Antonio Spilimbergo, and Jeromin Zettelmeyer.

Daniel Leigh and Pau Rabanal led the preparation of the report. The report draws on contributions from Gustavo Adler, Cian Allen, Giovanni Ganelli, Keiko Honjo, Luciana Juvenal, Christina Kolerus, Gian Maria Milesi-Ferretti (Brookings Institution), Cyril Rebillard, Charlotte Sandoz, and Niamh Sheridan. Important input was provided by country teams as well as by Mahir Binici, Russell Green, Yuko Hashimoto, Shakill Hassan, Adam Jakubik, Juan Manuel Jauregui, Parisa Kamali, Dimitre Milkov, Marco Rodriguez Waldo, Silvia Sgherri, and Hui Tong.

Excellent research and editorial assistance were provided by Rachelle Blasco, Luisa Calixto, Jane Haizel, Mariela Caycho Arce, Jair Rodriguez, Xiaohan Shao, and Rongjin Zhang.

Gemma Rose Diaz and Cheryl Toksoz from the Communications Department led the editorial team for the report, with production and editorial support from Lorraine Coffey, Christine Ebrahimzadeh, Lucy Morales, Joe Procopio, and AGS.

The analysis has benefited from comments and suggestions by staff members from other IMF departments, as well as by Executive Directors following their discussion of the report on July 16, 2021. However, both projections and policy considerations are those of the IMF staff and should not be attributed to Executive Directors or to their national authorities.

EXECUTIVE SUMMARY

After declining steadily since 2015, global current account balances—the sum of absolute deficits and surpluses—increased in 2020 and are set to widen further in 2021, amid diverging economic prospects across countries. The widening—from 2.8 percent of world GDP in 2019 to 3.2 percent of GDP in 2020—mainly reflects the unequal impact of the COVID-19 crisis, including on the travel, oil, medical goods, and household consumption goods sectors. It also reflects, in 2021, the larger fiscal expansions in advanced economies with current account deficits, notably the United States. Without these pandemic-related shifts and policy responses, global balances would have continued on their declining path. The stocks of external assets and liabilities remain near historic highs, with large valuation-induced changes and attendant risks for both creditor and debtor economies.

At the country level, the COVID-19 pandemic has triggered wide fluctuations in external positions, with uneven effects. Despite the global recovery in merchandise trade, spending on services remains subdued, with global tourism arrivals far below their 2019 levels and sharp falls in trade balances for tourism-exporting economies. Oil exporters also initially saw sharply falling trade balances, but these gradually recovered after mid-2020 with rising oil prices. The lockdown-induced shift in household spending from services to consumer goods and the health-emergency-induced trade in medical products have triggered further movements in exports and imports.

Unprecedented government borrowing to finance health care and economic support has had uneven effects on trade balances. As the analysis in Chapter 2 highlights, what happens to the current account depends on a country's relative fiscal policy stance compared with that of its trading partners. Countries with the largest budgetary expansions have caused their trade balances to fall, all else equal, while those with smaller fiscal expansions have had their trade balances rise. The movements in overall saving-investment (current account) balances as a share of GDP reflect these fiscal expansions, with falling public saving, and partially offset relatively stable investment rates and increases in private saving—especially by higher-income households. With richer economies borrowing relatively more than poorer economies to fund government spending, their current account balances have, on average, declined by more. This development suggests that the pandemic may have slowed the "downhill" flow of funds from richer to poorer countries, highlighting the unequal impact of the pandemic and potentially exacerbating the divergent speeds of recovery across income groups.

Currencies fluctuated widely early in the pandemic, with more moderate movements since mid-2020. Reserve currencies at first appreciated during the flight to safety at the onset of the crisis, but most have since depreciated amid exceptional policy support, including significant expansions in liquidity by central banks and expansionary fiscal packages, as well as positive vaccine news and global risk sentiment. Emerging market currencies that depreciated early in the crisis have, in many cases, rebounded, but some economies with external vulnerabilities have experienced continuing pressure on their currencies, along with declining foreign exchange reserves.

The IMF's multilateral approach suggests that excessive current account deficits and surpluses—deviations from desirable medium-term levels—were broadly unchanged in 2020 at about 1.2 percent of world GDP. Excessive current account imbalances can fuel trade tensions, become targets for protectionist measures, and increase the likelihood of disruptive asset price adjustments. The assessments for 2020 take into consideration the temporary impacts of the pandemic in a multilaterally consistent way, through the use of additional cyclical adjustors. About 72 percent of the excess balances in 2020 pertained to advanced economies, up from 69 percent in 2019. The largest contributors to lower-than-warranted current account balances—as a share of world GDP—were, in order, the United States, France, the United Kingdom, and Canada. The largest contributors to larger-than-warranted current account balances were Germany, The Netherlands, Mexico, Poland, and Russia.

The relatively large fiscal expansions of some economies affected their trading partners' external positions and assessments.

The outlook for global current account balances is a gradual narrowing during 2022–26, mainly reflecting a narrowing of the US deficit and China's surplus to below pre-pandemic levels. Numerous uncertainties surround this forecast. The path depends crucially on fiscal policy developments (Chapter 2). A resurgence of the pandemic could make the aforementioned sectoral effects of the crisis more persistent than currently expected. A tightening of global financial conditions could further slow the downhill flow of capital. A retreat from trade integration could weaken growth prospects, especially for economies integrated into supply chains. On the upside, expedited vaccinations, including in lagging regions, would improve confidence and contribute to unwinding crisis-induced current account movements.

In the near term, policy efforts should focus on averting downside risks by ending the pandemic globally. Strong international cooperation is needed to secure up-front financing for vaccinations and public health measures. If further external shocks materialize, economies with flexible exchange rates should allow them to adjust, where feasible, although for economies with adequate reserves, exchange rate intervention can alleviate disorderly market conditions, particularly if there are shallow foreign currency markets and large balance sheet mismatches.

Multilateral efforts should intensify to resolve trade and technology tensions and to modernize international taxation. Priorities include phasing out tariff and nontariff barriers, including on medical products, and addressing gaps in the rules-based multilateral trading system. Tariffs negatively affect business sentiment and consumers and do not effectively address policy gaps and structural distortions to lower external imbalances.

Over the medium term, collective action is needed to reduce global imbalances in a growth-friendly manner. Where excess current account deficits reflect larger-than-desirable fiscal deficits, fiscal consolidation would promote debt sustainability, reduce the current account gap, and facilitate raising international reserves. Countries with export competitiveness challenges would benefit from productivity-raising reforms, including to enhance education outcomes and innovation. In economies with excess current account surpluses and remaining fiscal space, policies should support the recovery and medium-term growth, including through greater public investment in digitalization, upgrading infrastructure, and climate change mitigation. Intensifying reforms to encourage private investment and discourage excessive precautionary saving may also be warranted, including by reducing informality and expanding social safety nets.

IMF EXECUTIVE BOARD DISCUSSION SUMMARY

The following remarks were made by the Chair at the conclusion of the Executive Board's discussion of the External Sector Report *on July 16, 2021.*

Executive Directors broadly agreed with the findings of the 2021 External Sector Report (ESR) and its policy recommendations. They noted that global balances are expected to rise further in 2021, mainly reflecting the unequal impact of the COVID-19 crisis across economic sectors and countries. Meanwhile, excess current account imbalances in 2020 remained broadly unchanged and concentrated in advanced economies. Directors observed that favorable global financial conditions had facilitated the financing of current account deficits, but that the pandemic may have slowed the downhill flow of capital from richer to poorer economies. Stocks of foreign assets and liabilities have fluctuated but are still near historic highs, with attendant risks to both debtor and creditor countries.

Directors observed that the pandemic has had varying effects across the membership in terms of trade, capital flows, and exchange rates. Despite the recovery in merchandise trade, spending on services remains subdued, implying lower trade balances for tourism-exporting economies. Directors noted that the unprecedented government borrowing to finance health care and economic support has had uneven effects on trade balances: economies with relatively large budgetary expansions saw their trade balances fall, while economies with smaller fiscal expansions experienced rising trade balances. Currencies fluctuated widely early in the pandemic, with more moderate movements since mid-2020, amid exceptional policy support and rising global risk sentiment.

Directors generally shared the view that global imbalances would narrow over the medium term under baseline policies, although numerous uncertainties surround this forecast. The path depends crucially on fiscal policy developments. A resurgence of the pandemic could make its impact on external positions more persistent, further slowing the flow of capital toward poorer economies. On the upside, expedited vaccinations, including in lagging regions, would contribute to unwinding pandemic-induced current account movements.

Directors considered that near-term policy efforts should focus on ending the pandemic, including through strong international cooperation to secure up-front financing for vaccinations and public health measures. A synchronized global investment push would also help the recovery, with limited effects on global current account balances. Directors welcomed in this context the Fund's recently proposed general SDR allocation, which can help countries meet international liquidity needs. Exchange rate intervention and capital flow management measures can complement macroprudential measures in addressing financial stability risks, which could arise if further external shocks materialize, guided by the Institutional View and the Integrated Policy Framework. Directors underscored that multilateral efforts should intensify to resolve trade tensions and to modernize international taxation, including by phasing out tariff and nontariff barriers, especially in the medical sector, and addressing gaps in the rules-based multilateral trading system. Some Directors also recommended avoiding measures that entangle trade and currency issues.

Directors underlined that, over the medium term, collective action by both excess surplus and excess deficit economies is needed to reduce excess global imbalances in a growth-enhancing manner. For economies in which current account deficits reflect larger-than-desirable fiscal deficits, fiscal consolidation over the medium term would promote debt sustainability, reduce the current account gap, and facilitate raising international reserves. Economies with export competitiveness challenges would benefit from productivity-raising reforms, including to enhance education outcomes and innovation. In economies with excess current account surpluses and remaining fiscal space, policies should support the recovery and medium-term growth, including through greater public investment in digitalization, infrastructure, and climate change mitigation and adaptation. Directors noted that, in some cases, intensifying reforms to encourage private investment and discourage excessive precautionary saving may also be warranted, including by reducing informality and expanding social safety nets.

Directors appreciated the consideration of temporary pandemic-induced factors in external sector assessments and encouraged continued efforts to refine the External Balance Assessment methodologies, including to reflect more persistent effects of the pandemic on external positions and address other limitations of the model. They reiterated the need to ensure transparency, consistency, and evenhandedness of external assessments across countries, while adequately taking account of country-specific circumstances. They also highlighted the importance of continued careful communication of the results of such assessments. Directors also welcomed the discussion of the pandemic's impact on non-ESR countries and encouraged such coverage in the future.

CHAPTER 1

EXTERNAL POSITIONS AND POLICIES

Uneven Crisis Impact on External Positions

The COVID-19 pandemic has moved trade, currencies, capital flows, and current accounts widely and unevenly across economies. After declining steadily since 2015, global current account balances—the sum of absolute deficits and surpluses—increased in 2020 and are set to widen further in 2021. Numerous uncertainties surround the outlook.

Goods Trade Recovery, Subdued Trade in Services

The COVID-19 crisis has had a sharp but generally short-lived impact on trade in goods (Figure 1.1). After contracting by 4.7 percent in 2020, global goods trade has recovered to above pre-pandemic levels, reflecting pent-up consumer demand and exceptional policy support, especially in advanced economies. The July 2021 *World Economic Outlook* (WEO) *Update* forecasts goods trade volume to grow by 9.9 percent in 2021. The rapid manufacturing-based recovery, in conjunction with supply shortages, including of containers, has resulted in rising shipping rates, rising input prices, and higher costs of oil and other commodities, such as metals. In addition, as WTO (2021) notes, the positive outlook for goods trade is marred by regional disparities.

Trade in services—especially travel-related services, such as tourism—remains subdued, reflecting the ongoing pandemic. International tourism arrivals were about 86 percent below their 2019 level in April 2021. Overall services trade, which comprises about one-fifth of global trade, contracted by 17.7 percent in 2020, and the July 2021 WEO *Update* forecasts only 5.8 percent growth in 2021, implying a wide shortfall compared with the pre-pandemic path. The external travel shock has sharply reduced the trade balances of hard-hit tourism-dependent economies (Box 1.1).

Fluctuations in Currencies, Capital Flows, and Currency Reserves

Currency movements have mirrored shifts in global financial conditions during the COVID-19 crisis (Figure 1.2). Reserve currencies appreciated during the flight to safety at the onset of the crisis, but most have depreciated since mid-March 2020 amid exceptional policy support, including significant expansions in liquidity by central banks (including via unconventional monetary policies) and expansionary fiscal packages, which, together with positive vaccine news, lifted global risk sentiment overall. Emerging market and developing economy currencies that depreciated early in the crisis during the sudden stop in capital flows have, in many cases, rebounded. Some emerging markets with external vulnerabilities saw pressures on their currencies continue in 2020 with declining foreign exchange reserves, including, for example, Argentina and Turkey, although reserves have in some cases increased somewhat thus far in 2021. Some advanced economies, such as Singapore and Switzerland, have had reserve accumulation in the context of appreciation pressures (Figure 1.3).

Foreign direct investment flows to emerging markets have been less affected than other types of flows—especially in comparison with nonresident portfolio flows—during the COVID-19 crisis, mainly reflecting inflows to Asia (Figure 1.4). By contrast, in advanced economies, foreign direct investment flows declined in 2020, reflecting drops in intra-firm flows and corporate restructuring (UNCTAD 2021). Several emerging market and developing economies sold foreign currency reserves during the sudden stop in early 2020 but rebuilt buffers later when capital flow pressures subsided. Other investment net flows have more recently declined, with this development driven by Chinese banks increasing overseas deposits and lending operations.

Fluctuations in Current Account Balances

Current account deficits and surpluses exhibited wider fluctuations in 2020 than in recent years (Figure 1.5). Exceptional sectoral shocks have driven these movements, with asymmetric effects across economies.

- *Role of travel shock:* The pandemic has led to a sharp decline in tourism arrivals, with significantly lower travel services and current account balances for Spain, Thailand, and Turkey and even larger declines for smaller tourism-dependent economies (Box 1.1).

Figure 1.1. Global Trade and the COVID-19 Crisis

Global trade in goods has recovered to pre-pandemic levels amid rising economic activity and commodity prices. Services trade, including tourism, remains subdued, reflecting the evolution of the COVID-19 pandemic. Shipping costs have increased since mid-2020, particularly for containers.

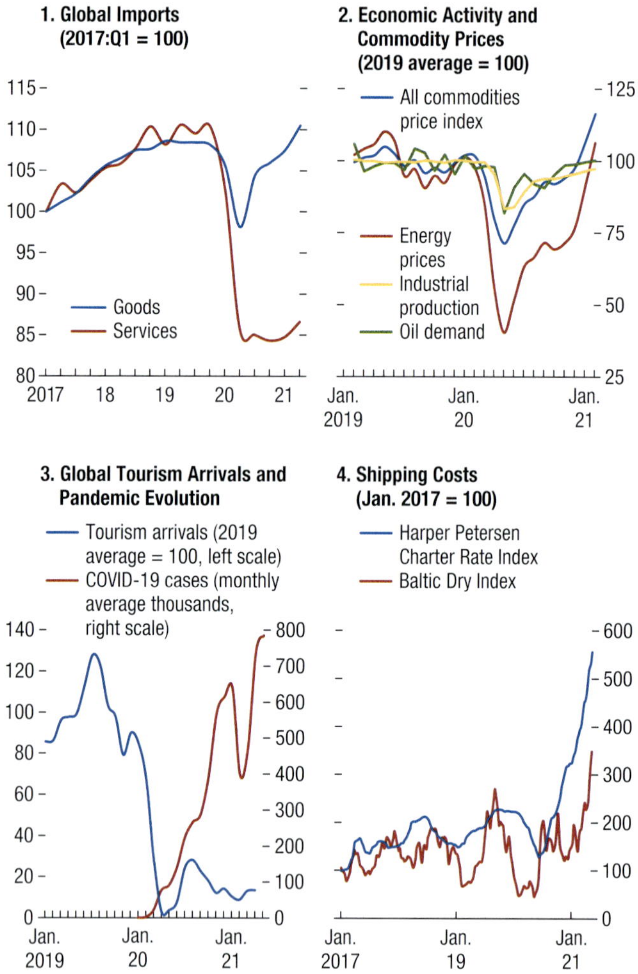

Sources: CEIC, Global Economic Data, Indicators, Charts & Forecasts; IMF, Primary Commodity Price System; Joint Organisations Data Initiative; World Tourism Organization; and *Our World in Data*, national government reports.
Note: Global imports in volumes.

Figure 1.2. Currency Movements: Nominal Effective Exchange Rate

(Percent change)

Reserve currencies appreciated at the onset of the COVID-19 crisis, while several emerging market currencies depreciated. These movements were partially unwound in most cases, although some emerging market currencies kept depreciating during the remainder of 2020 and early 2021.

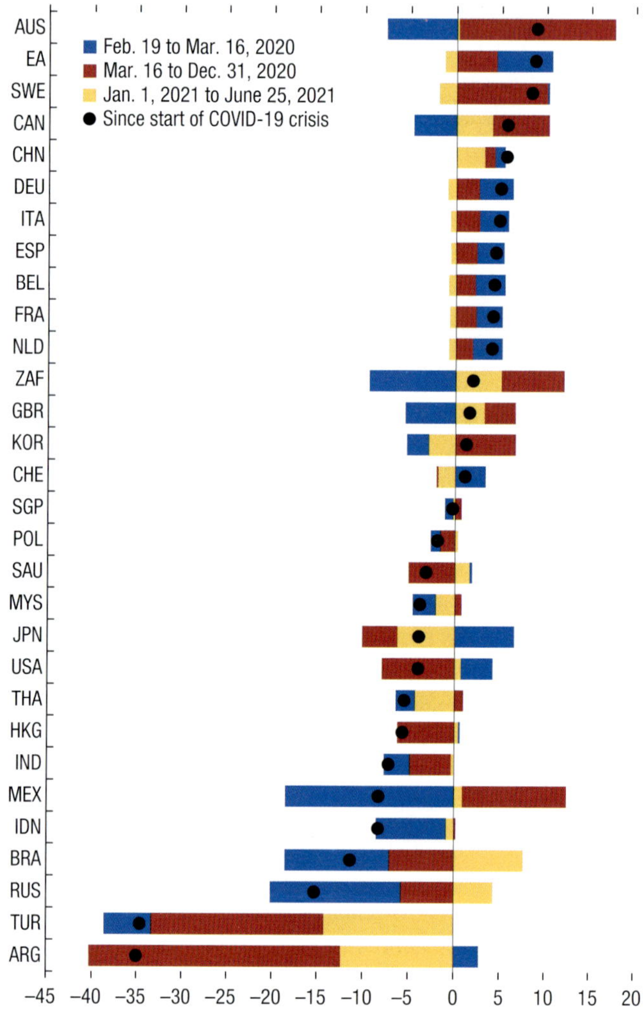

Sources: IMF, Global Data Source; and IMF staff calculations.
Note: EA = euro area. Data labels use International Organization for Standardization (ISO) country codes.

The counterpart to these declines has been a smaller rise in travel services balances spread across numerous economies that are net importers of travel services (for example, China, Germany, and Russia, among major economies).

- *Role of oil trade shock:* The collapse in oil demand and energy prices early in the crisis was relatively short-lived, with oil prices recovering in the second half of 2020. Nonetheless, oil-exporting economies saw their current account balances decline sharply (Russia and Saudi Arabia, among major economies, also due to production cuts), with corresponding increases in oil trade balances spread across many net oil-importing economies.
- *Role of trade in medical products:* The COVID-19 medical emergency has triggered demand for medical products, including medicine, medical supplies and equipment, and personal protective equipment, with implications for imports and exports, including

Figure 1.3. Estimated Change in Foreign Exchange Reserves[1] and Nominal Effective Exchange Rate Change

(March 2020–April 2021)

Some emerging market and developing economies with currency depreciation have had substantial declines in foreign exchange reserves. Some advanced economies with currency appreciation pressures have had substantial increases in foreign exchange reserves.

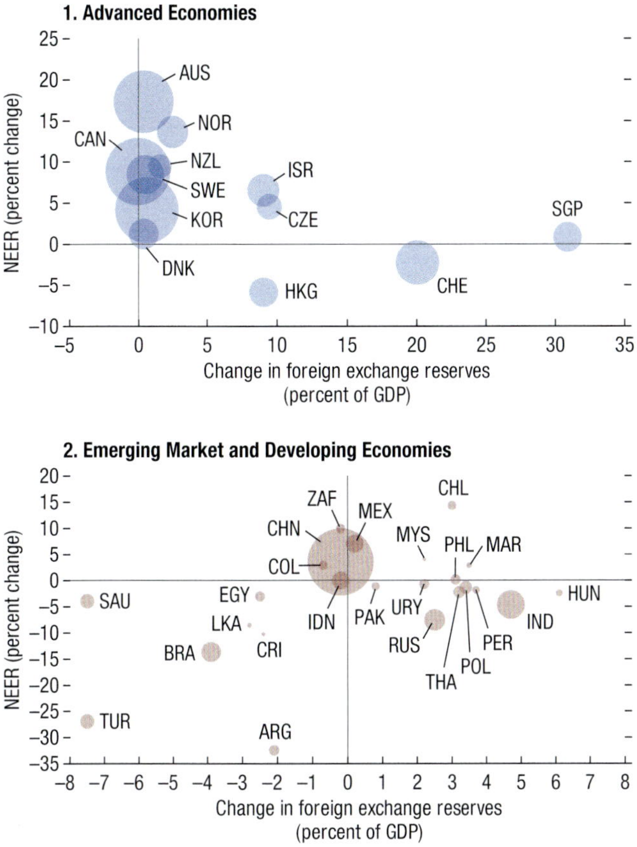

Sources: Adler and others (2021); IMF, *International Financial Statistics*; IMF, Information Notice System; and IMF staff calculations.

Note: NEER = nominal effective exchange rate. Data labels use International Organization for Standardization (ISO) country codes.

[1]The change in foreign exchange reserves is based on the change in the stock of reserves, adjusted for valuation changes, reserve income flows, and changes in foreign exchange assets and liabilities vis-à-vis residents and nonresidents, and operations with foreign exchange derivatives. It may differ from actual foreign currency market transactions data when available.

of intermediate inputs used in the production of medical goods.

- *Role of shift in household consumption composition:* The pandemic has shifted the composition of household consumption from services toward consumer goods. In advanced economies, the composition shift has been toward both durable and nondurable goods (Figure 1.6). For durable goods, the shift involves an increased preference for such items as cars and electrical appliances, including to accommodate the shift

Figure 1.4. Capital Flows to Emerging Market and Developing Economies and the VIX

Portfolio flows to emerging market and developing economies have rebounded since the spike in the VIX in March 2020. Foreign direct investment flows have been relatively stable throughout the pandemic. International reserves declined in early 2020 but have generally rebounded since then.

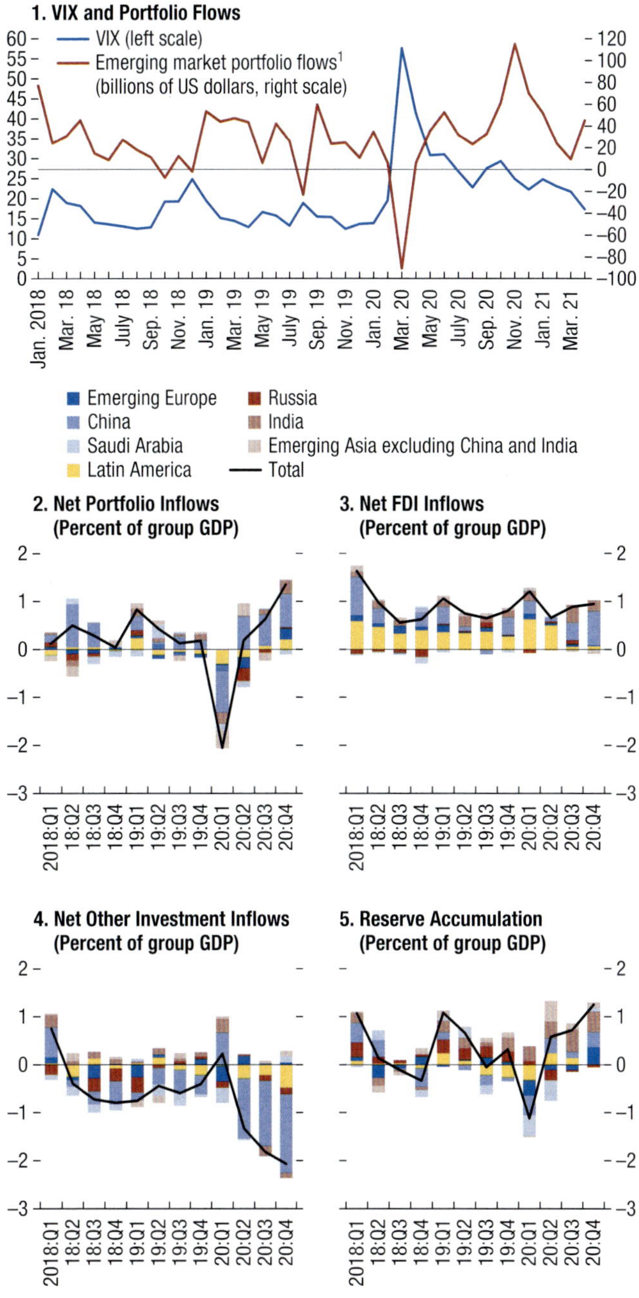

Sources: IMF, *International Financial Statistics*; Institute of International Finance; and IMF staff calculations.

Note: For panels 2–4, positive numbers represent net inflow of capital. FDI = foreign direct investment; VIX = Chicago Board Options Exchange Volatility Index.

[1]Net nonresident purchases of emerging market stocks ("portfolio equity flows") and bonds ("portfolio debt flows") in billions of US dollars, proxy for portfolio flows as measured in the balance of payments.

Figure 1.5. Current Account Movements
(Percent of GDP)

Current account movements were larger in 2020 than in recent years and are expected to moderate in 2021. A large share of the changes in current account balances between 2019 and 2020 can be explained by sectoral shocks associated with the COVID-19 crisis.

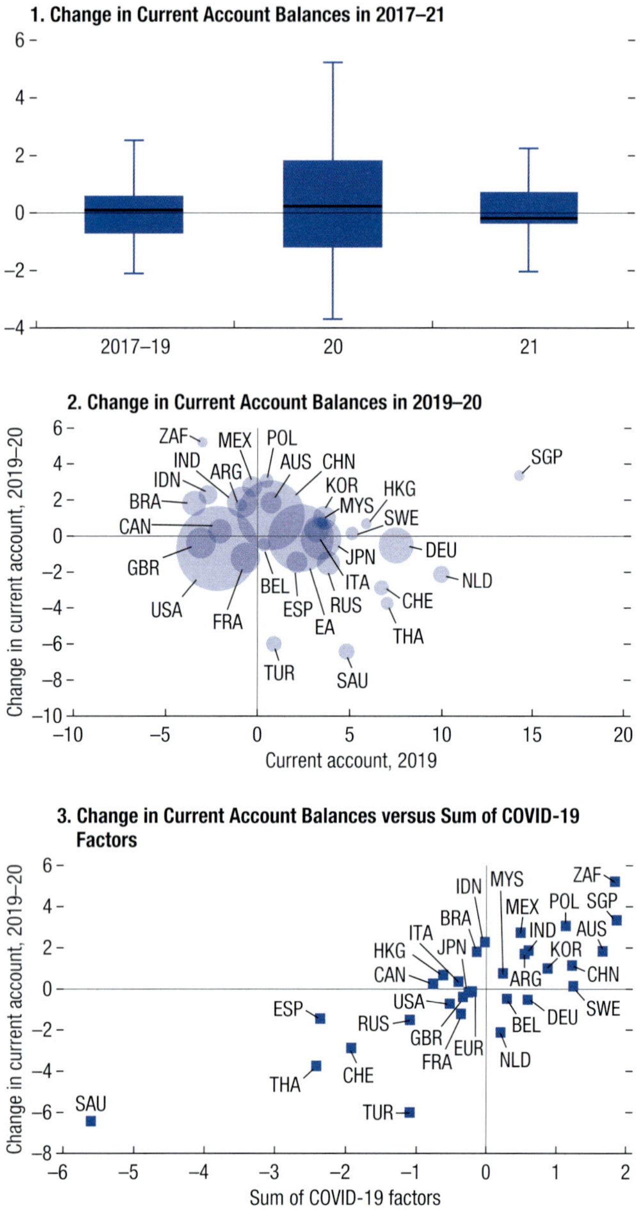

Sources: IMF, *International Financial Statistics*; IMF, *World Economic Outlook*; and IMF staff calculations.

Note: Bubble size is relative to 2019 nominal GDP in US dollars. Sample includes IMF, *External Sector Report* sample economies. Data labels use International Organization for Standardization (ISO) country codes. See the chapter text for the definition of sectoral shocks associated with the COVID-19 crisis.

Figure 1.6. Household Consumption Composition Shift
(Percent of household consumption)

Consumption has shifted from services toward consumer goods in real terms during the pandemic, especially in advanced economies. This pattern contrasts sharply with previous recessions, during which consumption shifted away from durable goods. In emerging market and developing economies, the shift has been less pronounced.

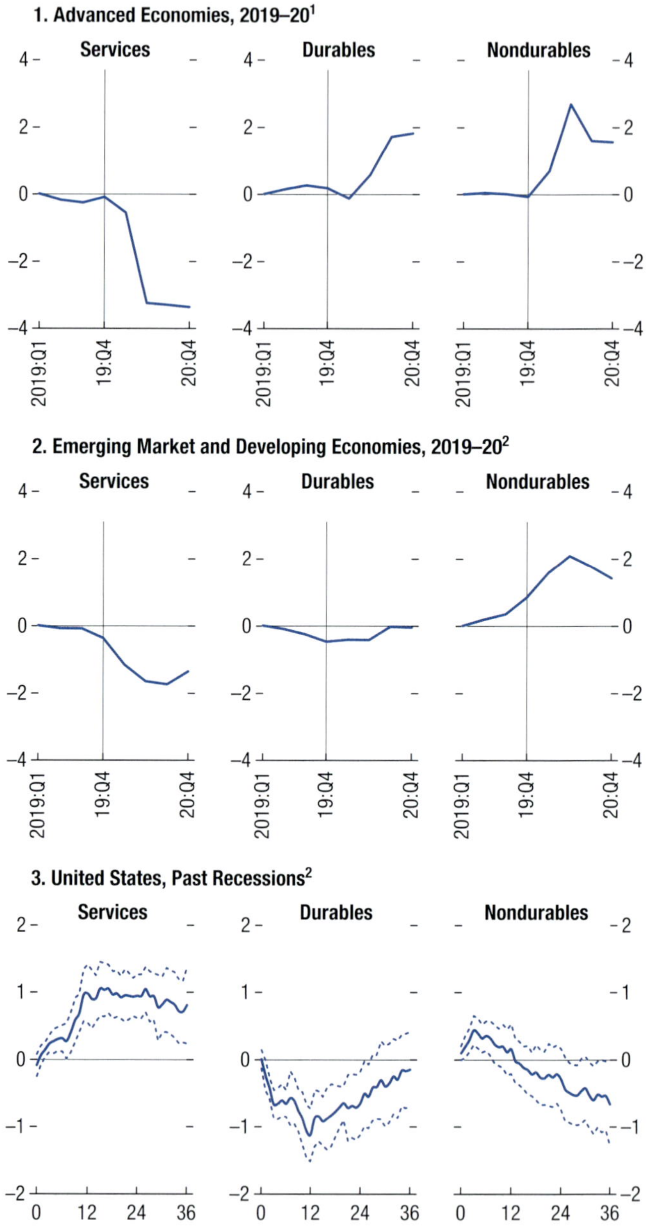

Sources: Haver Analytics; National Bureau of Economic Research (NBER); US Bureau of Economic Analysis; and IMF staff estimates.

Note: Data labels use International Organization for Standardization (ISO) country codes.

[1]Change in consumption shares from 2019:Q1, quarterly data. The panel shows the GDP-weighted average for 14 advanced economies (AUS, CAN, DEU, DNK, ESP, FRA, GBR, ISR, ITA, JPN, KOR, NZL, SWE and USA) and 7 emerging market and developing economies (CHN, CHL, IDN, MEX, THA, TUR and ZAF).

[2]Estimates of Jordà (2005) and local projections for NBER-dated US recessions since 1958, excluding the COVID-19 crisis; monthly data. Dashes indicate 90 percent confidence bands. Units on the *x*-axis are months.

toward teleworking and virtual learning (see Box 1.1 in the April 2021 WEO). This development contrasts with past recessions, during which the consumption share of durable goods has typically declined. In emerging market and developing economies, the shift away from services also occurred but was not as pronounced and was mainly offset by an increased consumption share of nondurables. The shift is currently expected to be a transitory development, driven by the pandemic and associated lockdowns and involving some purchases—such as home office equipment—that depreciate slowly.

Additional country-specific factors have also contributed to the sharp movements in current accounts. For instance, some economies with large foreign direct investment liabilities experienced sharp increases in their income balances and current accounts due to lower dividend payments to foreign investors (for Australia, Poland, and South Africa, for example). In other cases, increased global demand for gold, a traditional safe asset in times of heightened global risk aversion, led to sharp increases in gold imports (for Switzerland, for example) and exports for gold producers (South Africa, for example). Remittance flows declined sharply in early 2020, affecting emerging market and developing economies such as India and Mexico, as well as numerous smaller ones (Figure 1.7).

However, remittances have since recovered faster than anticipated and have become an important consumption smoothing mechanism for the recipient households, forming a significant (private) element of global social protection systems (World Bank 2021). Kpodar and others (2021) find that remittances were greater in migrants' home economies with higher COVID-19 infection rates.

Overall, these special COVID-19–related factors explain a substantial share of the movement in current account balances in 2020 (Figure 1.5). Online Annex 1.1[1] provides a quantification of the impact of these factors on current account balances. About 66 percent of the movement of current account balances for major economies is explained by the sum of these factors (Figure 1.5).[2]

[1]All annexes are available at www.imf.org/en/Publications/ESR.

[2]The relationship depicted in Figure 1.15, $\Delta CA_i = \alpha + \beta$Sum of COVID-19 Factors$_i + \varepsilon_i$, where ΔCA_i is the change in the current account-to-GDP ratio for economy i in 2020 has, for the 30 economies with ESR assessments, an R-squared of 66 percent.

Figure 1.7. Remittances during the COVID-19 Crisis
(US dollars; 2019 = 100)

Flows of remittances to emerging market and developing economies were resilient in 2020 and early 2021, with most economies having experienced a sustained increase since May 2020, which reversed the decline observed at the onset of the COVID-19 crisis.

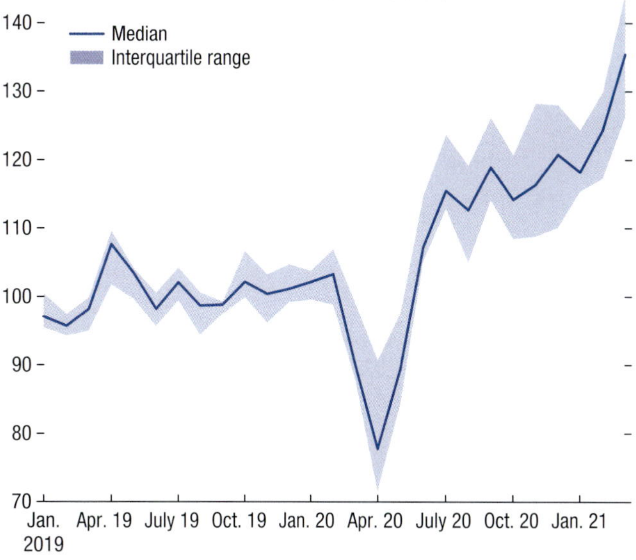

Sources: National authorities; and IMF staff calculations.
Note: Country sample: Bangladesh, Colombia, Dominican Republic, El Salvador, Georgia, Guatemala, Kenya, Lebanon, Mexico, Morocco, Pakistan, Paraguay, Philippines, Sri Lanka, Thailand.

In addition, as the analysis in Chapter 2 suggests, the unprecedented fiscal expansion is having significant effects on current account balances, although what happens to the current account depends on a country's relative fiscal policy stance compared with that of its trading partners. For economies with relatively limited fiscal expansions during the COVID-19 crisis compared with those of their trading partners, consequences include a rise in their current account balances (such as in Mexico).

Impact on "Downhill" Flow of Capital, Saving, and Investment

In 2020 poorer economies saw, on average, larger unexpected increases in their current account balances than did richer economies, compared with pre-pandemic forecasts (Figure 1.8), highlighting the unequal impact of the pandemic and potentially exacerbating the divergent speeds of recovery across income groups. A doubling in income per capita is associated with more than a 1 percentage point of GDP

Figure 1.8. Income Levels and Current Account Forecast Errors, 2020
(Percent of GDP)

Current account forecast errors in 2020 are negatively associated with income levels, implying an "uphill" flow of capital from poorer to richer economies relative to previous forecasts. This reflects mainly larger negative forecast errors in public net lending in richer economies.

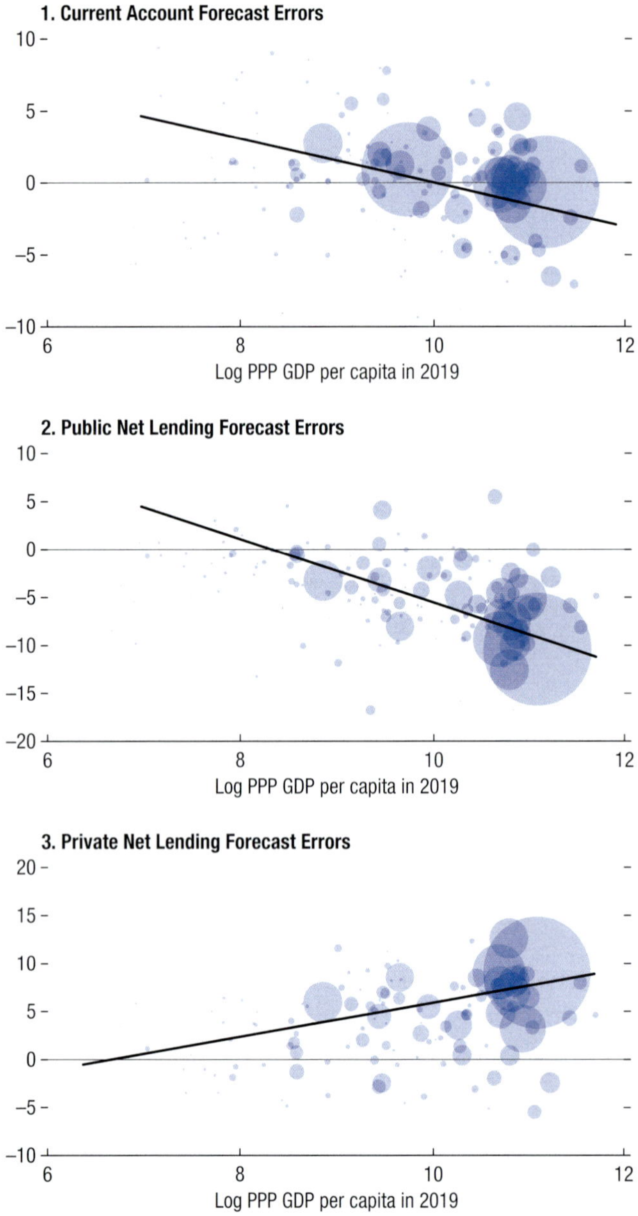

Sources: IMF, *International Financial Statistics*; IMF, *World Economic Outlook* (WEO); and IMF staff calculations.
Note: Forecast errors are defined as outcomes minus the January 2020 WEO forecast. Bubble sizes are proportional to US dollar GDP. The vertical axis for chart 1 is cut off at ±10 percent of GDP. Current account balances outside this range sum to less than 0.1 percent of world GDP. PPP = purchasing power parity.

reduction in the current account balance compared with pre-pandemic forecasts (see Online Annex 1.2).[3] The relationship suggests that the COVID-19 crisis may have slowed the downhill flow of capital from richer to poorer economies that occurred during the decade following the global financial crisis. After that crisis, deleveraging and associated investment declines led to lower net inflows into richer economies, and the global flow of loanable funds supported investment in poorer economies (Boz, Cubeddu, and Obstfeld 2017).

This development regarding the direction of capital flows, which is expected to gradually unwind over the coming years, reflects larger declines in public saving–investment balances in richer economies associated with their larger fiscal expansions (see the April 2021 *Fiscal Monitor* and Online Annex 1.2). The fall in public saving–investment balances has been partly offset by higher private saving–investment balances, which have increased in most economies but by more in richer ones. Despite this average result, for a number of lower- and middle-income economies, there were sharp declines in current account balances, especially for those with significant exports of travel services or oil, as already mentioned (Box 1.1).

Sectoral data for advanced economies suggest that the rise in private saving–investment balances mainly reflects record household saving rates (Figure 1.9) due to lockdown-induced consumption reductions, the saving of government transfers, and precautionary motives (Box 1.2). The increase in household saving and the fall in government saving have been much larger than during the global financial crisis. Corporate saving movements have been relatively modest, reflecting offsetting effects of falling profits and government support to companies. Household and corporate

[3]As Figure 1.8 indicates (and Online Annex 1.2 documents in further detail), the forecast error for the current account balance in percentage of GDP in 2020 compared with the January 2020 WEO forecast is negatively correlated with the initial (2019) log of purchasing-power-parity (PPP) GDP per capita for a global sample of economies. The slope coefficient (–1.05) implies that a doubling in income per capita is associated with a 1.05 percentage point of GDP reduction in the current account balance compared with pre-pandemic forecasts. Excluding China and the United States from the analysis decreases the coefficient modestly (in absolute terms) to –0.99. This result is both statistically and economically significant. Additional analysis (Online Annex 1.2) confirms that countries with lower per capita income had, on average, lower current account balances during 2010–19: a doubling in per capita income for that decade is associated with a 1.02 percentage point of GDP *rise* in the current account balance.

Figure 1.9. Private and Public Sector Saving Rates in Advanced Economies
(Percent of GDP, quarters on x-axis)

Compared with the global financial crisis, the COVID-19 crisis led to larger (and offsetting) shifts in household and public saving, with a smaller impact on corporate saving and investment.

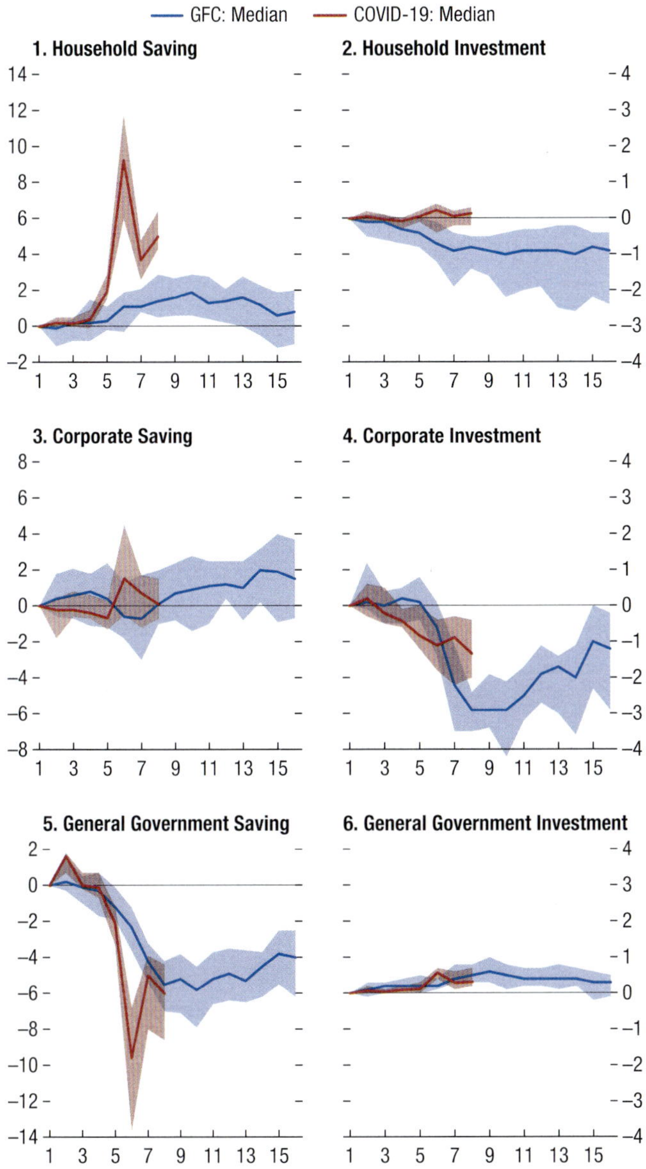

Sources: Eurostat; national authorities; Refinitiv Datastream; and IMF staff calculations.
Note: Countries are Australia, Austria, Belgium, Canada, the Czech Republic, Denmark, Finland, France, Germany, Greece, Ireland, Italy, The Netherlands, Norway, Poland, Portugal, Romania, Slovenia, Spain, Sweden, the United Kingdom, the United States. The global financial crisis (GFC) and COVID-19 series are rebased to zero in 2007:Q3 and 2019:Q1, respectively. In both cases, Q = 6 corresponds to the peak of the crisis.

investment has been relatively resilient, which differs from past recessions, with private investment typically contracting, especially following credit booms (Box 1.3), as was the case following the global financial crisis, which came after real-estate booms in a number of economies.

Widening Global Current Account Balances

Global current account deficits and surpluses widened in 2020 compared with 2019 and are set to widen further in 2021 (Figure 1.10 and Table 1.1). The aforementioned sectoral COVID-19 factors explain the entire widening in global current account balances in 2020 (Figure 1.11). Net of these factors, the global current account balance in 2020 is slightly *lower* than in 2019 (Figure 1.11).

The widening of global balances in 2020–21, which is expected to be temporary, contrasts with developments in the aftermath of the global financial crisis and earlier global downturns, during which global balances narrowed. Factors that explain the different dynamics observed this time include, in addition to the aforementioned sectoral shocks, the highly synchronized nature of the pandemic recession and relatively limited precrisis domestic and external imbalances, with relatively few associated financial crises (Box 1.3). In addition, the ongoing fiscal expansions, which tend to raise current account deficits, are especially large for economies with current account deficits, such as the United States, and this distribution of fiscal expansions across economies contributes to further widening global balances in 2021 (Chapter 2). Overall, forecasts of global current account balances for the coming years have been revised up (Figure 1.11) and their currently expected declining path over the medium term is subject to upside risks, as discussed in what follows, which would further add to the stock of external assets and liabilities.

Creditor and debtor stock positions remain historically high (Figure 1.12). The largest debtor economy remains the United States, whose net international investment position declined from –51 percent of GDP in 2019 to –67 percent of GDP in 2020 (Table 1.2). Other large debtor economies include Spain, the United Kingdom, and Australia, while the largest creditor economies remain Japan, Germany, Hong Kong SAR, and China. Foreign currency reserves remain adequate in most emerging

Figure 1.10. Global Current Account Balances, 1990–2026
(Percent of world GDP)

Global current account deficits and surpluses, which had been on a declining trend for a number of years, increased in 2020 and are set to widen further in 2021.

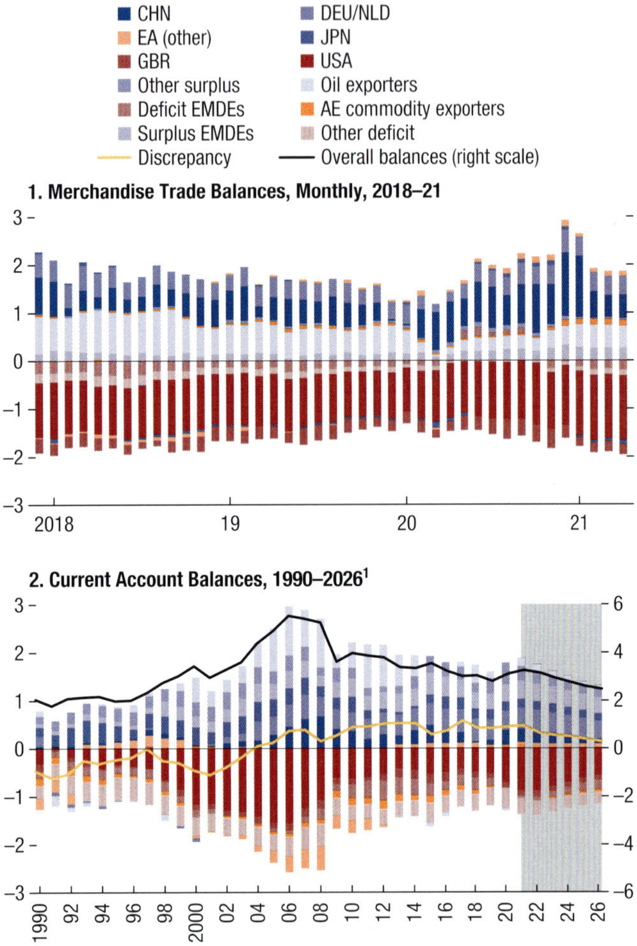

Sources: IMF, *International Financial Statistics*; IMF, *World Economic Outlook* (WEO); and IMF staff calculations.
Note: The shaded area indicates forecasts. AE = advanced economies; EA = euro area; EMDEs = emerging market and developing economies. Data labels use International Organization for Standardization (ISO) country codes.
[1]Overall balance is the absolute sum of global surpluses and deficits. AE commodity exporters comprise Australia, Canada, and New Zealand; deficit EMDEs comprise Brazil, Chile, India, Indonesia, Mexico, Peru, South Africa, and Turkey; oil exporters comprise WEO definition plus Norway; surplus AEs comprise Hong Kong SAR, Korea, Singapore, Sweden, Switzerland, and Taiwan Province of China. Other deficit (surplus) comprise all other economies running current account deficits (surpluses).

Figure 1.11. Global Current Account Balances and COVID-19 Factors
(Percent of world GDP)

Sectoral shocks associated with the COVID-19 crisis explain the increase in global current account balances—the sum of absolute deficits and surpluses—in 2020. Forecasts of global current account balances for the coming years have been revised up.

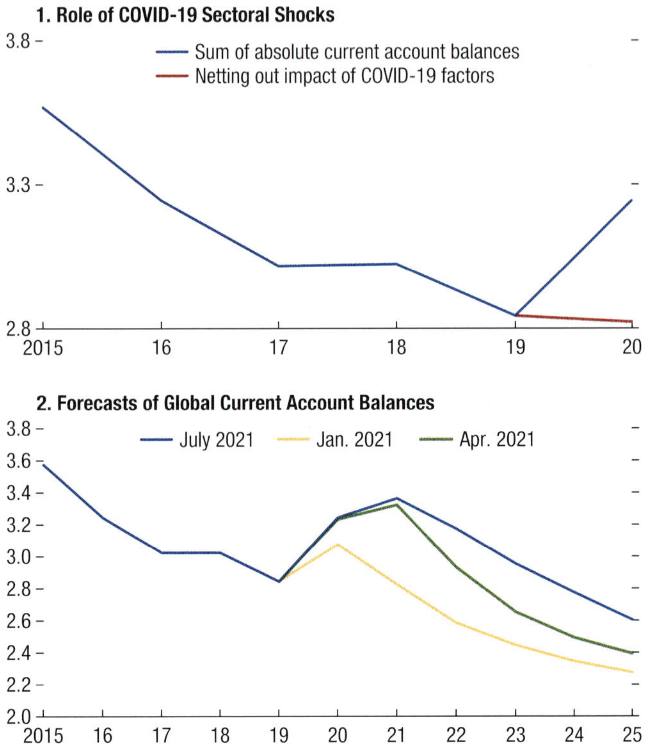

Sources: Census and Economic Information Center; IMF, Information Notice System; IMF, *International Financial Statistics*; IMF, *World Economic Outlook*; and IMF staff calculations.
Note: See the chapter text for the definition of sectoral shocks associated with the COVID-19 crisis. Forecast dates refer to vintages of the IMF, *World Economic Outlook*.

market and developing economies (Annex Table 1.1.1). Valuation effects drove changes in the net international investment position of major advanced and emerging market economies. The United States experienced the largest valuation losses in percent of GDP, which are mainly explained by asset price valuation losses as a result of the increase in domestic stock prices, which affects the value of US external equity liabilities. Currency-induced valuation effects for the United States are relatively small. Among emerging markets, Turkey experienced large currency-induced valuation losses, particularly on debt, driven by the large depreciation of the Turkish lira. These valuation losses were only partially offset by asset price valuation gains. Brazil had currency-induced valuation losses on external debt positions, but these losses were offset by gains on equity positions and asset prices. By contrast, South Africa experienced large net foreign valuation gains (in terms of smaller net foreign liabilities) due to declining asset price valuations (see Online Annex 1.3 for the methodology on computing valuation effects).

Table 1.1. Selected Economies: Current Account Balance, 2018–21

	Billions of US Dollars				Percent of World GDP				Percent of GDP			
	2018	2019	2020	2021 Projection	2018	2019	2020	2021 Projection	2018	2019	2020	2021 Projection
Advanced Economies												
Australia	−30	9	35	38	0.0	0.0	0.0	0.0	−2.1	0.7	2.5	2.4
Belgium	−4	2	−1	−5	0.0	0.0	0.0	0.0	−0.8	0.3	−0.2	−0.9
Canada	−40	−36	−30	−15	0.0	0.0	0.0	0.0	−2.3	−2.1	−1.8	−0.8
France	−16	−18	−50	−62	0.0	0.0	−0.1	−0.1	−0.6	−0.7	−1.9	−2.1
Germany	292	274	265	327	0.3	0.3	0.3	0.4	7.4	7.1	7.0	7.6
Hong Kong SAR	14	21	23	20	0.0	0.0	0.0	0.0	3.7	5.7	6.5	5.5
Italy	52	60	67	74	0.1	0.1	0.1	0.1	2.5	3.0	3.5	3.5
Japan	177	188	165	195	0.2	0.2	0.2	0.2	3.5	3.7	3.3	3.6
Korea	77	60	75	77	0.1	0.1	0.1	0.1	4.5	3.6	4.6	4.2
The Netherlands	99	90	63	91	0.1	0.1	0.1	0.1	10.8	9.9	7.0	9.0
Singapore	58	53	60	55	0.1	0.1	0.1	0.1	15.4	14.3	17.6	14.6
Spain	27	30	8	14	0.0	0.0	0.0	0.0	1.9	2.1	0.7	1.0
Sweden	15	27	31	31	0.0	0.0	0.0	0.0	2.6	5.1	5.7	5.0
Switzerland	49	49	28	56	0.1	0.1	0.0	0.1	6.7	6.7	3.8	6.7
United Kingdom	−105	−88	−95	−121	−0.1	−0.1	−0.1	−0.1	−3.7	−3.1	−3.5	−3.9
United States	−450	−480	−616	−876	−0.5	−0.6	−0.7	−0.9	−2.2	−2.2	−2.9	−3.9
Emerging Market and Developing Economies												
Argentina	−27	−4	3	10	0.0	0.0	0.0	0.0	−5.2	−0.9	0.8	2.3
Brazil	−42	−51	−24	−9	0.0	−0.1	0.0	0.0	−2.2	−2.7	−1.7	−0.6
China	24	103	271	274	0.0	0.1	0.3	0.3	0.2	0.7	1.8	1.6
India[1]	−57	−25	26	−36	−0.1	0.0	0.0	0.0	−2.1	−0.9	1.0	−1.2
Indonesia	−31	−30	−5	−15	0.0	0.0	0.0	0.0	−2.9	−2.7	−0.4	−1.3
Malaysia	8	12	14	15	0.0	0.0	0.0	0.0	2.2	3.4	4.2	3.8
Mexico	−25	−4	26	22	0.0	0.0	0.0	0.0	−2.1	−0.3	2.4	1.8
Poland	−8	3	21	13	0.0	0.0	0.0	0.0	−1.3	0.5	3.5	2.0
Russia	116	65	34	67	0.1	0.1	0.0	0.1	7.0	3.8	2.3	3.9
Saudi Arabia	72	38	−20	23	0.1	0.0	0.0	0.0	9.2	4.8	−2.8	2.8
South Africa	−13	−11	7	3	0.0	0.0	0.0	0.0	−3.5	−3.0	2.2	1.0
Thailand	28	38	16	2	0.0	0.0	0.0	0.0	5.6	7.0	3.3	0.5
Turkey	−22	7	−37	−21	0.0	0.0	0.0	0.0	−2.8	0.9	−5.1	−2.7
Memorandum item:[2]												
Euro Area	393	307	285	401	0.5	0.4	0.3	0.4	2.9	2.3	2.2	2.8
Global Current Account Balance	2,590	2,477	2,736	3,141	3.0	2.8	3.2	3.4	…	…	…	…
Statistical Discrepancy	317	339	362	348	0.4	0.4	0.4	0.4	…	…	…	…
Overall Surpluses	1,453	1,388	1,497	1,742	1.7	1.6	1.8	1.9	…	…	…	…
Of which: Advanced Economies	1,041	1,007	1,022	1,225	1.2	1.2	1.2	1.3	…	…	…	…
Overall Deficits	−1,136	−1,049	−1,135	−1,394	−1.3	−1.2	−1.3	−1.5	…	…	…	…
Of which: Advanced Economies	−670	−684	−813	−1,104	−0.8	−0.8	−1.0	−1.2	…	…	…	…

Sources: IMF, *World Economic Outlook;* and IMF staff calculations.
Note: "…" indicates that data are not available or not applicable.
[1]For India, data are presented on a fiscal year basis.
[2]Overall surpluses and deficits (and the "of which" advanced economies) include non-*External Sector Report* economies.

Figure 1.12. Net International Investment Positions, 1990–2021

Stocks of foreign assets and liabilities remain at historically high levels. In 2020 changes in the net foreign asset position were larger than explained by current account balances in a number of cases, reflecting large valuation changes, including those driven by asset price and currency movements.

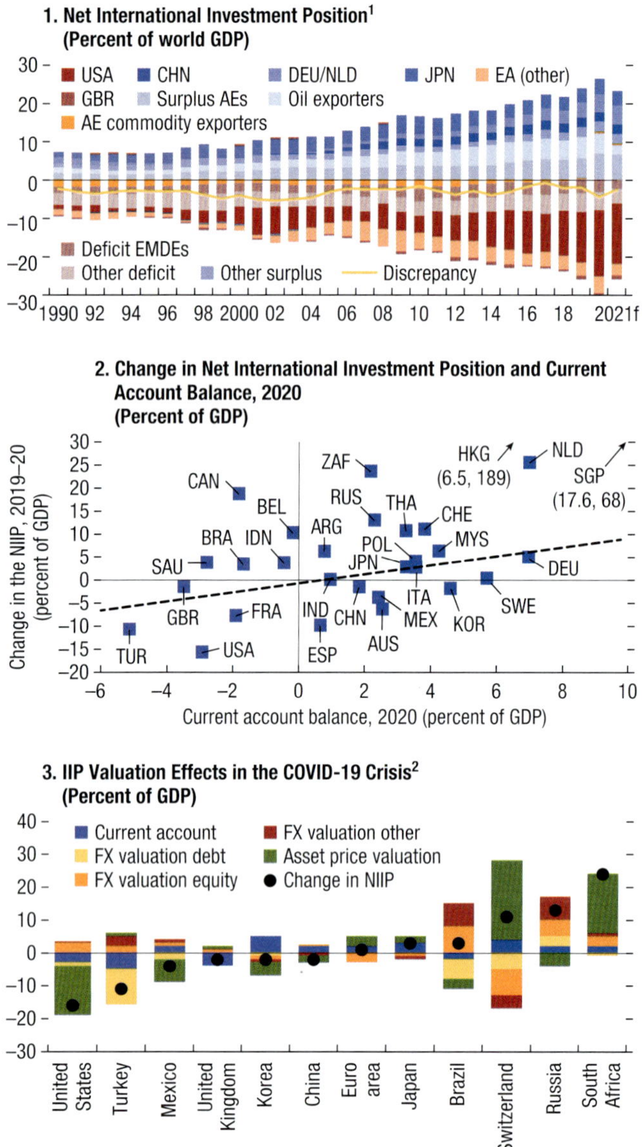

Sources: Bénétrix and others (2019); External Wealth of Nations database; Hale and Juvenal (2020); IMF, *International Financial Statistics*; IMF, *World Economic Outlook* (WEO); and IMF staff calculations.

Note: AEs = advanced economies; EA = euro area; EMDEs = emerging market and developing economies; "f" = IMF staff forecasts; FX = foreign exchange; IIP = international investment position; NFA = net foreign assets; NIIP = net international investment position. Data labels use International Organization for Standardization (ISO) country codes.

[1]AE commodity exporters comprise Australia, Canada, New Zealand; creditor AEs comprise Hong Kong SAR, Korea, Singapore, Sweden, Switzerland, Taiwan Province of China; deficit EMDEs comprise Brazil, Chile, India, Indonesia, Mexico, Peru, South Africa, and Turkey; oil exporters comprise WEO definition plus Norway.

[2]Euro area comprises Austria, Belgium, France, Germany, Italy, The Netherlands, Finland, Greece, Ireland, Portugal, and Spain.

Normative Assessment of External Positions in 2020

IMF staff external sector assessments for 2020 provide an analysis of how the COVID-19 crisis has affected external positions. The assessment of external positions requires a multilateral approach that matches positive and negative excess external imbalances. The IMF's external assessment framework combines numerical inputs from the latest vintage of the External Balance Assessment (EBA) models with a series of external indicators and analytically grounded judgment and country-specific insights (see Box 1.4). The EBA methodology produces multilaterally consistent estimates for current account and real exchange rate norms (benchmarks), which depend on country fundamentals and desired policies.[4] The IMF staff estimates current account and real effective exchange rate gaps by comparing actual current accounts (stripped of temporary components) and real effective exchange rates with their IMF staff–assessed norms, using analytically grounded judgment and country-specific insights, where appropriate. The IMF staff arrives at a holistic overall external sector assessment for 30 of the world's largest economies based on the estimated gaps as well as consideration of other external sector indicators, such as the net international investment position, capital flows, and foreign exchange reserves. Annex Table 1.1.2 summarizes the IMF staff–assessed current account and real effective exchange rate gaps and the external sector assessments for the 30 economies.

To strip out factors associated with the COVID-19 crisis and allow the IMF staff to assess the underlying current account position, special adjustments to EBA model estimates are provided (see Online Annex 1.1). These adjustors estimate the impact of the crisis on (1) the travel services balance (reflecting mostly tourism) due to the drop in international travel, (2) oil balances, (3) trade in medical products triggered by the health emergency, and (4) shifts in household consumption composition due to the shift from services toward durables and other consumer goods. Additional, more idiosyncratic adjustments related to the COVID-19 crisis, such as those involving sharp shifts

[4]For instance, advanced economies with higher incomes, older populations, and lower growth prospects have positive current account norms. Conversely, current account norms are negative for most emerging market and developing economies, as they are expected to import capital to invest and exploit their higher growth potential.

Table 1.2. Selected Economies: Net International Investment Position, 2017–20

	Billions of US Dollars				Percent of World GDP				Percent of GDP			
	2017	2018	2019	2020	2017	2018	2019	2020	2017	2018	2019	2020
Advanced Economies												
Australia	–756	–738	–643	–714	–0.9	–0.9	–0.7	–0.8	–54.6	–51.9	–46.2	–52.6
Belgium	288	187	186	231	0.4	0.2	0.2	0.3	57.3	34.5	34.9	45.1
Canada	569	547	742	1,007	0.7	0.6	0.9	1.2	34.5	31.8	42.6	61.3
France	–547	–506	–507	–694	–0.7	–0.6	–0.6	–0.8	–21.1	–18.1	–18.6	–26.4
Germany	2,174	2,410	2,756	2,905	2.7	2.8	3.2	3.4	59.0	60.8	71.4	76.3
Hong Kong SAR	1,421	1,283	1,579	2,154	1.8	1.5	1.8	2.5	416.5	354.6	431.8	621.0
Italy	–158	–98	–18	34	–0.2	–0.1	0.0	0.0	–8.1	–4.7	–0.9	1.8
Japan	2,915	3,033	3,271	3,347	3.6	3.5	3.8	4.0	59.1	60.2	63.5	66.3
Korea	262	436	501	465	0.3	0.5	0.6	0.6	16.1	25.3	30.3	28.4
The Netherlands	523	633	810	1,038	0.6	0.7	0.9	1.2	62.7	69.2	89.3	113.9
Singapore	867	770	896	1,046	1.1	0.9	1.0	1.2	252.6	204.8	239.3	307.8
Spain	–1,114	–1,127	–1,037	–1,082	–1.4	–1.3	–1.2	–1.3	–84.9	–79.2	–74.4	–84.5
Sweden	–7	43	94	97	0.0	0.0	0.1	0.1	–1.2	7.7	17.7	18.0
Switzerland	676	751	609	705	0.8	0.9	0.7	0.8	95.9	102.0	83.2	94.2
United Kingdom	–372	–432	–814	–820	–0.5	–0.5	–0.9	–1.0	–13.9	–15.1	–28.7	–30.3
United States	–7,622	–9,674	–11,051	–14,090	–9.5	–11.3	–12.7	–16.7	–39.0	–46.9	–51.6	–67.3
Emerging Market and Developing Economies												
Argentina	17	65	115	122	0.0	0.1	0.1	0.1	2.7	12.6	25.8	32.0
Brazil	–645	–595	–786	–552	–0.8	–0.7	–0.9	–0.7	–31.3	–31.1	–41.9	–38.3
China	2,065	2,108	2,300	2,150	2.6	2.5	2.6	2.5	16.8	15.2	16.0	14.5
India	–424	–437	–375	–341	–0.5	–0.5	–0.4	–0.4	–16.0	–16.2	–13.1	–13.1
Indonesia	–323	–317	–338	–281	–0.4	–0.4	–0.4	–0.3	–31.8	–30.4	–30.2	–26.5
Malaysia	–8	–18	–5	16	0.0	0.0	0.0	0.0	–2.4	–4.9	–1.5	4.8
Mexico	–553	–584	–648	–590	–0.7	–0.7	–0.7	–0.7	–47.7	–47.8	–51.0	–54.9
Poland	–350	–315	–298	–273	–0.4	–0.4	–0.3	–0.3	–66.4	–53.7	–49.9	–45.9
Russia	280	374	359	504	0.3	0.4	0.4	0.6	17.8	22.6	21.2	34.2
Saudi Arabia	624	658	675	623	0.8	0.8	0.8	0.7	90.6	83.6	85.1	88.8
South Africa	35	45	31	98	0.0	0.1	0.0	0.1	9.9	12.3	8.9	32.4
Thailand	–31	–6	2	55	0.0	0.0	0.0	0.1	–6.7	–1.1	0.3	11.0
Turkey	–462	–370	–348	–404	–0.6	–0.4	–0.4	–0.5	–53.8	–47.5	–45.7	–56.4
Memorandum item:												
Euro Area	–1,097	–587	–35	111	–1.4	–0.7	0.0	0.1	–8.7	–4.3	–0.3	0.8
Statistical Discrepancy	–1,173	–2,556	–2,318	–3,407	–1.5	–3.0	–2.7	–4.0	...	...	...	...
Overall Creditors[1]	15,611	16,308	18,188	20,156	19.4	19.0	20.9	23.9	...	...	...	...
Of which: Advanced Economies	12,180	12,628	14,300	16,217	15.1	14.7	16.4	19.2	...	...	...	...
Overall Debtors[1]	–16,785	–18,863	–20,506	–23,563	–20.8	–22.0	–23.5	–27.9	...	...	...	...
Of which: Advanced Economies	–12,033	–14,153	–15,633	–19,074	–14.9	–16.5	–17.9	–22.6	...	...	...	...

Sources: IMF, World Economic Outlook; US Bureau of Economic Analysis; and IMF staff calculations.
Note: "..." indicates that data are not available or not applicable.
[1]Overall creditors and debtors (and the "of which" advanced economies) include non-External Sector Report economies.

in the income balance, gold balance, and remittances, are included. As already mentioned, these COVID-19–related factors explain a large share of the movement in current account balances in 2020, implying that, without their use, the 2020 external sector assessments would be distorted and harder to interpret. Annex Table 1.1.3 reports the overall set of IMF staff adjustments to reflect both the COVID-19 factors and other country-specific factors.

Current Account Norms in 2020

Current account norms in 2020 reflected, as in 2019, economic fundamentals and desirable policies (Figure 1.13, panel 1). IMF staff adjustments to norms include those for demographic characteristics not captured by the EBA models (Canada, Germany, Indonesia, South Africa) and to enhance external debt sustainability (Argentina and Spain).

Norm changes in 2020 compared with 2019 mainly reflect changes in medium-term desirable fiscal policy settings—the level of the general government cyclically adjusted fiscal balance in five years recommended by the IMF staff (Figure 1.13, panel 2). Changes in other desired policy settings contributed little to changes in current account norms. In the near term, departures from medium-term policy settings can be desirable, as in the case of the 2020 necessary fiscal expansions. In most cases, the IMF staff reduced the medium-term desirable fiscal policy settings compared with those for the 2020 *External Sector Report* (ESR) to avoid an excessively sharp adjustment over the subsequent five years. In some cases, the IMF staff increased the desirable fiscal medium-term fiscal policy setting, to ensure stabilization or decline in government debt to GDP by 2026. Additional analysis indicates that all normative medium-term fiscal policy is consistent with either debt stabilization or, more often, debt reduction by 2026.[5]

Figure 1.13. External Balance Assessment Current Account Norms, 2020
(Percent of GDP)

The External Balance Assessment methodology produces multilaterally consistent estimates for current account norms, which depend on country fundamentals and desirable policies. Current account norm changes in 2020 mainly reflected changes in medium-term fiscal policy settings.

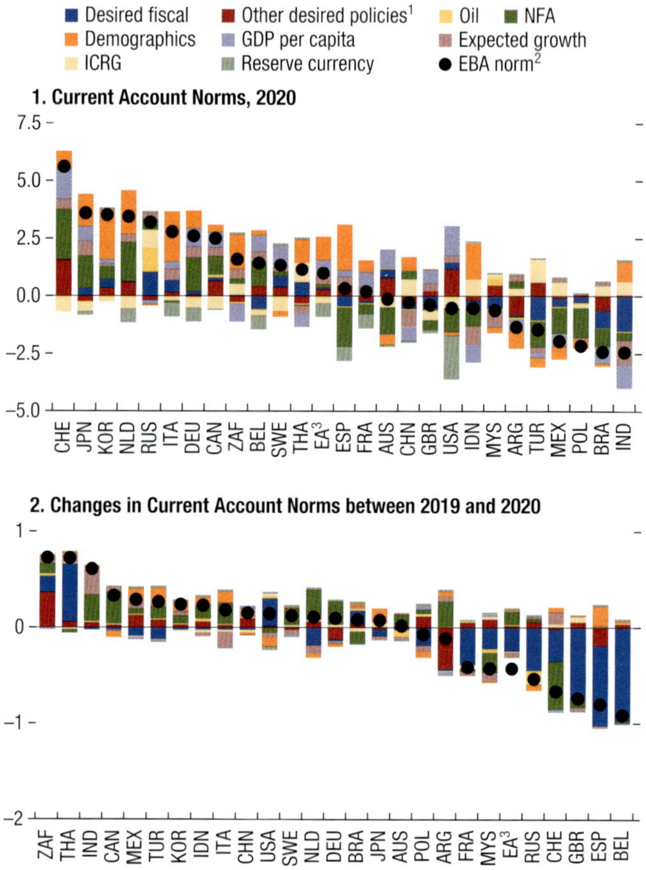

Source: IMF, External Balance Assessment (EBA) estimates.
Note: The figure excludes Hong Kong SAR, Saudi Arabia, and Singapore as they are not included in the EBA regression model. Data labels use International Organization for Standardization (ISO) country codes. EA = euro area; ICRG = *International Country Risk Guide*; NFA = net foreign assets.
[1]Other desired policies also includes intercept and multilateral consistency adjustment.
[2]The EBA current account norm is multilaterally consistent and cyclically adjusted.
[3]The current account norm is corrected for reporting discrepancies in intra-area transactions, since the current account of the entire euro area is about 0.71 percent of GDP less than the sum of the individual 11 countries' balances (for which no such correction is available).

Changes in External Assessments in 2020

Almost half of the 30 economy assessments changed categories in 2020 compared with 2019 (Figure 1.14, Annex Table 1.1.2, and Annex Table 1.1.3). Economies with estimated excess current account surpluses (deficits) generally also had an undervalued (overvalued) real effective exchange rate, according to IMF staff estimates (Figure 1.15, panel 2, Annex Table 1.1.2, and

[5]In particular, the medium-term desirable policy settings (P*) for the fiscal balance in 2026 reported in Annex Table 1.1.5 are all at or above the level of fiscal balances compatible with a constant government-debt-to-GDP ratio in 2026.

Figure 1.14. The Evolution of External Sector Assessments, 2012–20

External sector assessments have generally persisted over time. In 2020, almost half of the 30 economy assessments changed categories compared with 2019.

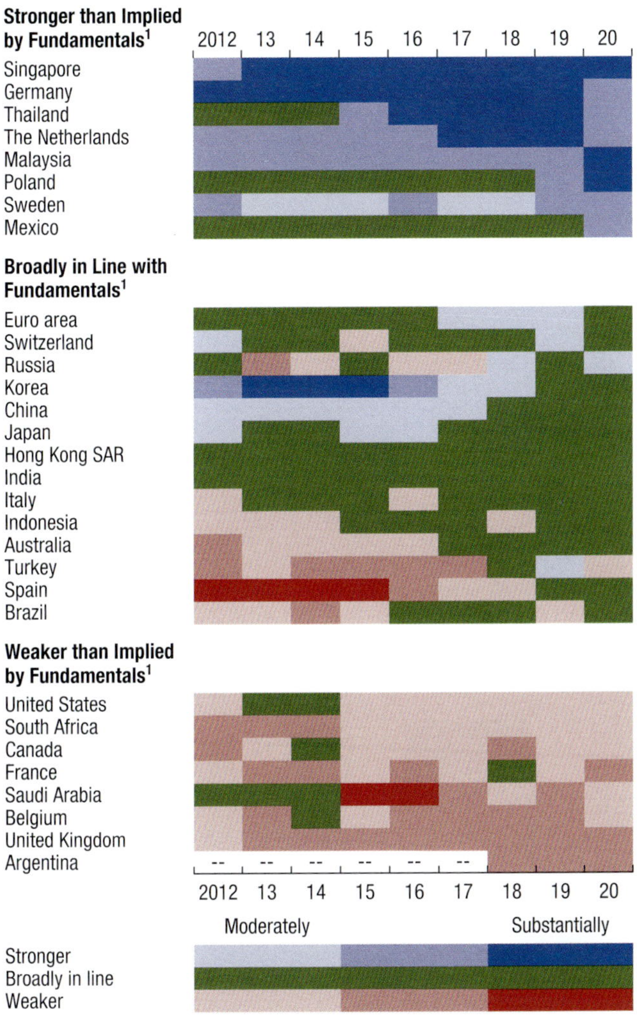

Source: IMF staff assessments.
[1]Grouping and ordering based on economies' average excess imbalance during 2019–20. Coverage of Argentina in the *External Sector Report* started in the 2018 *External Sector Report.*

Figure 1.15. IMF Staff and External Balance Assessment Current Account and Real Exchange Rate Gaps, 2020

The IMF staff combines the numerical inputs from the External Balance Assessment methodology with country-specific judgment and other indicators to arrive at multilaterally consistent assessments of the 29 largest systemically important economies and the euro area.

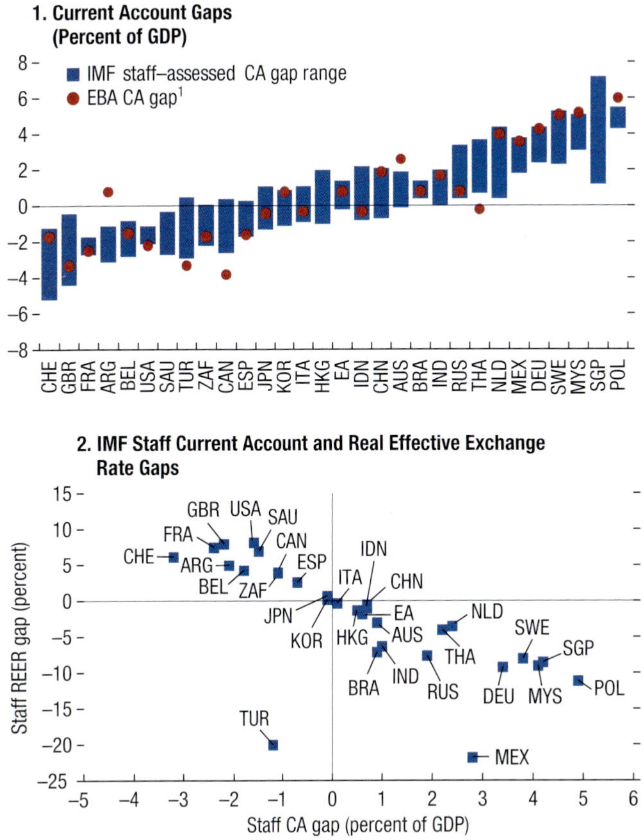

Source: IMF staff assessments.
Note: REER gap is based on 2020 External Sector Report; CA = current account; EBA = IMF External Balance Assessment model; REER = real effective exchange rate. Data labels use International Organization for Standardization (ISO) country codes.
[1]There are no EBA estimates for Hong Kong SAR, Saudi Arabia, and Singapore.

Annex Table 1.1.4).[6] External positions compared with the levels consistent with medium-term fundamentals and desirable policies were as follows:

- *Moderately stronger, stronger, or substantially stronger than the level consistent with medium-term fundamentals and desirable policies:* The nine economies with such positions are Germany, Malaysia, The Netherlands, Poland, Sweden, Thailand, and Singapore, as well as Mexico and Russia, which entered this category in 2020, driven by increases in their current account gaps, reflecting, in part, a smaller fiscal policy expansion compared with those of major trading partners (see Annex Table 1.1.5). These results indicate how relatively large fiscal expansions in some economies affected their trading partners' external positions and assessments, such as in Mexico and Russia.

[6]Figure 1.14 reports the ranges for IMF staff–assessed current account gaps as well as the EBA model–based current account gap estimates. As reported in Annex Table 1.1.3, the EBA and staff-assessed current account gaps differ in a number of cases, reflecting the use of country specific judgment and COVID-19 adjustors.

- *Moderately weaker or weaker than the level consistent with medium-term fundamentals and desirable policies:* The nine economies with such positions are Argentina, Belgium, Canada, France, Saudi Arabia, South Africa, the United Kingdom, the United States, and Turkey, which entered this category in 2020.
- *Broadly in line with the level consistent with medium-term fundamentals and desirable policies:* The 12 economies with such positions are Australia, China, Hong Kong SAR, India, Indonesia, Italy, Japan, Korea, and Spain, as well as Brazil, the euro area, and Switzerland, which entered this category in 2020.[7]

Multilateral consistency of the IMF staff–assessed current account gaps holds for 2020 when taking into account the shift in balances between economies covered in the ESR assessments and other (non-ESR) economies covered in the EBA exercise. Overall, ESR economies had an excess current account deficit of 0.1 percent of world GDP in 2020, lower than the 2019 near-zero excess, with the counterpart being an aggregate excess current account surplus of 0.1 percent of world GDP for non-ESR EBA economies (see Annex Table 1.1.3). IMF staff–assessed real effective exchange rate gaps were generally consistent with IMF staff–assessed current account gaps (Figure 1.15, panel 2; Annex Table 1.1.2 and Annex Table 1.1.4). For Turkey, a larger-than-expected negative exchange rate gap—implying undervaluation, based on the IMF staff–assessed current account gap—reflects the sharp lira depreciation in 2020, which is expected to support the current account adjustment over the coming years.

IMF staff–assessed current account gaps narrowed for several euro area economies, such as Belgium, Germany, and The Netherlands, as well as for the currency union as a whole, and for other advanced economies, such as Switzerland and the United Kingdom (Figure 1.15). These changes largely mirrored increased current account gaps for emerging market and developing economies, such as Malaysia, Mexico, and Poland. Overall, IMF staff–assessed current account gaps—which incorporate the IMF staff adjustments—changed substantially less in 2020 than did headline current account balances (Figure 1.16).

[7]The change in the assessment for Switzerland between 2019 and 2020 is subject to higher-than-usual uncertainty related to recent large downward statistical revisions to historical current account balances. The IMF staff–assessed current account gap for China reflects, as in 2019, offsetting policy gaps and structural distortions.

Figure 1.16. Evolution of IMF Staff–Assessed Current Account Gaps

IMF Staff-assessed current account gaps changed by less than headline current account balances in 2020. The global sum of absolute excessive current account imbalances compared with their desirable medium-term levels was broadly unchanged, while the sum of absolute headline current account balances increased by 0.4 percentage point of world GDP.

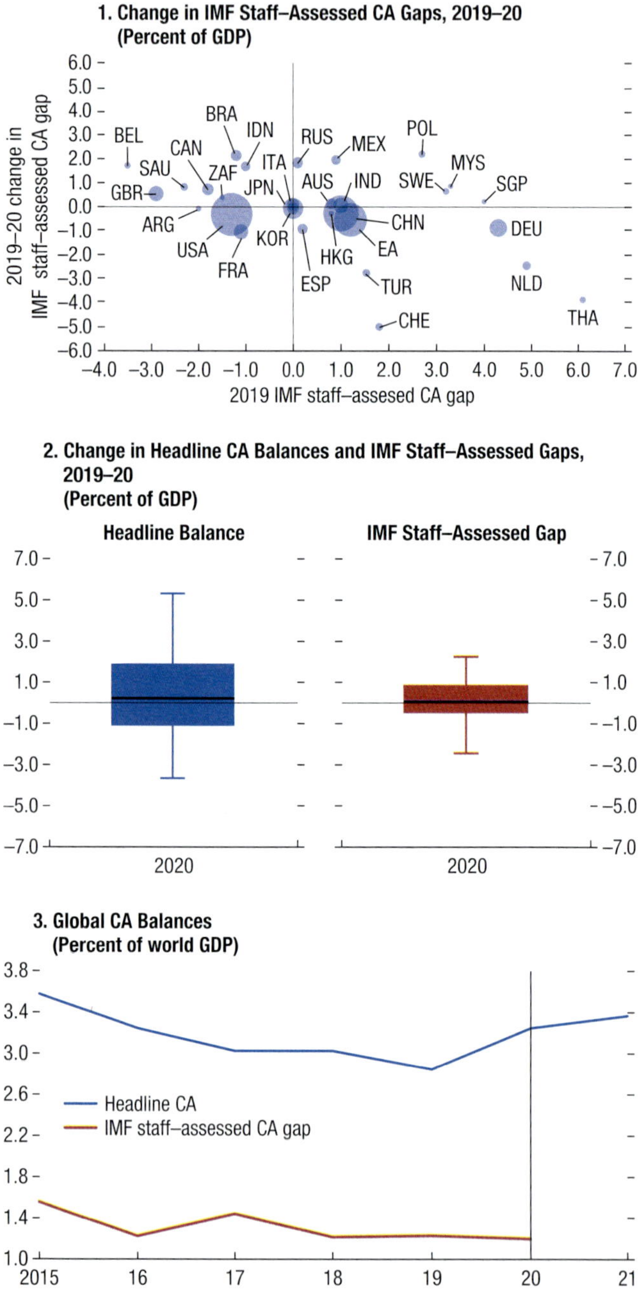

Source: IMF staff calculations.
Note: The box plots indicate median, interquartile range and adjacent values, with outside values excluded. CA = current account. Data labels use International Organization for Standarization (ISO) country codes.

Global *excessive* imbalances—the sum of absolute current account gaps compared with their desirable medium-term levels—were broadly unchanged in 2020 at about 1.2 percent of world GDP. By contrast, the sum of absolute headline current account balances rose by 0.4 percentage point of world GDP to 3.2 percent of world GDP. About 70 percent of the excess balances in 2020 pertained to advanced economies, up from 69 percent in 2019. The largest contributors to lower-than-warranted current account balances—as a share of world GDP—were, in order, the United States, France, the United Kingdom, and Canada. The largest contributors to larger-than-warranted current account balances were Germany, The Netherlands, Mexico, Poland, and Russia.

Figure 1.17. Global Saving-Investment Balances, 2019–26
(Change from 2019, percent of World GDP)

After rising in 2020–21, global current account balances are expected to narrow over the medium term, with private and public saving returning toward their pre-pandemic levels.

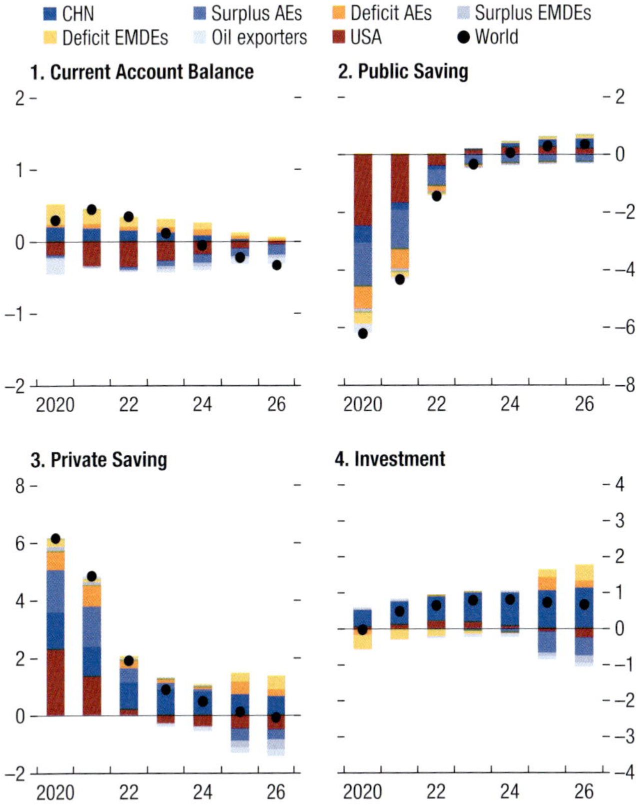

Sources: IMF, World Economic Outlook; and IMF staff calculations.
Note: Data labels use International Organization for Standardization (ISO) country codes. AEs = advanced economies; EMDEs = emerging market and developing economies.

Outlook for Current Account Balances and Risks

Medium-Term Current Account Forecasts

The latest IMF staff forecasts underpinning the July 2021 WEO *Update* imply a gradual decline in global current account balances during 2022–26, mainly reflecting a narrowing in the US deficit and the China surplus, to below pre-pandemic levels, reaching 2.5 percent of world GDP by 2026 (Figure 1.17). As the pandemic is brought under control, a substantial withdrawal of fiscal stimulus—with a corresponding rise in public saving—is projected, in particular in the United States, euro area member countries, and other advanced economies. Meanwhile, private saving is expected to decline in tandem as the conditions that led to more saving during the pandemic fade. The outlook for the investment-to-GDP ratio at the global level is more stable, with a modest rise in the medium term driven by emerging market and developing economies, especially China.

Within these aggregate trends, projected changes in current account balances for major economies vary widely (Table 1.1).

- *Advanced economies:* In the United States, continued fiscal expansion in response to the COVID-19 crisis in 2021 will more than offset the impact of higher private sector saving, resulting in a current account deficit of 3.7 percent of GDP, up from 2.2 percent of GDP in 2019. The US current account deficit is expected to start declining in 2023, falling below 3 percent of GDP in the medium term. The euro area current account surplus is projected to increase by 0.6 percent of GDP to 2.8 percent of GDP in 2021 and remain near that level in the medium term, reflecting high corporate and household saving and weak investment in some large creditor economies. Japan's current account surplus is projected to widen by 0.3 percent of GDP to 3.6 percent of GDP in 2021, before stabilizing at just above 3 percent in the medium term, reflecting a high saving-investment balance of the private sector and a sizable income balance owing to the large net foreign asset position.
- *Emerging market and developing economies:* China's current account surplus is projected to decline by 0.2 percentage point of GDP, to 1.6 percent of GDP in 2021, as the effects of the decline in outbound travel, lower commodity prices, and a surge in pandemic-related exports wane, and converge toward

about 0.5 percent of GDP over the medium term, with continued rebalancing toward consumption-driven growth. Current account balances are projected to decline in other economies as domestic demand recovers (India, Indonesia, Mexico, Poland, South Africa) under current policies.

Numerous Uncertainties

The outlook for trade, currencies, and current account balances remains uncertain, with numerous risks, including in relation to the following broad areas.

- *Path and scarring impact of the pandemic:* A pandemic resurgence due to vaccine-resistant strains could result in a slower recovery of economic activity, global trade, and commodity prices than currently assumed. A more protracted pandemic could also extend or renew the aforementioned sectoral effects of the COVID-19 crisis on travel services, oil balances, medical goods, and household consumption composition, making them more persistent than currently expected. If the crisis has lasting negative (scarring) effects on growth in poorer economies, which the crisis has so far hit harder than richer ones (see the April 2021 WEO), this could dim their investment prospects, raise their current account balances toward surplus, and further weaken the downhill flow of capital from richer countries. Conversely, an expedited vaccine rollout, even in regions that are currently moving slowly, would improve investor and consumer sentiment, contribute to an unwinding of the crisis-induced changes in current account positions, and strengthen capital flows toward poorer countries.
- *Financial conditions:* A reassessment of market fundamentals in response to COVID-19 developments or an increase in sovereign yields or expected policy interest rates of major advanced economy central banks—including as a result of a faster-than-expected pickup in inflation—could cause financing difficulties, capital outflows, and currency depreciation for emerging market economies (see Chapter 4 of the April 2021 WEO on monetary policy spillovers during the recovery from the COVID-19 crisis). At the same time, most emerging market and developing economies have accumulated reserve buffers to withstand shocks (Figure 1.18), and the capital-flows-at-risk analysis

Figure 1.18. Emerging Market and Developing Economies: External Vulnerabilities

At the end of 2020, most emerging market and developing economies held sizable foreign exchange reserves, in excess of their short-term financing needs, measured by the sum of short-term debt and the current account deficit in 2020. Changes with respect to 2019 were mostly driven by increases in reserves. Vulnerabilities to capital flow reversals remained, given that the sum of portfolio and other investment liabilities exceeded reserves in most emerging market and developing economies.

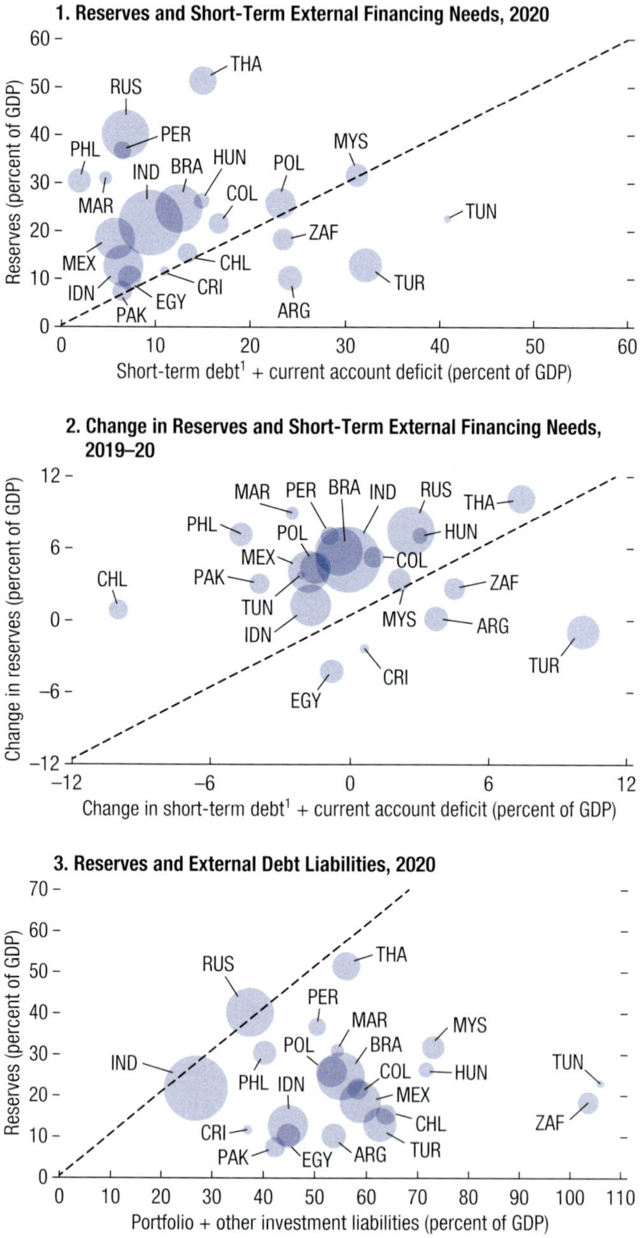

Sources: IMF, International Financial Statistics; IMF, World Economic Outlook; and IMF staff calculations

Note: Bubble sizes are proportional to US dollar GDP. Data labels use International Organization for Standardization (ISO) country codes.

[1]Short-term debt on a residual maturity basis. 2019 portfolio positions are reported when 2020 data are unavailable.

of the April 2021 *Global Financial Stability Report* suggests that risks of portfolio outflows are lower for economies with stronger fundamentals.

- *Fiscal policy path:* As discussed in Chapter 2, additional deficit-financed fiscal expansions by current account deficit economies, or a faster-than-expected pace of fiscal consolidation among current account surplus economies, could prevent the predicted narrowing in global balances over the coming years.
- *Cross-border integration:* Risks in this area include, in the near term, a proliferation of export curbs on vaccines and vaccine ingredients (Evenett and others 2021). A broader retreat from trade integration remains a risk that could thwart efforts to agree on a more open, stable, and transparent rules-based international trade system, including through a greater increase in protectionist measures and increased trade and foreign direct investment restrictions. Consequences would include a weakening in the recovery of global trade and of growth in poorer economies integrated into supply chains.

Box 1.5 considers alternative (out-of-baseline) scenarios that combine some of these risks, based on simulations of the IMF's G20 Model.

Policies for Escaping the Crisis and Promoting External Rebalancing

Ending the Pandemic

Ending the pandemic is a precondition for ensuring a lasting recovery in global economic well-being. It is also essential in order to avoid further divergence of economic recovery and capital flows between richer and poorer economies and long-term damage to trade, especially in services, and to pave the way for external rebalancing.

Many governments have already taken unprecedented action to fight the pandemic, as have such institutions as the World Health Organization, World Bank, Global Alliance for Vaccines and Immunization, and African Union. At the same time, as the IMF staff's recent proposal to end the pandemic (Agarwal and Gopinath 2021) emphasizes, up-front financing and vaccine donations and investments to diversify and increase vaccine production remain essential for handling downside risks, including from the spread of new virus variants. Grants, national government resources, and concessional financing are needed to pay for such investments and to ensure widespread testing and tracing, maintain adequate stocks of therapeutics, and enforce public health measures in places where vaccine coverage is low.

Fiscal policy should remain supportive until the recovery is firmly in place, conditional on available space, with programs targeted at the most affected sectors, aided by monetary accommodation, where possible. Facilitating a synchronized global investment push—including by ensuring that financially constrained economies have adequate access to international liquidity—could hasten the recovery and convergence to higher levels of per capita income with, as Chapter 2 explains, limited effects on global current account balances. At a time when financially constrained economies face difficult choices between meeting essential health and social spending needs, supporting their economies more broadly, and fulfilling obligations on external borrowing, the IMF's proposal for a General Allocation of Special Drawing Rights (SDRs) equivalent to US$650 billion will ease some of the constraints and help them better manage the trade-offs. Implementing clear health and safety protocols will complement these efforts by promoting a seamless return to contact-intensive sectors, including travel and tourism. Ensuring the continued resilience of remittance flows will require collecting timely and granular data and efforts to lower costs by offering incentives (such as subsidies) to remittance service providers and supporting innovative technologies and market competition (World Bank 2021).

Managing External Shocks and Capital Flows

Facing the risk of further external shocks, such as an unexpected increase in global interest rates as a result of a faster-than-expected pickup in inflation, countries should take advantage of favorable financing conditions to improve the composition of their debt structure (for example, by extending maturities and locking in the currently historically low interest rates) and reverse any departures from sound public debt management that may have occurred during the pandemic (for example, by reducing reliance on the domestic banking system). In the event that such shocks materialize, economies with flexible exchange rates should allow them to adjust as needed, where feasible. For economies that have built buffers with adequate reserves (Annex Table 1.1.1), exchange rate intervention can be appropriate to alleviate disorderly market conditions and limit financial stress, particularly where there are shallow foreign currency markets and large balance sheet mismatches. For some currencies, foreign exchange intervention may be used to partially mitigate appreciation pressure that would otherwise push the economy toward deflation, particularly during periods of economic weakness, but this should not preclude secular real appreciation.

Inflow capital flow management measures can be useful to manage surges in certain circumstances without substituting for warranted macroeconomic adjustments. Inflow measures can be useful, together with macroprudential tools, when the room for macroeconomic policy adjustment is limited, financial stability is at risk, or appropriate policy adjustments take time to be implemented and become effective. Capital flow management measures should be implemented in a transparent manner and should be temporary and targeted, while preferably avoiding discrimination by residency.

In imminent crisis circumstances, countries with limited reserves and facing reversals of external financing could use capital flow management measures on outflows as part of a broad package, provided they do not substitute for warranted macroeconomic and structural policy actions. In those cases, capital flow management measures would generally need to be broad-based and tightly enforced to effectively reduce capital outflows. If introduced, such measures should be implemented in a transparent manner, clearly communicated to the public, temporary, and eliminated once crisis conditions abate.

Resolving Trade Tensions

Countries have imposed numerous new export and import restrictions in 2020–21, data from the Global Trade Alert suggest, with a large share relating to medical products (Figure 1.19). WTO (2020) reports that the stock of new import restrictions in force has nearly tripled since 2016, now covering products representing nearly 10 percent of world imports. More than half of current export curbs in the medical goods and medicine sectors are scheduled to remain in place through the end of 2021, based on Global Trade Alert data. Such restrictions and policies, which encourage companies to repatriate their supply chains, could lead to retaliation in many countries across interlinked economic sectors and could slow the recovery. US-China trade distortions, including tariffs, introduced over the past four years, remain largely in place (Figure 1.20). The continued imposition of import tariffs and expanded preferences for domestic producers in procurement do not directly address the underlying drivers of external imbalances.

Figure 1.19. New Trade Restrictions, 2009–21

Countries have imposed numerous new export and import restrictions in 2020–21, with a large share relating to medical products. More than half of current export curbs in the medical goods and medicine sectors are scheduled to remain in place through the end of 2021.

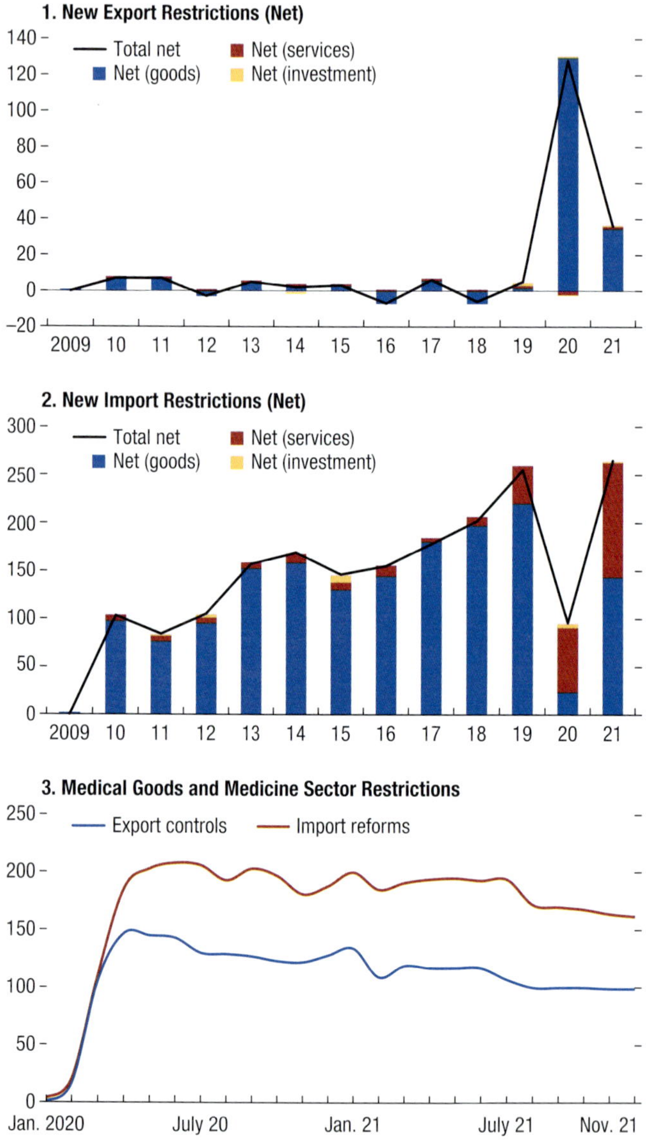

Source: Global Trade Alert (https://www.globaltradealert.org/).
Note: "Net" is defined as the difference between harmful and liberalizing interventions. Annual totals refer to numbers reported by May 25 each year. Export controls includes export restricting measures, while import reforms includes import liberalizing measures in the medical goods and medicine sectors. See Evenett (2021) for details.

Figure 1.20. US and Chinese Tariffs
(Percent)

US-China tariff increases introduced during 2019 and 2020 remain largely in place.

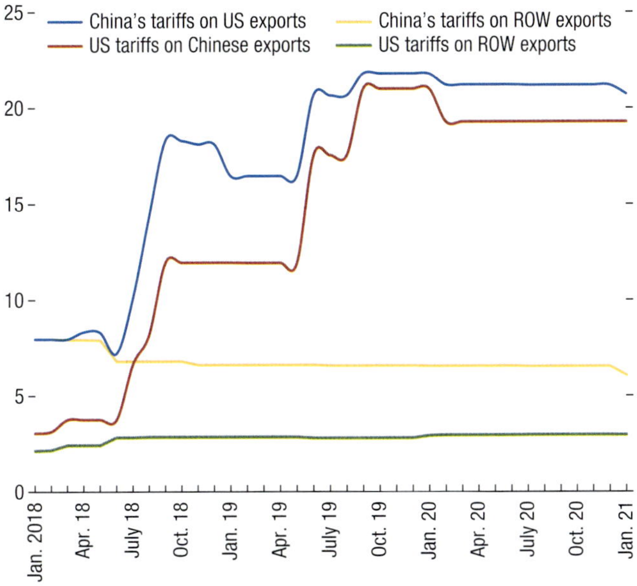

Source: Data collected by Chad Bown of the Peterson Institute for International Economics using China's Ministry of Finance announcements and United States Trade Representative announcements, available at (https://www.piie.com/research/piie-charts/us-china-trade-war-tariffs-date-chart).
Note: Trade-weighted average tariffs are computed from product-level tariff and trade data, weighted by US exports to the world and China's exports to the world in 2017. ROW = rest of the world.

Avoiding export curbs on vaccines and vaccine ingredients, rolling back restrictions to trade, and strengthening the rules-based multilateral trade system would sustain the recovery and strengthen cross-border supply chains, including for the production and provision of vaccines and medical goods. Further collaboration on phasing out tariff and nontariff barriers to trade, including in medical equipment and supplies, would be useful for addressing the present pandemic and help prepare for future health emergencies by ensuring versatile, diversified, and resilient supply chains for vital medical supplies.

Strong multilateral cooperation is also needed to resolve underlying trade and technology tensions as well as gaps in the rules-based multilateral trading system. Countries should work together to modernize rules to address underlying sources of conflict, including in the areas of technology transfer policies and practices, farm and industrial subsidies, and digital trade, and to modernize international taxation and measures to limit cross-border profit shifting. Ensuring a smoothly functioning international trade dispute settlement system, including by restoring effective WTO dispute settlement, would facilitate the resolution of such long-standing global trade and investment distortions.

Entangling trade and currency issues in international agreements and disputes poses significant risks to the multilateral trade and international monetary systems and should be avoided. In 2020, the previous US administration imposed currency-based countervailing duties on China and Vietnam. The adoption of currency-based countervailing duties is counterproductive for the country adopting such measures as, all else equal, it further appreciates its currency and can lead to retaliation by other countries. Furthermore, other countries might pursue a similar approach to link trade and currency, perhaps using their own standards and methodologies, with the potential for a broadening use of trade restrictions and a further increase in trade tensions. The threat of trade penalties could also impinge on monetary policy decisions and discourage exchange rate flexibility while complicating effective dialogue and analysis regarding the underlying structural and policy distortions affecting external positions, which is necessary to resolve trade tensions.

Promoting External Rebalancing

Following exceptional policy support to address the COVID-19 crisis in the near term, reforms can contribute to external rebalancing over the medium term in a number of ways in a manner conducive to sustained growth. Excessive current account imbalances can fuel trade tensions among countries, become targets for protectionist measures, and increase the likelihood of disruptive currency and asset price adjustments, with negative implications for global growth. Policies for fostering external rebalancing differ, based on individual economies' external positions and needs, as detailed in the Individual Economy Assessments in Chapter 3 and summarized in Annex Table 1.1.6. In particular,

- *Economies with weaker-than-warranted external positions:* Where excess current account deficits in 2020 partially reflected fiscal deficits above desirable medium-term levels (as in the United States) and where such imbalances persist, fiscal consolidation once the pandemic is over will be critical to support external rebalancing and bring the current account balance closer to its norm. It should, however, be implemented in a way that prevents long-term scarring from the crisis, including by protecting spending for infrastructure, health care, and education. In a number of emerging market and developing economies with weaker-than-warranted external positions in 2020, fiscal consolidation once the pandemic is over (such as in Argentina and South Africa) and a strong commitment to a firm monetary policy stance to help durably lower inflation and increase monetary policy credibility (Turkey) would also support raising international reserves to more adequate levels. Structural policies to increase productivity—and, in the case of commodity exporters (such as Saudi Arabia), diversification—would further support rebalancing. Countries with lingering competitiveness challenges would also need to address structural challenges, including through labor, product market, and other reforms, to promote green, digital, and inclusive growth.

- *Economies with stronger-than-warranted external positions:* In economies where excess current account surpluses persist, intensifying reforms that encourage investment and discourage excessive private saving is warranted. In economies with remaining fiscal space (such as Germany and The Netherlands), policies should avoid a rush to consolidate, thereby supporting the recovery with a growth-oriented fiscal policy, including through greater public sector investment in digitalization, infrastructure, and green transition, which would crowd in private investment, make the economy more resilient, and help narrow the excess current account surplus. In some cases, fostering corporate investment and using active labor market policies to facilitate sectoral transitions, with structural reforms focused on raising potential growth (as in Poland, where public investment is expected to rise, supported in part by Next Generation EU funds, and in Mexico), would also help reduce external imbalances. In some cases, reforms to discourage excessive precautionary saving by expanding social safety nets (Malaysia, Thailand) and tackling widespread informality (Thailand) would also help reduce excess current account surpluses.
- *Economies with external positions broadly in line with fundamentals:* In such cases, policies should continue to address domestic imbalances to prevent excessive external imbalances. Former excess surplus countries should, where relevant, address domestic imbalances by gradually narrowing larger-than-desirable fiscal deficits while boosting domestic private investment, including through state-owned enterprise reform, opening markets to more competition, and creating a more market-based and robust financial system (as in China). Former excess deficit countries (including Spain) should, where relevant, carefully manage the public debt load, boost competitiveness, and facilitate post–COVID-19 sectoral adjustment, including through continued wage flexibility, reforms to address labor market duality, product and service market reforms, and measures to enhance education outcomes and innovation.

As more data become available to assess the recovery from the pandemic, comprehensive and multilaterally consistent analysis will remain necessary to promote a shared understanding of underlying distortions and reforms needed to continue rebalancing the global economy.

Box 1.1. The Travel Shock

From March 2020 onward, government restrictions on cross-border travel and behavioral changes triggered by the COVID-19 pandemic have resulted in a collapse in world travel activity. Tourism revenues from overseas (and the corresponding expenditures overseas by domestic residents) declined by about two-thirds on average compared with the previous year, and by close to 75 percent in the last three quarters of the year. Cross-border travel was more severely affected than domestic tourism, reflecting unprecedented travel restrictions and, in some cases, a strong preference for traveling domestically (see EC 2021).

The most severe economic losses were concentrated in countries that traditionally rely heavily on revenues from overseas travelers. Among the 31 economies with an average net travel trade surplus exceeding 5 percent of GDP between 2015 and 2019 and with detailed balance of payments data currently available for 2020, the median decline in the net travel balance as a share of GDP compared with its average over the previous five years was about 12 percentage points, and was reflected in sharp declines in real exports and the services balance (Figure 1.1.1). Tourism-dependent countries are mostly small island economies (the median economy had a GDP of roughly US$8 billion and about 600,000 inhabitants in 2019). However, the group also includes larger economies such as Thailand, Portugal, Greece, the Dominican Republic, Panama, and Croatia. Among the eight small island economies belonging to the Eastern Caribbean Currency Union, the aggregate surplus in travel services declined from US$3.1 billion in 2019 (40 percent of GDP) to US$1.1 billion in 2020 (17 percent of GDP). Pacific islands have also been severely hit, with net tourism revenues falling by 90 percent in Fiji in 2020 compared with 2019 (about 13 percentage points of GDP).

The authors of this box are Gian Maria Milesi-Ferretti and Charlotte Sandoz.

The repercussions of the travel shock for economic activity in these economies were very severe: as shown in Milesi-Ferretti (2021) countries with a higher share of tourism revenues in GDP experienced a much sharper GDP decline in 2020 when compared with pre-pandemic forecasts, after controlling for the severity of the domestic pandemic.[1]

With the collapse in travel revenues, economies more dependent on tourism also experienced a sharp current account deterioration. However, the net effect of the travel shock on the current account balance was partially offset by its induced repercussions on the domestic economy (Figure 1.1.2). In particular, the decline in domestic demand and the reduced spending of tourists on imported goods (particularly important for small island economies) led to a sharp improvement in the trade balance on goods. At the same time, net investment income payments overseas declined, reflecting in particular the much-reduced income of foreign-owned hotels, leading to an improvement in the investment income balance.

Projections for economic developments during the next few years are subject to particularly high uncertainty, as they crucially depend on health-related factors, including the evolution of the pandemic, the speed of vaccination outside advanced economies, and so on. The forecasts published in the July 2021 *World Economic Outlook Update* envisage a still-substantial impact of the travel shock in 2021, particularly in emerging market and developing economies (such as Fiji, Seychelles, Thailand) considering the expected slow normalization of cross-border travel. Over the medium term, as the pandemic fades and borders reopen, the external balances of tourism-dependent economies are expected to gradually recover. On average, their current account balances are expected to revert to their pre-COVID trend by 2025 (Figure 1.1.2, panel 6).

[1]Milesi-Ferretti (2021).

Box 1.1 *(continued)*

Figure 1.1.1. Change in Current Account Balance in 2020 vs. Pre-pandemic Travel Share
(Percent of GDP)

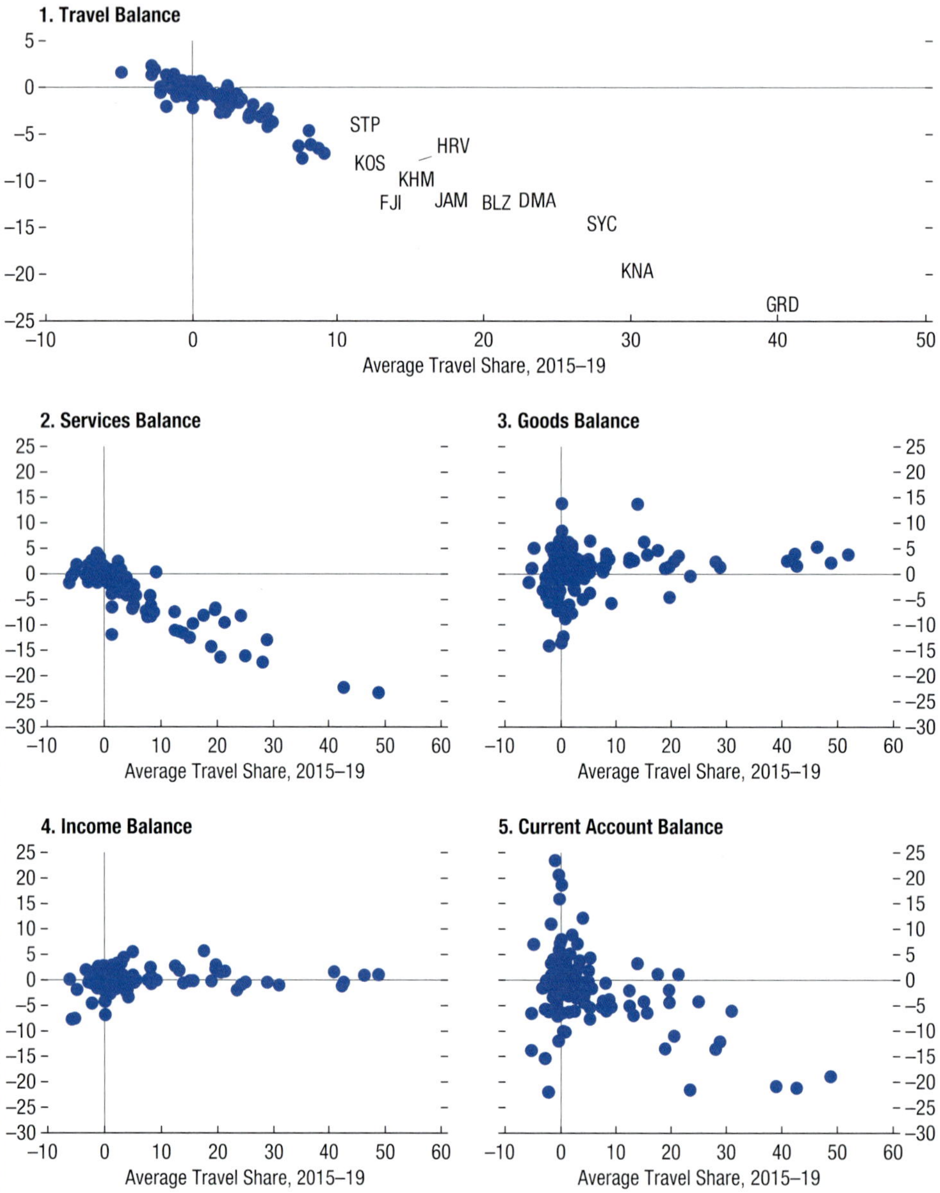

Sources: IMF, Balance of Payments Statistics; IMF, *World Economic Outlook*; and IMF staff calculations.
Note: Travel share is measured by the average net travel exports over GDP between 2015 and 2019. Change in balances in 2020 compared to 2019. Outliers are excluded based on Cook's distance. Data labels use International Organization for Standardization (ISO) country codes.

Box 1.1 *(continued)*

Figure 1.1.2. Predicted Level of Current Account Balances

(Deviation from precrisis trend)

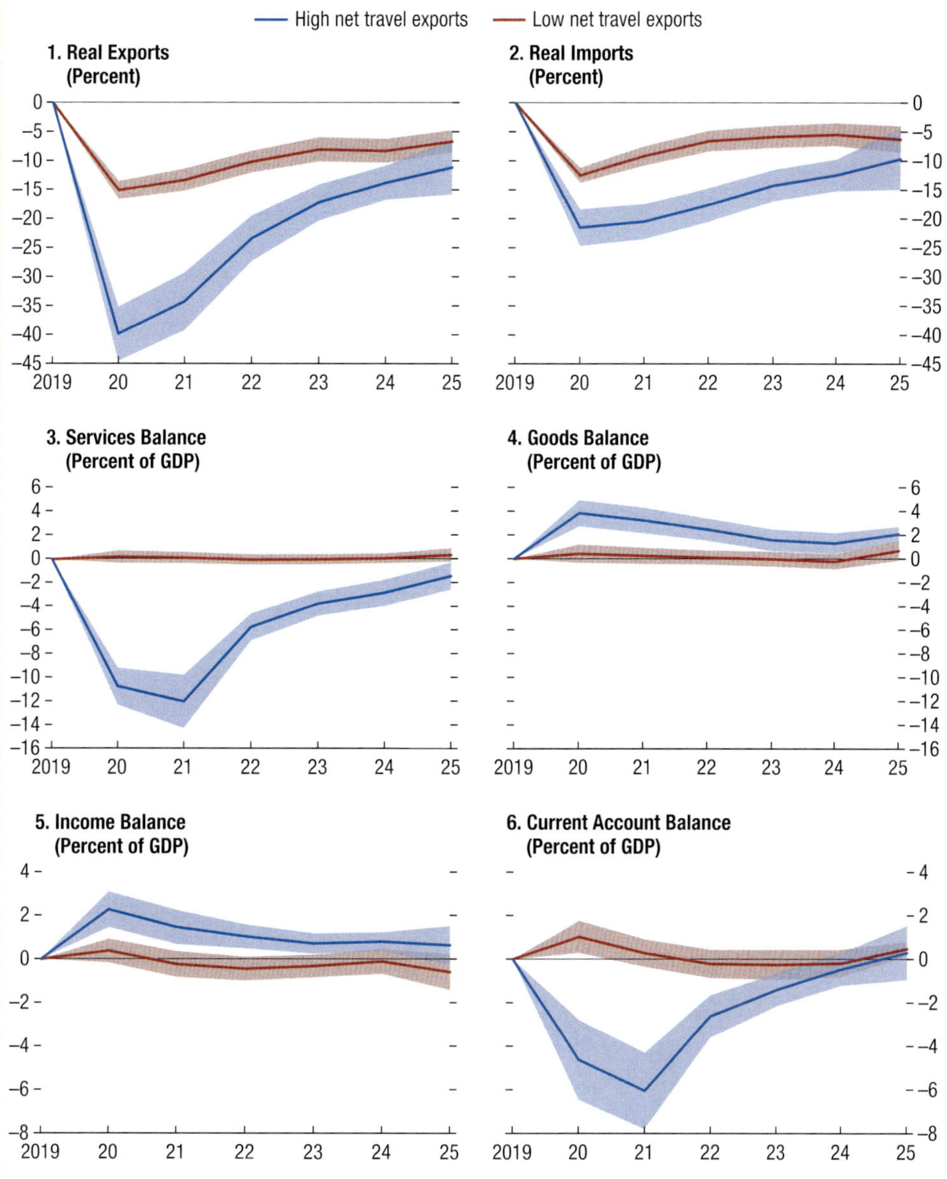

Sources: Eurostat; national authorities; Refinitiv Datastream; and IMF staff calculations.

Note: The figure shows the revision of balances in the latest *World Economic Outlook* (WEO) compared with before the crisis (January 2020 WEO Update). High net travel exports: economies with average net travel exports above 5 percent of GDP between 2015 and 2019. Shading indicates mean and 90 percent confidence interval. Outliers are excluded based on Cook's distance.

Box 1.2. The Household Saving Surge

Household saving increased sharply during the COVID-19 crisis, mainly in advanced economies, driven by lower consumption and increased disposable income from government transfers. It reflected both lockdown-induced saving and precautionary motives, with the effects differing markedly across countries and income groups.

Decomposition—income versus consumption: Household disposable income changed in response to two opposing forces. First, compensation of employees and other standard sources of income fell, reflecting the crisis and pandemic-related lockdowns. Second, government support to income increased, reflecting either higher social benefits or delayed payments of income taxes and social contributions, including via automatic stabilizers. Consumption cuts played an important role across countries in early 2020, but government transfer increases raised income by much more in the United States than elsewhere (Figure 1.2.1).

The authors of this box are Cian Allen and Cyril Rebillard.

Figure 1.2.1. Decomposing the Household Saving Surge: Disposable Income versus Consumption

(Percent of potential GDP)

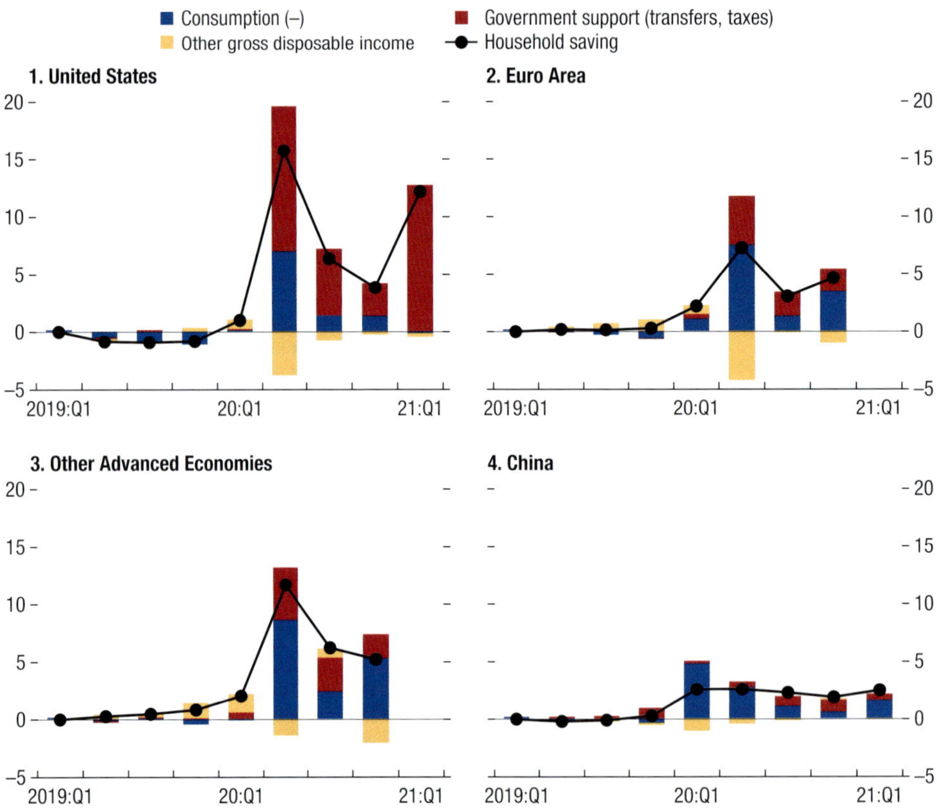

Sources: China, National Bureau of Statistics (household survey); Eurostat and national authorities (quarterly sector accounts);IMF, *World Economic Outlook*; and IMF staff calculations.

Note: Household saving and its components are shown as cumulated changes from 2019:Q1. Current taxes and transfers include taxes on income and wealth, social contributions, social benefits (especially government support), and other transfers. Other gross disposable income includes gross operating surplus and mixed income, compensation of employees, and net property income. Other advanced economies comprise Australia, Canada, the Czech Republic, Denmark, Norway, Slovenia, Sweden, and the United Kingdom. China's chart is based on household survey (rescaled to the whole economy), and may be less comparable to other charts based on national accounts.

Box 1.2 *(continued)*

Figure 1.2.2. Lockdowns versus Household Saving
(Percent of potential GDP)

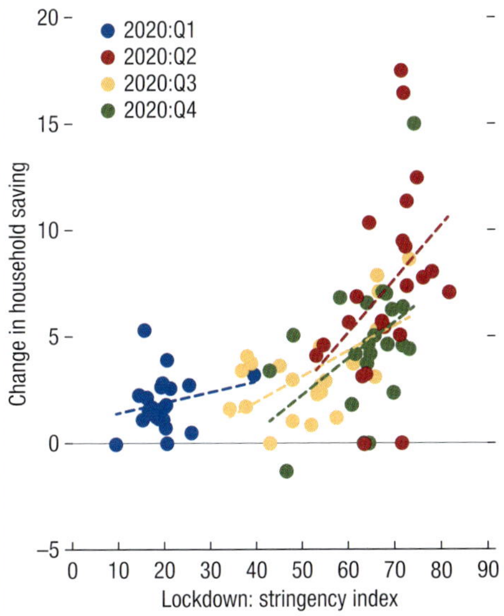

Sources: Eurostat; IMF, *World Economic Outlook*; national authorities (quarterly sector accounts); Stringency and Policy Indices, Oxford COVID-19 Government Response Tracker; and IMF staff calculations.
Note: Household saving is shown as cumulative changes from its 2019 average.

Figure 1.2.3. Unemployment Expectations versus Saving

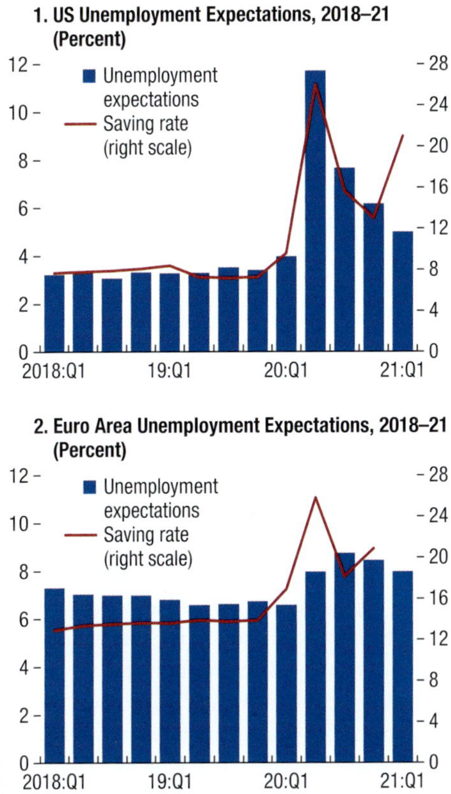

Sources: IMF, *International Financial Statistics*; IMF, *World Economic Outlook*; national authorities (customs data); and IMF staff calculations.
Note: Unemployment expectations are constructed following Carroll, Slacalek, and Sommer (2019) using fitted values from the regression of the four-quarter-ahead change in unemployment rate on the answer in the respective surveys on future unemployment.

Lockdowns and forced saving: The stringency of lockdowns was positively associated with household saving throughout the crisis, but the relationship seems to have weakened over time (Figure 1.2.2). This is consistent with the notion of "lockdown fatigue," which could include decreasing compliance over time with lockdown rules, as well as changing social patterns due to the pandemic, including working from home and greater use of e-commerce.

Unemployment risk and saving: The increase in household saving can also be partly explained by an increase in uncertainty regarding future labor market outcomes or the state of the economy, leading households to save more for precautionary reasons (in line with Mody, Ohnsorge, and Sandri 2012; Carroll, Slacalek, and Sommer 2019; and Coibion and others 2021). Indeed, household expectations about future unemployment risk (over a 12-month horizon) spiked in tandem with saving rates in both the United States and the euro area (see Figure 1.2.3).[1] In addition, surveys suggest that financial concerns have weighed on consumption (Christelis and others 2021). This could have important implications for the future path

[1]The indictors of household expectations about future unemployment are taken from Carroll, Slacalek, and Sommer (2019), constructed using the University of Michigan's Surveys of Consumers and the European Consumer survey for the euro area. Both indicators are based on answers to a question about households' expected level of unemployment in the coming 12 months.

Box 1.2 *(continued)*

of the household saving rate, as elevated uncertainty could still weigh on consumption, even as restrictions in the economy are lifted. While it is difficult to disentangle precautionary from forced saving, preliminary analysis in EU countries suggests that most of the early increase in saving was due to forced saving (Dossche and Zlatanos 2020). Additional statistical analysis for the United States based on an extension of Carroll, Slacalek, and Sommer (2019) confirms that, while unfavorable unemployment expectations can explain some of the increase in household saving in 2020, the impact of the fiscal expansion had a stronger effect on private saving. Indeed, while unemployment expectations decreased further in the United States in the first quarter of 2021(Figure 1.2.3), the saving rate rebounded, reflecting additional fiscal transfers as part of the American Rescue Plan Act of 2021.

Distribution of saving: While very little is known about how the increase in saving is distributed across households, studies based on credit card data show that it is likely concentrated at the top of the income distribution in nominal terms (see for instance Bachas and others 2020; Landais and others 2020). For the United States, the change in household net wealth by percentile, published by the Federal Reserve, can be used as a proxy for the distribution of saving (even though it also includes valuation effects).[2] While there was an overall increase in net wealth in percent of disposable income relative to before the pandemic (between the end of 2019 and the end of 2020), much of the benefit has accrued to people at the top of the distribution (with a large increase in corporate equities and mutual fund shares).

However, very little change in the distribution of wealth across groups was observed, given that changes in net wealth were in line with the pre-pandemic shares in the wealth distribution (see Figure 1.2.4, panel 2). In addition, the government response to the crisis may have contributed to an increase in saving by households at the top of the income distribution. For instance, Chetty and others (2020) show that the January 2021 stimulus payments substantially increased spending among lower-income households but had little impact on spending among higher-income households, in contrast with the April 2020 stimulus payments. These results are consistent with higher-income households having (1) a relatively smaller marginal propensity to consume than lower-income households; and (2) a larger share of their traditional consumption basket affected by lockdowns, including on travel and restaurant meals.

Figure 1.2.4. US Household Saving Increase, by Household Wealth Level

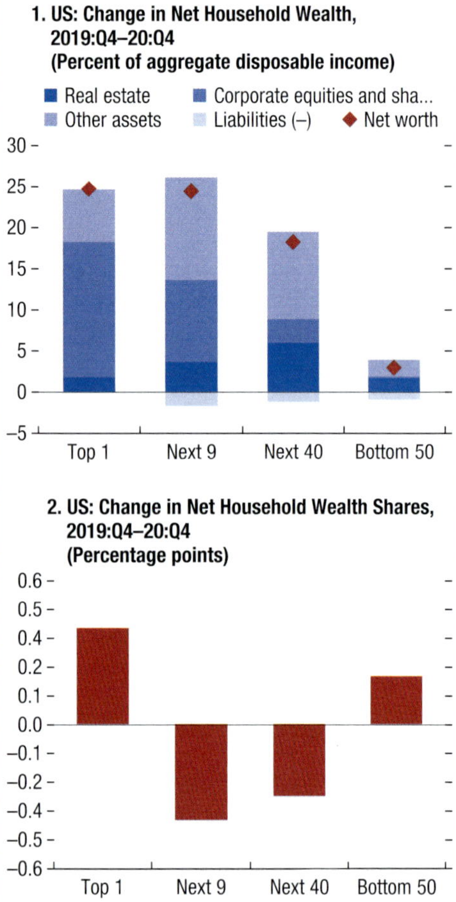

Sources: Federal Reserve, Distributional Financial Accounts; IMF, *International Financial Statistics*; IMF, *World Economic Outlook*; national authorities (customs data); and IMF staff calculations.
Note: Other assets include pension entitlement, private businesses, consumer durables, and other assets.

[2]The change in net household wealth is equal to the flow of saving plus valuation changes, especially changes in financial asset and real estate prices.

Box 1.3. Recessions and Current Account Movements

Unlike past severe economic downturns, the COVID-19 crisis has not reduced global balances—the absolute sum of current account deficits and surpluses. Global balances narrowed by about 1.5 percent of world GDP after the 2007–08 global financial crisis and the 1973–74 oil shock, but *widened* by 0.4 percent of world GDP in 2020 (Figure 1.3.1). Differences in precrisis external and internal imbalances, the high degree of synchronization of economic downturns across economies, and factors related to the nature of health crises explain this difference.

An analysis of 278 recessions in 49 advanced and emerging market and developing economies during 1960 to 2019 suggests that recessions typically raise an economy's current account balance by about 1.5 percent of GDP in a persistent manner, with lower investment and imports. Saving declines modestly, with government dissaving offsetting higher private saving (Figure 1.3.1, panels 2–4). But there are stark differences in the current account response, depending on underlying internal and external imbalances as well as the nature of the crisis.

Internal imbalances: Recessions associated with domestic imbalances, such as credit booms or higher public debt, come with sharper and more persistent current account adjustments than recessions in economies without such imbalances (Figure 1.3.2) and feature larger declines in investment and greater private saving. A similar finding holds for recessions associated with a financial crisis. Before the global financial crisis, private credit expansion and housing booms, including in the United States, and public borrowing in a number of European economies widened domestic imbalances, and the subsequent deleveraging fueled sustained narrowing in current account deficits. The COVID-19 shock, however, has not been accompanied by such financial sector turmoil and was not generally preceded by comparable levels of private or public sector borrowing in current account deficit economies. Accordingly, the investment response has

The author of this box is Christina Kolerus (with analysis based on Kolerus 2021).

Figure 1.3.1. External Accounts during Recessions
(Year on x-axis)

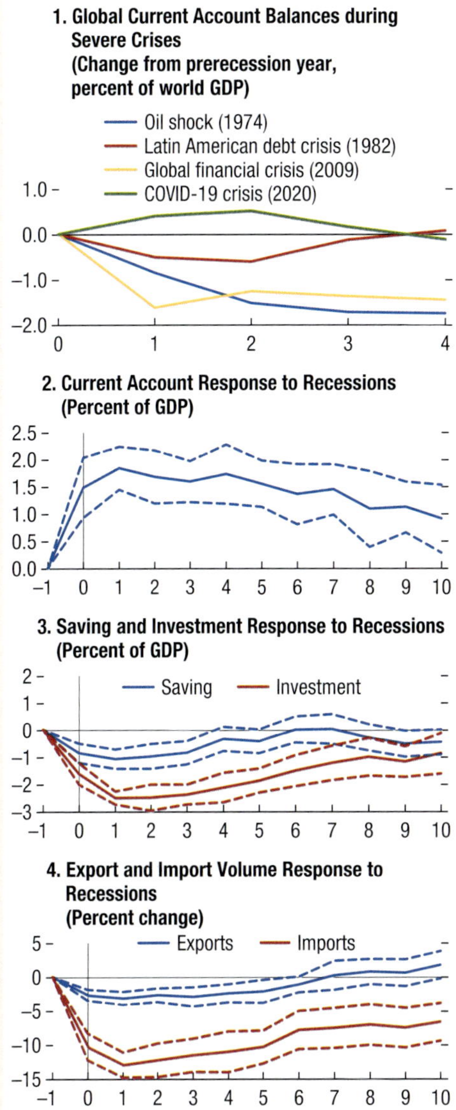

Sources: IMF, *World Economic Outlook*; and IMF staff calculations.
Note: Global imbalances are the absolute sum of surpluses and deficits. The figure reports estimated responses and 90 percent confidence bands derived from Jordà (2005) local projections. Recessions are defined as negative real GDP growth years.

Box 1.3 *(continued)*

Figure 1.3.2. Recessions and Credit Booms
(Percent of GDP; years on x-axis)

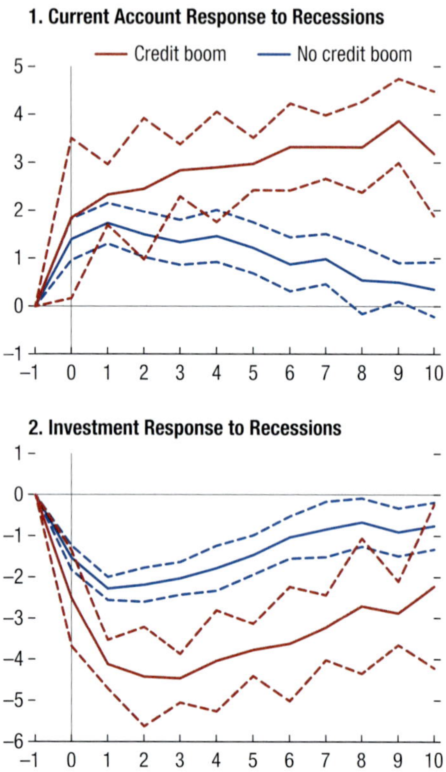

Source: IMF staff calculations.
Note: The figure reports estimated responses and 90 percent confidence bands derived from Jordà (2005) local projections. Recessions are defined as negative real GDP growth years. Credit booms are based on Dell'Ariccia and others (2020).

Figure 1.3.3. Recessions and Preexisting Deficits and Surpluses
(Percent of GDP; years on x-axis)

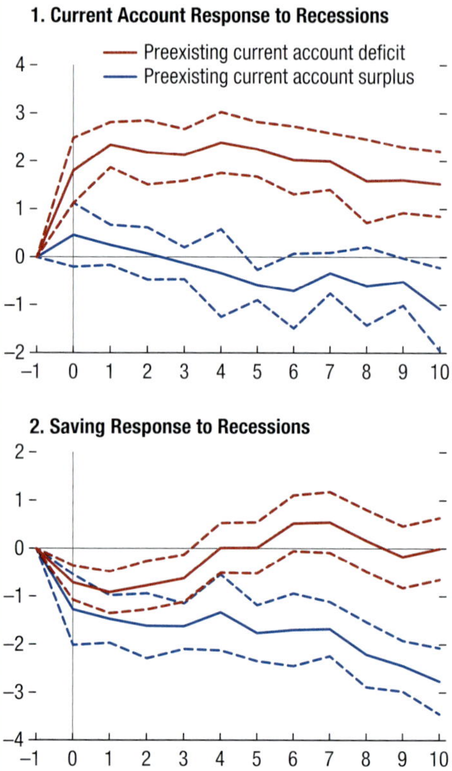

Source: IMF staff calculations.
Note: The figure reports estimated responses and 90 percent confidence bands derived from Jordà (2005) local projections. Recessions are defined as negative real GDP growth years.

been relatively modest during the COVID-19 crisis compared with the global financial crisis.

External imbalances: Economies with larger prerecession current account deficits typically experience sharper external adjustments than those with prerecession current account surpluses (Figure 1.3.3). This finding reflects a striking difference in saving responses: current account surplus economies draw down existing buffers, with significant dissaving during the recession and smaller declines in investment. These asymmetries explain why recessions are typically accompanied by a narrowing of global current account imbalances, as observed during the global financial crisis and other severe downturns. Additional analysis suggests that economies with higher external debt before the recession also experience sharper and more persistent current account adjustments. A similar finding holds for economies experiencing a sudden stop in capital flows. Current account deficits in the United States increased significantly in the run-up to the global financial crisis, as well as in many economies in Latin America and the Caribbean before the Latin American debt crisis. By contrast, for major economies, current account deficits and surpluses were smaller before the COVID-19 crisis.

Globally synchronized downturns, natural disasters, and pandemics: During previous globally synchronized downturns (with more than 25 percent of economies in recession), such as those associated with the 1973–74 oil crisis, the 1979 oil crisis, the

Box 1.3 *(continued)*

1982 Latin American debt crisis, and the 2007–08 global financial crisis, an economy's current account balance increased significantly less than during less globally synchronized recessions as exports fall in tandem with imports given declining domestic and global demand (Figure 1.3.4, panel 1). Large natural disasters or epidemics, which tend to affect an economy's supply side, tend to be associated with a decline in the current account balance, with import needs growing and exports declining (Figure 1.3.4, panel 2).

Overall, the COVID-19 crisis has been one of the most globally synchronized recessions on record, with the overwhelming majority of economies experiencing recession. Economies generally entered the 2020 crisis with fewer internal and external imbalances, and the source of the recession was a pandemic with sharp sectoral effects on travel, oil, medical products, and consumer goods. Together, these factors help explain the rise in global balances in 2020 instead of the sizable narrowing as in past global downturns.

Figure 1.3.4. Globally Synchronized Downturns and Epidemics
(Percent of GDP; years on x-axis)

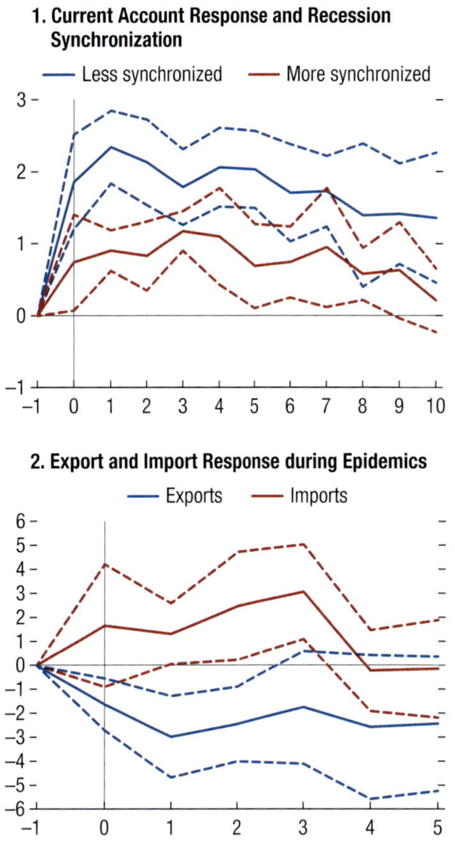

Source: IMF staff calculations.
Note: Less synchronized recessions correspond to episodes with <25 percent of countries in recession; more synchronized recessions correspond to >25 percent in recession. The figure reports estimated responses and 90 percent confidence bands derived from Jordà (2005) local projections. The sample period is 1870 to 2019; epidemics are those with high (90th percentile) impact. Responses are estimated using Cook's distance correction.

Box 1.4. External Assessments: Objectives and Concepts

Current account deficits and surpluses can be desirable from an individual country and global perspective. A country's ability to run current account deficits and surpluses at different times is important for absorbing country-specific shocks and facilitating a globally efficient allocation of capital. Some countries may need to save through current account surpluses (for example, because of an aging population); others may need to borrow via current account deficits (for example, to import capital and foster growth). Similarly, countries facing temporary positive (negative) terms-of-trade changes may benefit from saving (borrowing) to smooth out those income shocks. Thus, running a nonzero external current account balance is often desirable both from an individual country and a global standpoint.

To determine if current account balances are *excessive*, the IMF staff compares the actual current account (stripped of cyclical and temporary factors) to the level it assesses to be consistent with fundamentals and desirable policies. The resultant IMF staff–assessed gap reflects policy distortions vis-à-vis other economies identified using External Balance Assessment models as well as other policy and structural distortions not captured by the models.[1]

A current account balance that is *higher (lower)* than implied by fundamentals and desirable policies corresponds to a positive (negative) current account gap. Elimination of such a gap is desirable over the medium term, although there may be good reasons to have a temporary gap and to adjust gradually. These gaps can reflect domestic macroeconomic or structural policy distortions or similar policy distortions in the rest of the world (that is, foreign distortions).

Assessments also include a view of the real effective exchange rate (REER) that is normally consistent with the assessed current account gap. A positive (negative) REER gap implies an overvalued (undervalued) exchange rate. REER gaps do not necessarily predict future exchange rates and may occur in any economy, including in an economy with a floating exchange rate.

Although the overall assessment of a country's external position reflects the current account and real exchange rate in a given year, it also takes other indicators into consideration. These include the financial account balances, the international investment position, reserve adequacy, and other competitiveness measures, such as the unit-labor-cost-based REER. The overall external position is judged to be weaker (stronger) than warranted by fundamentals and desired policies depending on how low (high) the current account balance is compared with the IMF staff–assessed norm and how overvalued (undervalued) the REER is deemed to be. The external position is broadly in line with fundamentals and desired policies when the current account balance and the REER are at, or close to, their IMF staff–assessed norms. Assessments strive to be multilaterally consistent; negative IMF staff–assessed current account and REER gaps in some economies are matched by positive IMF staff–assessed gaps in others.

[1]See Cubeddu and others (2019) for a description of the External Balance Assessment models and complementary tools that help in applying analytically grounded judgment, as well as the external assessment process.

Box 1.5. Risk Scenarios: Implications for Trade and Current Account Balances

The IMF's G20 Model is used to illustrate the impact on trade and current account balances of two risk scenarios: (1) a new wave of COVID-19 in emerging market economies; and (2) faster vaccine distribution, particularly in emerging market economies. Results are presented in Figure 1.5.1 as deviations from the July 2021 WEO *Update* projections (the baseline) for advanced economies and emerging market economies.

Downside scenario—A new COVID-19 wave in emerging markets with additional financial tightening and scarring: The first scenario assumes that new, more infectious variants of COVID-19 generate an additional upsurge in infections in emerging market economies in late 2021. With vaccine supplies in many emerging markets increasing only gradually, mobility restrictions (mandated and voluntary) lead to slowing in growth in late 2021 and a more notable slowdown in 2022.

Although advanced economies experience some mild negative spillovers from the slower emerging market growth, inflation pressures prove to be more persistent than expected, and monetary policy normalization occurs faster than assumed in the baseline. This tightening, plus investor concern about emerging market prospects given the path of the virus, leads to a notable and persistent tightening in financial conditions in many emerging markets.

For emerging markets, the weaker growth and tighter financial conditions lead to more bankruptcies and additional persistent scarring on the supply side in many emerging market economies.

The combination of this negative supply-side impact and demand disruptions, as well as tighter global financial conditions, causes currency depreciation and a sharp contraction in imports peaking at –8 percent in 2022. Export capacity also contracts, but by less than imports, given the relatively resilient demand from advanced economies, resulting in an increase in the current account balance for emerging markets. For advanced economies, the negative spillovers from emerging markets depress exports, but, with relatively resilient overall demand, their current account balances decline.

Overall, the downside scenario exacerbates the increasingly unequal impact of the crisis, with a more divergent recovery and a further slowdown in capital flows from richer to poorer economies. At the same time, with a fall in current account balances occurring in both deficit and surplus advanced economies, there is little external rebalancing or widening in overall global current account balances.

Figure 1.5.1. Risk Scenarios: Implications for Trade and Current Account Balances
(Deviation from baseline)

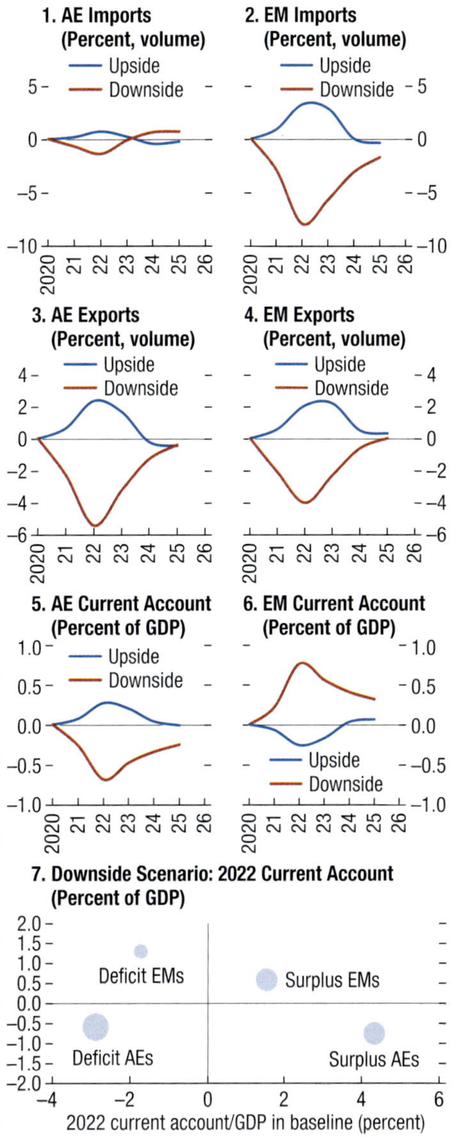

Sources: IMF, *World Economic Outlook*; and IMF staff estimates (G20 Model simulations).
Note: Size of bubbles based on GDP in US dollars. AEs = advanced economies; EMs = emerging market economies.

The authors of this box are Susanna Mursula and Daniel Leigh.

Box 1.5 *(continued)*

Upside scenario—Faster vaccine distribution, particularly in emerging market economies: In the second scenario, more concerted efforts to expand vaccine supply in emerging market economies leads to a faster normalization of mobility in late 2021 and into 2022, which allows for faster reopening of the high-contact sectors most affected by mobility restrictions. Growth rebounds above baseline mildly in 2021 and more notably in 2022. The faster recovery in emerging market economies helps unwind some of the scarring in the baseline in 2023 and beyond. Advanced economies experience positive trade spillovers from this faster recovery.

For emerging market economies, the faster recovery in domestic demand and easing of mobility restrictions, as well as the resulting increase in domestic interest rates and associated currency appreciation, raise import demand by about 3 percent by 2022. The faster recovery in supply in emerging markets, and the rise in global economic activity, raises exports in both emerging market and advanced economies by about 2 percent.

Overall, the faster recovery is associated with a decline in emerging market current account balances and a strengthening of capital flows from richer to poorer economies. At the same time, given the lack of correlation of emerging market economy status with current account surpluses or deficits, there is little impact on global current account balances.

Annex Table 1.1.1. Selected Economies: Foreign Reserves, 2017–20[1]

	Gross Official Reserves[2] (Billions of US Dollars)				Gross Official Reserves[2] (Percent of GDP)				IMF Staff-Estimated Change in Official Reserves[3] (Percent of GDP)				Gross Official Reserves in Percent of ARA Metric (2020)[4]	FXI Data Publication
	2017	2018	2019	2020	2017	2018	2019	2020	2017	2018	2019	2020		
Advanced Economies														
Australia	67	54	59	43	4.8	3.8	4.2	3.2	–0.1	0.1	–0.1	0.0	…	Yes/Daily
Canada	87	84	85	90	5.3	4.9	4.9	5.5	0.0	–0.1	–0.1	0.0	…	Yes/Monthly
Euro Area	803	823	914	1,078	6.3	6.0	6.8	8.3	0.1	0.3	0.1	0.1	…	Yes/Quarterly
Hong Kong SAR	431	425	441	492	126.4	117.4	120.7	141.9	9.3	0.6	1.7	0.4	…	Yes/Daily
Japan	1,264	1,270	1,322	1,391	25.6	25.2	25.7	27.5	0.3	0.5	0.5	–0.1	…	Yes/Monthly
Korea	389	403	409	443	24.0	23.4	24.8	27.1	0.7	0.1	0.1	1.1	99.0	Yes/Quarterly
Singapore	285	293	285	362	83.0	77.9	79.0	106.6	14.6	5.0	0.6	28.8	…	Yes/Semiannually
Sweden	62	61	56	59	11.5	10.9	10.4	10.9	0.0	–0.1	–1.3	0.1	…	Yes/Weekly
Switzerland	811	787	855	1,083	115.1	106.9	114.0	135.9	8.8	1.9	2.2	16.6	…	Yes/Quarterly
United Kingdom	151	173	174	180	5.7	6.0	6.1	6.6	0.4	0.8	–0.1	–0.1	…	Yes/Monthly
United States	451	450	517	628	2.3	2.2	2.4	3.0	0.0	0.1	0.0	0.0	…	Yes/Quarterly
Emerging Market and Developing Economies														
Argentina	55	66	45	39	8.6	12.8	10.1	10.3	2.3	–3.3	–8.5	–2.0	60.4	Yes/Daily
Brazil	374	375	357	356	18.1	19.5	19.0	24.8	0.3	–2.2	0.4	–2.4	160.8	Yes/Daily
China	3,236	3,168	3,223	3,357	26.4	22.9	22.5	22.6	1.1	0.1	–0.1	0.2	120.0	No
India	413	399	465	586	15.6	14.8	16.2	22.5	2.6	–1.3	2.5	4.4	197.2	Yes/Monthly
Indonesia	130	121	129	136	12.8	11.6	11.5	12.8	1.7	–1.4	0.7	0.5	121.4	No
Malaysia	102	101	104	108	32.1	28.3	28.4	30.6	0.7	–2.5	2.5	0.9	118.1	No
Mexico	175	176	183	199	15.1	14.4	14.4	18.5	–0.4	0.0	0.2	1.1	128.4	Yes/Monthly
Poland	113	117	128	154	21.5	19.9	21.5	25.9	–1.5	1.2	1.7	3.1	140.5	No
Russia	433	469	555	596	27.5	28.4	32.8	40.3	1.7	2.0	3.9	–0.9	360.7	Yes/Daily
Saudi Arabia	509	509	500	455	74.0	64.8	63.0	64.8	–5.8	0.1	0.6	–6.0	…	No
South Africa	51	52	55	55	14.5	14.0	15.7	18.2	0.4	–0.1	0.4	–0.3	74.4	No
Thailand	203	206	224	258	44.4	40.6	41.2	51.4	8.1	0.8	2.7	1.3	241.4	No
Turkey	108	93	106	93	12.5	11.9	13.9	13.0	–1.0	–1.5	–1.2	–10.8	73.5	Yes/Daily
Memorandum item:														
Aggregate[5]	10,703	10,674	11,191	12,242	13.2	12.4	12.8	14.4	0.5	0.1	0.2	0.3	…	…
AEs	4,801	4,821	5,117	5,850	5.9	5.6	5.9	6.9	0.2	0.2	0.1	0.3	…	…
EMDEs	5,902	5,852	6,074	6,392	7.3	6.8	7.0	7.5	0.3	–0.1	0.1	0.0	…	…

Sources: IMF, Assessing Reserve Adequacy data set; IMF, *International Financial Statistics* (IFS); IMF, International Reserves and Foreign Currency Liquidity (IRFCL); IMF, *World Economic Outlook* (WEO); and IMF staff calculations.

Note: "…" indicates that data are not available or not applicable. AEs = advanced economies; ARA = assessment of reserve adequacy; EMDEs = emerging market and developing economies; FX = foreign exchange; FXI = foreign exchange intervention.

[1] Sample includes *External Sector Report* economies excluding individual euro area economies. Euro area is reported as aggregate.

[2] Total reserves from IFS, includes gold reserves valued at market prices.

[3] This item is not necessarily equal to actual FXI, but it is used as an FXI proxy in External Balance Assessment model estimates. The estimated change in official reserves is equivalent to the change in reserve assets in the financial account series from the WEO (which excludes valuation effects, but includes interest income on official reserves) plus the change in off-balance-sheet holdings (short and long FX derivative positions and other memorandum items) from IRFCL minus net credit and loans from the IMF.

[4] The ARA metric reflects potential balance of payments FX liquidity needs in adverse circumstances and is used to assess the adequacy of FX reserves against potential FX liquidity drains (see IMF 2015). The ARA metric is estimated only for selected EMDEs and Korea, and includes adjustments for capital controls for China. For Argentina, the adjusted measure uses a four-year average to smooth the temporary effect of the sharp reductions in short-term debt and exports, and a collapse in the valuation of debt portfolio investments in the wake of the sovereign debt restructuring. Additional adjusted figures are available in the individual country pages in Chapter 3.

[5] The aggregate is calculated as the sum of *External Sector Report* economies only. The percent of GDP is calculated relative to total world GDP.

Annex Table 1.1.2. External Sector Report Economies: Summary of External Assessment Indicators, 2020

Economy	Overall Assessment	Current Account (Percent of GDP)		IMF Staff CA Gap (Percent of GDP)		IMF Staff REER Gap (Percent)		International Investment Position (Percent of GDP)			CA NFA Stabilizing (Percent of GDP)	SE of CA Norm (Percent)
		Actual	Cycl. Adj.	Midpoint	Range	Midpoint	Range	Net	Liabilities	Assets		
Argentina	Weaker	0.8	–0.5	–2.1	±1	5.0	±7.5	32	73	105	1.5	0.9
Australia	Broadly in line	2.5	2.4	0.9	±1	–3.0	±5	–53	224	171	–2.9	1.1
Belgium	Moderately weaker	–0.2	–0.1	–1.8	±1	4.3	±2.5	45	422	467	1.9	0.6
Brazil	Broadly in line	–1.7	–1.6	0.9	±0.5	–7.1	±7.5	–38	102	64	–1.9	0.8
Canada	Moderately weaker	–1.8	–1.3	–1.1	±1.5	3.9	±5.5	61	238	299	2.7	1.0
China	Broadly in line	1.8	1.7	0.7	±1.4	–0.5	±10	14	44	59	1.1	1.4
Euro Area[1]	Broadly in line	2.2	1.8	0.6	±0.8	–1.8	±2	1	268	268	0.0	0.8
France	Weaker	–1.9	–2.3	–2.2	±0.5	8.0	±2	–26	378	352	–1.2	0.6
Germany	Stronger	7.0	6.9	3.4	±1	–9.2	±5	76	232	308	3.2	0.9
Hong Kong SAR	Broadly in line	6.5	5.2	0.5	±1.5	–1.3	±4	621	1193	1814	. . .	. . .
India	Broadly in line	1.0	–0.8	1.0	±1	–6.3	±6.5	–13	46	33	–1.1	1.3
Indonesia	Broadly in line	–0.4	–0.8	0.7	±1.5	–1.0	±5	–27	65	38	–2.1	1.5
Italy	Broadly in line	3.5	2.5	0.1	±1	–0.3	±4	2	185	187	0.1	0.9
Japan	Broadly in line	3.3	3.2	–0.1	±1.2	0.7	±9	66	147	213	2.4	1.2
Korea	Broadly in line	4.6	4.3	–0.1	±1	0.2	±2.5	28	91	120	1.5	0.9
Malaysia	Substantially stronger	4.2	4.6	4.1	±1	–9.0	±2	5	130	135	0.4	0.8
Mexico	Stronger	2.4	1.7	2.8	±1	–21.8	±8	–55	118	63	–2.7	1.2
The Netherlands	Stronger	7.0	7.5	2.4	±2	–3.5	±3	114	1052	1166	5.2	0.9
Poland	Substantially stronger	3.5	3.9	4.9	±0.6	–11.1	±1.5	–46	103	58	–2.6	0.6
Russia	Moderately stronger	2.3	4.0	1.9	±1.5	–7.6	±6	34	71	105	1.6	1.5
Saudi Arabia	Moderately weaker	–2.8	–1.3	–1.5	±1.2	7.0	±6	89	76	165	. . .	. . .
Singapore	Substantially stronger	17.6	16.9	4.2	±3	–8.5	±6	308	1053	1361	. . .	. . .
South Africa	Moderately weaker	2.2	–0.1	–1.1	±1	4.0	±4	32	132	165	1.4	1.2
Spain	Broadly in line	0.7	–1.3	–0.7	±1	2.6	±4	–85	290	206	–3.8	0.8
Sweden	Stronger	5.7	6.4	3.8	±1.5	–8.0	±5	18	275	293	0.9	1.2
Switzerland	Broadly in line	3.8	3.9	–3.2	±2	6.2	±4	94	664	758	4.0	1.2
Thailand	Stronger	3.3	1.0	2.2	±1.5	–4.0	±2.5	11	109	120	0.7	1.5
Turkey	Moderately weaker	–5.1	–4.7	–1.2	±1.7	–20.0	±5	–56	90	34	–3.5	1.8
United Kingdom	Weaker	–3.5	–3.7	–2.4	±2	7.5	±7.5	–30	618	588	–1.4	0.7
United States	Moderately weaker	–2.9	–2.7	–1.6	±0.5	8.2	±3	–67	221	154	–3.1	0.9

Sources: IMF, *International Financial Statistics*; IMF, *World Economic Outlook*; US Bureau of Economic Analysis; and IMF staff assessments.

Note: CA = current account; Cycl. Adj. = cyclically adjusted; NFA = net foreign assets; SE = standard error; REER = real effective exchange rate.

[1]The IMF staff–assessed euro area CA gap is calculated as the GDP-weighted averages of IMF staff–assessed CA gaps for the 11 largest euro area economies.

Annex Table 1.1.3. External Sector Report Economies: Summary of IMF Staff–Assessed Current Account Gaps and IMF Staff Adjustments, 2020

(Percent of GDP)

							IMF Staff Adjustments[3]				
									Other		
Economy	Assessment 2020	Actual CA Balance [A]	Cycl. Adj. CA Balance [B]	EBA CA Norm [C]	EBA CA Gap[1] [D=B–C]	IMF Staff-Assessed CA Gap[2] [E=D+F]	Total [F=G+H-I]	Covid-19 [G]	CA [H]	Norm [I]	Comments on Non–COVID-19-related Adjustments
Argentina	Weaker	0.8	–0.5	–1.3	0.8	–2.1	–2.9	–0.5	0.0	2.4	NIIP/financing risk considerations
Australia	Broadly in line	2.5	2.4	–0.1	2.6	0.9	–1.7	–1.7	0.0	0.0	
Belgium	Moderately weaker	–0.2	–0.1	1.4	–1.5	–1.8	–0.3	–0.3	0.0	0.0	
Brazil	Broadly in line	–1.7	–1.6	–2.4	0.8	0.9	0.1	0.1	0.0	0.0	
Canada	Moderately weaker	–1.8	–1.3	2.5	–3.8	–1.1	2.7	0.8	1.5	–0.4	Measurement biases (CA); demographics (norm)
China	Broadly in line	1.8	1.7	–0.3	1.9	0.7	–1.2	–1.2	0.0	0.0	
Euro Area[4]	Broadly in line	2.2	1.8	1.0	0.8	0.6	–0.1	0.2	–0.1	0.3	Country-specific adjustments
France	Weaker	–1.9	–2.3	0.2	–2.5	–2.2	0.4	0.4	0.0	0.0	
Germany	Stronger	7.0	6.9	2.6	4.3	3.4	–0.9	–0.6	0.0	0.4	Demographics (uncertainty related to large and sudden immigration)
India	Broadly in line	1.0	–0.8	–2.4	1.7	1.0	–0.6	–0.6	0.0	0.0	
Indonesia	Broadly in line	–0.4	–0.8	–0.5	–0.3	0.7	0.9	0.0	0.0	–0.9	Demographics (high mortality risk)
Italy	Broadly in line	3.5	2.5	2.8	–0.3	0.1	0.4	0.4	0.0	0.0	
Japan	Broadly in line	3.3	3.2	3.6	–0.4	–0.1	0.3	0.3	0.0	0.0	
Korea	Broadly in line	4.6	4.3	3.5	0.8	–0.1	–0.9	–0.9	0.0	0.0	
Malaysia	Substantially stronger	4.2	4.6	–0.6	5.2	4.1	–1.0	–0.2	–0.8	0.0	One-off large transaction in the income balance
Mexico	Stronger	2.4	1.7	–1.9	3.6	2.8	–0.8	–0.5	–0.3	0.0	Effects of trade diversion
The Netherlands	Stronger	7.0	7.5	3.4	4.0	2.4	–1.6	–0.2	–1.4	0.0	Measurement biases
Poland	Substantially stronger	3.5	3.9	–2.1	6.0	4.9	–1.1	–1.1	0.0	0.0	
Russia	Moderately stronger	2.3	4.0	3.2	0.8	1.9	1.1	1.1	0.0	0.0	
South Africa	Moderately weaker	2.2	–0.1	1.6	–1.7	–1.1	0.6	–1.8	1.4	–1.0	SACU transfers and measurement biases (CA); demographics (high mortality risk, norm)
Spain	Broadly in line	0.7	–1.3	0.3	–1.6	–0.7	0.9	2.4	0.0	1.5	NIIP/financing risk considerations
Sweden	Stronger	5.7	6.4	1.3	5.1	3.8	–1.2	–1.2	0.0	0.0	
Switzerland	Broadly in line	3.8	3.9	5.6	–1.7	–3.2	–1.5	1.9	–3.4	0.0	Measurement biases
Thailand	Stronger	3.3	1.0	1.2	–0.2	2.2	2.4	2.4	0.0	0.0	
Turkey	Moderately weaker	–5.1	–4.7	–1.5	–3.3	–1.2	2.1	1.1	1.0	0.0	Temporarily high demand for gold imports (uncertainty)

(*Continued*)

Annex Table 1.1.3. *(continued)*

Economy	Assessment 2020	Actual CA Balance [A]	Cycl. Adj. CA Balance [B]	EBA CA Norm [C]	EBA CA Gap[1] [D=B–C]	IMF Staff-Assessed CA Gap[2] [E=D+F]	IMF Staff Adjustments[3] Total [F=G+H-I]	Covid-19 [G]	Other CA [H]	Other Norm [I]	Comments on non–COVID-19-related adjustments
United Kingdom	Weaker	–3.5	–3.7	–0.4	–3.3	–2.4	0.9	0.3	0.6	0.0	Measurement biases
United States	Moderately weaker	–2.9	–2.7	–0.5	–2.2	–1.6	0.5	0.5	0.0	0.0	
Hong Kong SAR	Broadly in line	6.5	5.2	. . .	. . .	0.5	. . .	. . .	. . .	. . .	
Singapore	Substantially stronger	17.6	16.9	. . .	. . .	4.2	. . .	. . .	. . .	. . .	
Saudi Arabia	Weaker	–2.8	–1.3	. . .	. . .	–1.5	. . .	. . .	. . .	. . .	
Absolute sum of excess surpluses and deficits[5]		. . .	. . .	. . .	1.7	1.2	. . .	. . .	. . .	. . .	
Discrepancy for all EBA/ESR economies[6]		. . .	. . .	. . .	. . .	0.0	. . .	. . .	. . .	. . .	
Of which: ESR economies		. . .	. . .	. . .	. . .	–0.1	. . .	. . .	. . .	. . .	
Of which: Non-ESR economies		. . .	. . .	. . .	. . .	0.1	. . .	. . .	. . .	. . .	

Source: IMF staff estimates.

Note: CA = current account; Cycl. Adj. = cyclically adjusted; EBA = external balance assessment; ESR = *External Sector Report*; NIIP = net international investment position; SACU = Southern African Customs Union. ". . ." indicates that data are not available or not applicable.

[1]Figures may not add up due to rounding effects.

[2]Refers to the midpoint of the IMF staff–assessed CA gap.

[3]Total IMF staff adjustments include rounding in some cases. See Online Annex 1.1 for a description of COVID-19 adjustors.

[4]The EBA euro area CA norm is calculated as the GDP-weighted average of norms for the 11 largest euro area economies, adjusted for reporting discrepancies in intra-area transactions. The IMF staff–assessed CA gap is calculated as the GDP-weighted average of IMF staff–assessed gaps for the 11 largest euro area economies.

[5]Sum of absolute value of IMF staff CA gaps in percent of aggregate GDP for economies included in the ESR exercise.

[6]Sum of IMF staff–assessed CA gaps in percent of aggregate GDP for economies included in the EBA and/or ESR exercise.

Annex Table 1.1.4. External Sector Report Economies: Summary of IMF Staff–Assessed Real Effective Exchange Rate and External Balance Assessment Model Gaps, 2020

Economy	IMF Staff-Assessed REER Gap[1]	REER Gap Implied from IMF Staff-Assessed CA Gap[2]	EBA REER-Level Gap	EBA REER-Index Gap	CA/REER Elasticity[3]	REER (Percent Change) Average 2020/ Average 2019	May 2021/ Average 2020
Argentina	5.0	15.3	. . .	−2.9	0.14	2.3	0.9
Australia	−3.0	−4.5	9.8	−2.1	0.20	−0.8	8.2
Belgium	4.3	4.3	18.2	9.6	0.42	1.4	0.3
Brazil	−7.1	−7.1	−21.3	−36.6	0.13	−20.6	−3.5
Canada	3.9	3.9	−6.5	2.6	0.28	−1.1	7.5
China	−0.5	−3.1	13.0	−0.3	0.23	2.1	3.0
Euro Area	−1.8	−1.8	−0.6	5.3	0.35	2.1	1.7
France	8.0	8.0	2.9	−2.3	0.27	1.0	0.3
Germany	−9.2	−9.2	−15.4	5.6	0.37	1.3	1.8
India	−6.3	−6.3	6.6	10.9	0.17	0.4	−1.8
Indonesia	−1.0	−3.9	−11.6	2.1	0.17	−1.3	−2.1
Italy	−0.3	−0.3	2.5	7.7	0.25	0.5	0.6
Japan	0.7	0.7	−12.0	−20.2	0.13	0.9	−8.7
Korea	0.2	0.2	−12.0	−3.7	0.36	−1.9	0.8
Malaysia	−9.0	−9.0	−42.0	−31.5	0.46	−3.6	−1.0
Mexico	−21.8	−21.8	−10.0	−20.9	0.13	−7.6	7.0
The Netherlands	−3.5	−3.5	4.2	17.8	0.70	2.0	0.6
Poland	−11.1	−11.1	−19.1	−2.7	0.44	0.7	1.0
Russia	−7.6	−7.6	−20.8	−12.3	0.25	−7.4	−3.8
South Africa	4.0	4.0	−10.5	−20.9	0.28	−9.2	13.2
Spain	2.6	2.6	4.0	6.2	0.28	0.5	1.4
Sweden	−8.0	−10.9	−16.8	−18.4	0.35	2.4	3.4
Switzerland	6.2	6.2	26.4	15.4	0.52	3.8	−2.9
Thailand	−4.0	−4.0	−5.2	10.8	0.56	−2.6	−3.7
Turkey	−20.0	4.9	−30.8	−34.5	0.24	−10.0	−9.0
United Kingdom	7.5	10.0	−3.8	−12.2	0.24	0.2	4.1
United States	8.2	8.2	12.4	8.3	0.20	1.4	−3.9
Hong Kong SAR	−1.3	−1.3	. . .	. . .	0.40	−0.6	−5.0
Singapore	−8.5	−8.4	. . .	. . .	0.50	−2.6	−0.3
Saudi Arabia	7.0	. . .	. . .	. . .	0.20	2.5	−2.3
Discrepancy[4]	1.1	. . .	. . .	. . .	. . .	. . .	. . .

Sources: IMF, Information Notice System; and IMF staff estimates.
Note: CA = current account; EBA = External Balance Assessment; REER = real effective exchange rate. ". . ." indicates that data are not available or not applicable.
[1]Refers to the midpoint of the IMF staff-assessed REER gap.
[2]Implied REER gap = −(IMF staff-assessed CA gap/CA-to-REER elasticity).
[3]CA-to-REER semi-elasticity used by IMF country teams.
[4]GDP-weighted average sum of IMF staff-assessed REER gaps.

Annex Table 1.1.5. Selected External Sector Report Economies: External Balance Assessment Current Account Regression Policy Gap Contributions, 2020

(Percent of GDP)

	EBA Gap				Fiscal Gap					Public Health Expenditure Gap					Private Credit Gap					Foreign Exchange Intervention Gap					Other (K-Controls)	
						Domestic					Domestic					Domestic					Domestic					
Economy	Total[1]	Identified	Dom[2]	Residual	Total[1]	Dom[3]	Coeff	P	P*	Total[1]	Dom[3]	Coeff	P	P*	Total[1]	Dom[3]	Coeff	P	P*	Total[1]	Dom[3]	Coeff	P	P*	Total[1]	Dom[3]
Argentina	0.8	0.2	–2.0	0.6	2.1	–0.3	0.3	–2.5	–1.5	–0.1	0.0	–0.4	6.5	6.5	0.1	0.1	–0.1	–0.5	0.0	–1.5	–1.5	0.8	–2.0	1.0	–0.4	–0.3
Australia	2.6	–0.6	–2.8	3.1	–0.6	–3.0	0.3	–9.1	0.0	–0.1	0.0	–0.4	7.0	6.9	0.3	0.2	–0.1	–2.3	0.0	0.0	0.0	0.8	0.0	0.0	–0.1	0.0
Belgium	–1.5	–0.6	–2.8	–0.9	0.3	–2.1	0.3	–9.4	–2.9	–0.2	–0.1	–0.4	7.9	7.7	–0.6	–0.6	–0.1	6.2	0.0	0.0	0.0	0.8	–0.1	0.0	–0.1	0.0
Brazil	0.8	–0.5	–2.7	1.3	–0.6	–3.0	0.3	–12.6	–3.5	0.1	0.2	–0.4	3.9	4.4	0.4	0.4	–0.1	–3.5	0.0	–0.5	–0.5	0.8	–2.4	0.0	0.0	0.1
Canada	–3.8	–1.3	–3.5	–2.5	–0.5	–2.9	0.3	–9.5	–0.7	–0.5	–0.4	–0.4	8.1	7.0	–0.1	–0.1	–0.1	1.4	0.0	0.0	0.0	0.8	0.0	0.0	–0.1	0.0
China	1.9	0.0	–2.2	2.0	–0.2	–2.6	0.3	–9.9	–2.0	0.2	0.2	–0.4	3.4	4.0	–0.3	–0.4	–0.1	3.9	0.0	0.0	0.1	0.8	0.2	0.0	0.3	0.4
Euro Area[4]	0.8	0.6	–1.6	0.2	1.1	–1.4	0.3	–5.0	–0.9	–0.1	0.0	–0.4	8.2	8.2	–0.2	–0.2	–0.1	1.2	–0.8	0.0	0.0	0.8	0.0	0.0	–0.1	0.0
France	–2.5	–0.3	–2.5	–2.2	0.7	–1.7	0.3	–6.6	–1.5	–0.2	–0.1	–0.4	9.3	9.1	–0.7	–0.8	–0.1	7.4	0.0	0.0	0.0	0.8	0.2	0.0	–0.1	0.0
Germany	4.3	0.6	–1.6	3.8	1.6	–0.8	0.3	–2.9	–0.5	–0.2	–0.1	–0.4	9.8	9.6	–0.7	–0.8	–0.1	6.4	–1.0	0.0	0.0	0.8	0.0	0.0	–0.1	0.0
India	1.7	3.7	1.5	–2.0	1.1	–1.3	0.3	–9.7	–5.8	–0.1	0.0	–0.4	1.5	1.6	0.5	0.4	–0.1	–4.1	0.0	1.6	1.6	0.8	4.4	0.0	0.5	0.7
Indonesia	–0.3	2.4	0.2	–2.6	1.6	–0.8	0.3	–5.0	–2.5	0.5	0.6	–0.4	1.6	3.0	0.0	–0.1	–0.1	0.7	0.0	0.1	0.1	0.8	0.5	0.0	0.2	0.3
Italy	–0.3	0.8	–1.4	–1.1	0.1	–2.3	0.3	–6.4	0.5	0.0	0.1	–0.4	6.6	6.8	0.8	0.8	–0.1	–7.5	0.0	0.0	0.0	0.8	0.2	0.0	–0.1	0.0
Japan	–0.4	–2.0	–4.2	1.6	–0.8	–3.2	0.3	–9.8	–0.1	–0.1	0.0	–0.4	9.1	9.1	–0.9	–1.0	–0.1	9.5	0.0	0.0	0.0	0.8	–0.1	0.0	–0.1	0.0
Korea	0.8	1.5	–0.7	–0.7	1.9	–0.5	0.3	–1.5	0.0	0.3	0.4	–0.4	4.9	5.8	–0.5	–0.6	–0.1	5.5	0.0	0.0	0.0	0.8	1.1	0.0	–0.1	0.0
Malaysia	5.2	2.5	0.3	2.7	1.7	–0.7	0.3	–4.6	–2.6	0.7	0.8	–0.4	2.0	4.1	–0.1	–0.2	–0.1	1.9	0.0	0.2	0.3	0.8	0.9	0.0	–0.1	0.1
Mexico	3.6	2.6	0.4	1.0	2.2	–0.3	0.3	–3.3	–2.5	0.3	0.3	–0.4	2.7	3.6	–0.2	–0.2	–0.1	2.3	0.0	0.3	0.3	0.8	1.1	0.0	0.1	0.2
The Netherlands	4.0	2.9	0.7	1.1	1.7	–0.7	0.3	–3.2	–1.0	0.1	0.2	–0.4	8.2	8.8	1.3	1.2	–0.1	–12.0	0.0	0.0	0.0	0.8	–0.1	0.0	–0.1	0.0
Poland	6.0	2.2	–0.1	3.9	1.1	–1.3	0.3	–5.9	–2.0	0.1	0.2	–0.4	4.9	5.4	0.5	0.4	–0.1	–4.1	0.0	0.5	0.6	0.8	3.1	0.0	–0.1	0.0
Russia	0.8	1.4	–0.8	–0.6	0.3	–2.1	0.3	–4.5	2.0	0.7	0.8	–0.4	3.5	5.5	0.8	0.7	–0.1	–6.7	0.0	–0.2	–0.2	0.8	–0.9	0.0	–0.1	0.0
South Africa	–1.7	0.2	–2.0	–1.9	0.6	–1.8	0.3	–6.6	–1.0	–0.1	0.0	–0.4	4.2	4.1	0.2	0.1	–0.1	–1.3	0.0	–0.4	–0.4	0.8	–0.3	3.0	0.0	0.2
Spain	–1.6	0.8	–1.4	–2.4	1.3	–1.1	0.3	–5.8	–2.5	–0.1	0.0	–0.4	6.3	6.3	–0.3	–0.3	–0.1	1.0	–2.0	0.0	0.0	0.8	0.0	0.0	–0.1	0.0
Sweden	5.1	0.7	–1.5	4.4	1.0	–1.4	0.3	–4.0	0.3	–0.2	–0.1	–0.4	9.3	9.0	0.1	0.0	–0.1	0.0	0.0	0.0	0.0	0.8	0.1	0.0	–0.1	0.0
Switzerland	–1.7	1.1	–1.1	–2.8	2.1	–0.3	0.3	–1.9	–1.0	–0.2	–0.1	–0.4	7.8	7.5	–0.7	–0.7	–0.1	7.1	0.0	0.0	0.0	0.8	16.6	0.0	–0.1	0.0
Thailand	–0.2	1.3	–0.9	–1.5	1.2	–1.3	0.3	–3.1	0.7	0.0	0.1	–0.4	3.8	4.1	–0.3	–0.4	–0.1	3.9	0.0	0.3	0.4	0.8	1.3	0.0	0.1	0.3
Turkey	–3.3	–4.1	–6.3	0.8	2.3	–0.1	0.3	–4.7	–4.3	0.0	0.0	–0.4	3.5	3.6	–3.0	–3.1	–0.1	30.0	0.0	–3.2	–3.2	0.8	–10.8	1.2	0.0	0.1
United Kingdom	–3.3	1.6	–0.6	–4.8	–0.3	–2.7	0.3	–11.3	–3.0	–0.1	0.0	–0.4	7.8	7.8	2.2	2.1	–0.1	–20.3	0.0	0.0	0.0	0.8	–0.1	0.0	–0.1	0.0
United States	–2.2	–1.2	–3.4	–1.0	–1.2	–3.6	0.3	–11.0	–0.2	–0.1	0.0	–0.4	8.4	8.4	0.2	0.2	–0.1	–1.8	0.0	0.0	0.0	0.8	0.0	0.0	–0.1	0.0

Source: IMF staff estimates.

Note: EBA = External Balance Assessment; K-controls = capital controls; Dom = domestic; Coeff = coefficient.

[1]Total contribution after adjusting for multilateral consistency.

[2]Includes the contribution of domestic policy gaps to the identified gap. The total foreign policy gap contribution is constant and equal to 2.4 percent for all countries. Foreign contributions are estimated as follows: fiscal = 2.6 percent of GDP; public health = –0.1 percent of GDP; private credit = –0.1 percent of GDP; foreign exchange intervention = 0.0 percent of GDP.

[3]Total domestic contribution is equivalent to coefficient*(P-P*).

[4]The euro area EBA CA gap and policy gap contributions are calculated as the GDP-weighted averages of EBA CA gaps and policy gap contributions for the 11 largest euro area economies.

Annex Table 1.1.6. 2020 Individual Economy Assessments: Summary of Policy Recommendations

Economy	Overall 2020 Assessment	Policy Recommendations
Argentina	Weaker	Implement growth-friendly fiscal consolidation and prudent monetary policies to maintain strong trade surplus, rebuild international reserves, and regain market access; introduce reforms to strengthen competitiveness and export capacity.
Australia	Broadly in line	Maintain adequate monetary and fiscal policy support, including scaling up public investment, to promote domestic demand and keep the external position in line with fundamentals.
Belgium	Moderately weaker	Strengthen competitiveness by addressing structural challenges, including labor and product market reforms, to foster green, digital, and inclusive growth. Rebuild fiscal space.
Brazil	Broadly in line	Implement fiscal consolidation accompanied by measures to support public and private investment and structural reforms to reduce cost of doing business and strengthen competitiveness. Stand ready for prudent FX interventions to alleviate possible disorderly market conditions.
Canada	Moderately weaker	Develop credible medium-term fiscal consolidation plan; boost nonenergy exports through improved labor productivity, investment in R&D and public infrastructure.
China	Broadly in line	Accelerate structural reforms (by further opening domestic markets, reforming SOEs, and ensuring competitive neutrality with private firms), reduce high household savings (by strengthening the social safety net), and promote green investment to accelerate the transition to more balanced, inclusive, and green growth. Further increase exchange rate flexibility to facilitate the adjustment to economic shocks.
Euro Area	Broadly in line	Implement area-wide initiatives (banking and capital markets union and fiscal capacity for macro-stabilization) to further reinvigorate investment and reduce the aggregate CA surplus; see member country-specific recommendations to reduce internal and external imbalances.
France	Weaker	Improve competitiveness by reinvigorating structural reforms and rebuilding fiscal space over the medium term.
Germany	Stronger	Pursue growth-oriented fiscal policy with greater public sector investment in digitalization, infrastructure, and climate mitigation; implement structural reforms to foster entrepreneurship that would also stimulate investment; introduce additional tax relief for lower-income households; adopt pension reforms prolonging working lives.
Hong Kong SAR	Broadly in line	Ensure fiscal sustainability given rapidly aging population and maintain policies that support wage and price flexibility to preserve competitiveness.
India	Broadly in line	Implement fiscal consolidation in the medium term and step up efforts to improve the business climate, ease domestic supply bottlenecks, and liberalize trade and investment to attract FDI and improve the CA financing mix. Continue ER flexibility as the main shock absorber, with interventions limited to addressing disorderly market conditions.
Indonesia	Broadly in line	Pursue planned fiscal consolidation while boosting competitiveness and allowing for higher infrastructure and social spending to foster human capital development; facilitate sectoral adjustment; ease non-tariff trade barriers and FDI restrictions; improve labor market flexibility. Continue ER flexibility with FX interventions limited to disorderly market conditions.
Italy	Broadly in line	Raise productivity and improve the business climate through higher investment and structural reforms, including by upskilling the workforce and increasing the quality of infrastructure and the effectiveness of the public administration. Improve budget efficiency to lower vulnerabilities associated with the rollover of external debt.
Japan	Broadly in line	Implement gradual fiscal consolidation within a well-specified medium-term fiscal framework, accommodative monetary policy, and structural reforms to mobilize investment, reduce debt, and support reflation and growth. Focus on reforms to increase labor supply, boost productivity and wages, reduce barriers to entry, and accelerate agricultural and professional services sector deregulation.
Korea	Broadly in line	Continue accommodative fiscal and monetary policies. Implement structural policies to stimulate investment and facilitate rebalancing of the economy toward services and other new growth drivers, by reducing barriers to entry and deregulating the nonmanufacturing sector; strengthen the social safety net. ER should remain market determined, with intervention limited to preventing disorderly market conditions.

(*Continued*)

Annex Table 1.1.6. *(continued)*

Economy	Overall 2020 Assessment	Policy Recommendations
Malaysia	Substantially stronger	Strengthen the social safety net, encourage private investment, and boost productivity growth.
Mexico	Stronger	Implement structural reforms to deliver stronger investment and strong, durable, and inclusive growth. Implement credible medium-term tax reform. Continue using floating ER as the main shock absorber, with FX interventions used only to prevent disorderly market conditions.
The Netherlands	Stronger	Promote the recovery and support investment in physical and human capital to foster robust potential growth.
Poland	Substantially stronger	Boost public investment by deploying Next Generation EU funds to help tackle infrastructure gaps, digitalization, and climate change; use public policies to help foster corporate investment and productivity; implement active labor market policies to facilitate sectoral transition and structural reforms to raise potential growth.
Russia	Moderately stronger	Pursue structural reforms to improve the business climate and address inefficiencies in the state-owned enterprise sector; promote investment in infrastructure, health, and education, to lift potential growth and diversify the economy away from oil and gas exports.
Saudi Arabia	Moderately weaker	Implement further consolidation, including energy price reforms and restraint of current spending, as well as structural reforms to diversify the economy and boost the non-oil tradable sector.
Singapore	Substantially stronger	Increase public investment, including on health care, physical infrastructure, and human capital, to address structural transformations in light of a rapidly aging population, transition to digital economy, and climate change; introduce structural reforms to improve productivity.
South Africa	Moderately weaker	Implement structural reforms to ameliorate competitiveness and pursue gradual but substantial fiscal consolidation, once the pandemic is over, while providing space for infrastructure and social spending; focus on improving governance, efficiency of key product markets (by crowding in the private sector), and functioning of labor markets; seize opportunities to build up reserves.
Spain	Broadly in line	Support investment, including through leveraging Next Generation EU funds, and foster competitiveness to raise potential growth and support decarbonization and digitalization while carefully managing the public debt load. Achieve productivity gains through continued wage flexibility and reforms to address labor market duality, product and service market reforms, and actions to enhance education and innovation.
Sweden	Stronger	Support greener and growth-enhancing private and public investments to facilitate structural transformation and support domestic demand; implement structural reforms to boost potential output.
Switzerland	Broadly in line	Ensure balanced domestic and external contributions to growth and improve the public-private mix in financial outflows, easing pressures on the franc; continue supportive fiscal policy and enhance efforts to foster green, digital transformation and productivity gains to address competitveness and aging.
Thailand	Stronger	Embark on fiscal expansion to revitalize domestic demand, through targeted social transfers as well as infrastructure investment; continue reforming social safety nets and addressing widespread informality to reduce precautionary saving and support consumption. Ensure ER flexibility as the key shock absorber, with intervention limited to disorderly market conditions.
Turkey	Moderately weaker	Further reining in of credit growth and strong commitment to and delivery of a firm monetary policy stance; enhance the fiscal anchor with a credible commitment to future consolidation; and take additional steps to build policy credibility to encourage capital inflows, support de-dollarization, and buildup of reserves.
United Kingdom	Weaker	Implement structural reforms to boost productivity and international competitiveness, including supporting reallocation to fast-growing sectors by upgrading the skill base and ensuring appropriate access to finance, as well as encouraging firm digitalization and innovation.
United States	Moderately weaker	Use fiscal space to increase infrastructure investment and facilitate the transition to a lower-carbon economy in the near term and embark on fiscal consolidation in the medium term, to put the debt-GDP ratio on a downward path; implement structural policies to increase competitiveness, including enhancing schooling, training, and mobility of workers, and labor force participation. Roll back tariff barriers, and resolve trade and investment disagreements supporting a global trading system.

Source: 2020 Individual External Balance Assessments.
Note: CA = current account; ER = exchange rate; FDI = foreign direct investment; FX = foreign exchange; R&D = research and development; SOE = state-owned enterprise.

References

Adler, Gustavo, Kyun Suk Chang, Rui Mano, and Yuting Shao. 2021. "Foreign Exchange Intervention: A Dataset of Public Data and Proxies." IMF Working Paper 2021/047, International Monetary Fund, Washington, DC.

Agarwal, Ruchir, and Gita Gopinath. 2021. "A Proposal to End the COVID-19 Pandemic." IMF Staff Discussion Note 21/04, International Monetary Fund, Washington, DC.

Bachas, Natalie, Peter Ganong, Pascal J. Noel, Joseph S. Vavra, Arlene Wong, Diana Farrell, and Fiona E. Greig. 2020. "Initial Impacts of the Pandemic on Consumer Behavior: Evidence from Linked Income, Spending, and Savings Data." NBER Working Paper 27617, National Bureau of Economic Research, Cambridge, MA.

Bénétrix, Agustin S., Deepali Gautam, Luciana Juvenal, and Martin Schmitz. 2019. "Cross-Border Currency Exposures." IMF Working Paper 19/299, International Monetary Fund, Washington, DC.

Boz, Emine, Luis Cubeddu, and Maurice Obstfeld. 2017. "Revisiting the Paradox of Capital." Vox: CEPR Policy Portal, March 9. http://voxeu.org/article/ revisiting-paradox-capital.

Carroll, Christopher D., Jiri Slacalek, and Martin Sommer. 2019. "Dissecting Saving Dynamics: Measuring Wealth, Precautionary, and Credit Effects." NBER Working Paper 26131, National Bureau of Economic Research, Cambridge, MA.

Chetty, Raj, John N. Friedman, Nathaniel Hendren, Michael Stepner, and the Opportunity Insights Team. 2020. "The Economic Impacts of COVID-19: Evidence from a New Public Database Built Using Private Sector Data." NBER Working Paper 27431, National Bureau of Economic Research, Cambridge, MA.

Christelis, Dimitris, Dimitris Georgarakos, Tullio Jappelli, and Geoff Kenny. 2021. "Heterogenous Effects of Covid-19 on Households' Financial Situation and Consumption: Cross-Country Evidence from a New Survey." Vox: CEPR Policy Portal, June 8. https://voxeu.org/article/heterogenous-effects-covid-19-households-financial-situation-and-consumption.

Coibion, Olivier, Dimitris Georgarakos, Yuriy Gorodnichenko, Geoff Kenny, and Michael Weber. 2021. "The Effect of Macroeconomic Uncertainty on Household Spending." NBER Working Paper 28625, National Bureau of Economic Research, Cambridge, MA.

Cubeddu, Luis, Signe Krogstrup, Gustavo Adler, Pau Rabanal, Mai Chi Dao, Swarnali Ahmed Hannan, Luciana Juvenal, and others. 2019. "The External Balance Assessment Methodology: 2018 Update." IMF Working Paper 19/65, International Monetary Fund, Washington, DC.

Dell'Ariccia, Giovanni, Ehsan Ebrahimy, Deniz Igan, and Damien Puy. 2020. "Discerning Good from Bad Credit Booms: The Role of Construction." IMF Staff Discussion Note 20/02, International Monetary Fund, Washington, DC.

Dossche, Maarten, and Stylianos Zlatanos. 2020. Abstract: "COVID-19 and the Increase in Household Savings: Precautionary or Forced?" European Central Bank *Economic Bulletin Boxes* 6 (5).

European Commission (EC). 2021. "A Challenging Winter, but Light at the End of the Tunnel." *Economic Forecast* (Winter).

Evenett, Simon. 2021. "The Trade and Government Procurement Policy Nexus: Before and after the COVID-19 Pandemic." In *Public Procurement in (a) Crisis: Global Lessons from the COVID-19 Pandemic*, edited by Sue Arrowsmith, Luke Butler, and Christopher Yukins Oxford: Hart Publishing.

Evenett, Simon, Bernard Hoekman, Nadia Rocha, and Michele Ruta. 2021. "The COVID-19 Vaccine Production Club: Will Value Chains Temper Nationalism?" World Bank Policy Research Working Paper 9565, World Bank, Washington, DC.

Hale, Galina B., and Luciana Juvenal. 2020. "Currency-Induced External Balance Sheet Effects at the Onset of the COVID-19 Crisis." CEPR Discussion Paper 15170, Center for Economic Policy Research, Washington, DC.

International Monetary Fund (IMF). 2015. "Assessing Reserve Adequacy-Specific Proposals." IMF Policy Paper, Washington, DC.

Jordà, Òscar. 2005. "Estimation and Inference of Impulse Responses by Local Projections." *American Economic Review* 95 (1): 161–82.

Kolerus, Christina. 2021. "What Shapes Current Account Adjustment During Recessions?" IMF Working Paper 21/198, International Monetary Fund, Washington, DC.

Kpodar, Kangni, Montfort Mlachila, Saad Quayyum, and Vigninou Gammadigbe. 2021. "Defying the Odds: Remittances during the COVID-19 Pandemic." Unpublished. International Monetary Fund, Washington, DC.

Landais, Camille, David Bounie, Youssouf Camara, Etienne Fize, John W. Galbraith, Chloe Lavest, Tatiana Pazem, and Baptiste Savatier. 2020. "Consumption Dynamics in the COVID Crisis: Real Time Insights from French Transaction & Bank Data." CEPR Discussion Paper 15474, Center for Economic Policy Research, Washington, DC.

Lane, Philip R., and Gian Maria Milesi-Ferretti. 2007. "The External Wealth of Nations Mark II: Revised and Extended Estimates of Foreign Assets and Liabilities, 1970–2004." *Journal of International Economics* 73 (2): 223–50.

Milesi-Ferretti, Gian Maria. 2021. "The Travel Shock." Unpublished. Brookings Institution, Washington, DC.

Mody, Ashoka, Franziska Ohnsorge, and Damiano Sandri. 2012. "Precautionary Savings in the Great Recession." *IMF Economic Review* 60 (1): 114–38.

United Nations Conference on Trade and Development (UNCTAD). 2021. *World Investment Report* 2021. United Nations, Geneva.

World Bank. 2021. "Resilience: COVID-19 Crisis through a Migration Lens." *Migration and Development Brief* 34 (May).

World Trade Organization (WTO). 2020. "Overview of Developments in the International Trading Environment." Annual Report by the Director General, Geneva.

World Trade Organization (WTO). 2021. Global Trade Barometer, Geneva.

CHAPTER 2

FISCAL POLICY AND EXTERNAL ADJUSTMENT: WHAT'S COMING?

This chapter examines how the unprecedented ongoing global fiscal expansion and the expected consolidation in the coming years will affect economies' external positions. Based on a historical analysis of fiscal policy changes in 33 economies over the past 40 years and IMF G20 Model simulations, it finds that fiscal consolidation—tax hikes and government spending cuts—strongly and persistently raises current balances and results in real exchange rate depreciation. Most of the current account adjustment comes from a decline in economic activity, investment, and imports. At the same time, what happens to the current account and real exchange rate depends on a country's relative fiscal policy stance compared with that of its trading partners. For economies with relatively limited fiscal expansions during the COVID-19 crisis, compared with those of their trading partners, consequences include a rise in their current account balances and currency depreciation. At the global level, the highly synchronized fiscal expansions in 2020 imply a modest net impact on the global balances—the sum of absolute current account deficits and surpluses. In 2021–22, fiscal expansions are more concentrated among current account deficit economies, resulting in wider global balances. Over the medium term, current account deficit economies are expected to implement more fiscal consolidation, resulting in a reduction in global balances to below pre–COVID-19 levels. However, additional deficit-financed fiscal expansions by current account deficit economies, or a faster-than-expected pace of fiscal consolidation among current account surplus economies, could forestall this reduction. A synchronized global investment push to support the recovery would have minimal implications for global balances.

The authors of this chapter are Gustavo Adler, Cian Allen, Giovanni Ganelli (co-lead), Keiko Honjo, and Daniel Leigh (co-lead), with support from Mariela Caycho, Jair Rodriguez, Shao Xiaohan, and Rongjin Zhang. Luisa Calixto and Jane Haizel provided editorial assistance. The chapter also benefited from discussions with Alan Taylor and Stefan Zeugner and from comments by internal seminar participants and reviewers.

Introduction

How will the unprecedented fiscal policy expansion in response to the COVID-19 crisis and the expected fiscal consolidation over the coming years affect economies' trade balances and exchange rates? Textbook economic models, such as the Mundell-Fleming model, suggest that tax hikes or government spending cuts that reduce fiscal deficits cause a reduction in demand, an exchange rate depreciation, and a rise in the trade balance.[1] Despite those textbook results, there is a lack of consensus among economists on the size and persistence of the effect of fiscal policy changes. In a 2017 poll of leading economists by the University of Chicago Booth School of Business, only 33 percent agreed that a reduction in the US fiscal deficit would reduce the US trade deficit.[2] Several studies of the historical relationship between fiscal policy changes and external current account balances and exchange rates also find weak or inconclusive results.[3] A central challenge in estimating this relationship is that fiscal policy decisions are often motivated by responding to developments that also affect trade and currency movements, such as a recession, which confounds estimates of causal effects.[4] Another difficulty is that the relationship between the fiscal deficit and the current account depends on a country's relative fiscal policy stance compared with that of its trading partners, with potential *direct* effects on individual economies' current account balances differing from *overall* effects in cases of synchronization across economies.

[1]This prediction also emerges from calibrated open-economy general equilibrium models with non-Ricardian features, such as overlapping generations, as discussed in Obstfeld and Rogoff (1996).

[2]Economists were asked to comment on the following statement: "If the US reduced its fiscal deficit, then its trade deficit would also shrink." Of the survey participants, 33 percent agreed, 39 percent were uncertain or had no opinion, 2 percent disagreed, and 26 percent did not answer. The survey is available at https://www.igmchicago.org/surveys/deficits.

[3]See, for example, the surveys of the literature in Kim and Roubini (2008) and Abbas and others (2011).

[4]Additional challenges include, as discussed in Bluedorn and Leigh (2011), the potential simultaneous effect of nonpolicy developments, such as asset price booms, on investment, imports, and the current account balance—giving rise to omitted variable biases.

Moreover, with much of the policy debate currently focused on how the ongoing changes in fiscal policy will affect economic activity and inflation, there has been relatively little analysis so far of implications for the global constellation of current account deficits and surpluses. Understanding such implications is, however, important, including to anticipate the evolution of current account deficits and surpluses, which can—if they become excessive—pose challenges for policymakers. If current account balances widen excessively, they can fuel trade tensions among countries, become targets for protectionist measures, and increase the likelihood of disruptive currency and asset price adjustments. As Chapter 1 explains, many factors affect current account balances. This chapter focuses on the impact of fiscal policy changes.

To shed light on these issues, this chapter addresses the following questions:

- Do changes in fiscal policy affect an economy's external current account balance, and how persistent is the effect? Through what channels does the adjustment occur? What happens to exchange rates, exports, and imports?
- Does the impact depend on the composition of policy changes across taxes and government spending, the synchronization of the policy changes across economies, and structural economic characteristics?
- Will the recently implemented and prospective changes in fiscal policy during 2020–26 affect the global constellation of current account deficits and surpluses?
- Would alternative fiscal policy paths affect global current account balances, including different paths of fiscal consolidation than currently envisaged or additional fiscal expansions?

This chapter addresses these issues using both historical analysis of fiscal policy changes in 33 economies over the past 40 years and—to address the unprecedented nature of the ongoing changes in fiscal policy, especially its highly synchronized nature—using simulations of the IMF's multi-country general equilibrium model (the G20 Model).[5] For the historical analysis, the chapter addresses challenges in identifying causal effects using a Romer and Romer (2010) narrative approach. The analysis focuses on changes in fiscal policy that historical documents suggest are not motivated by responding to prospective macroeconomic conditions, building on earlier related work (for example, Chapter 3 of the October 2010 *World Economic Outlook* [WEO]) by extending the sample to include the decade since the global financial crisis as well as additional economies.

The main findings of the chapter are as follows:

- Changes in taxes and government spending strongly and persistently affect current account balances and exchange rates. A 1 percent of GDP fiscal consolidation raises the current account, on average, by about 0.6 percent of GDP, with the real effective exchange rate depreciating by about 1.8 percent. Most of the current account adjustment comes from a decline in economic activity, investment, and imports.
- The current account and exchange rate effects of fiscal policy changes are broadly comparable across tax and spending instruments, with the exception of changes in capital income taxation and public investment, which have larger effects. The effects are especially strong for economies that are more open to trade, have a greater share of liquidity-constrained households that cannot smooth consumption in response to shocks, and have less flexible exchange rates. At the same time, what happens to the current account and real exchange rate depends crucially on the *relative* fiscal policy stance compared with trading partners, given that not all economies can experience currency depreciation at the same time.
- The 2020–21 fiscal expansions had sizable *direct* effects on individual economies' current account balances but more limited *overall* effects, given the high degree of synchronization across economies. For economies with relatively limited tax reductions and spending increases compared with those of their trading partners, consequences include a rise in their current account balances and currency depreciation. At the global level, the high degree of synchronization of fiscal expansions in 2020 implies a modest net impact on the global balances—the sum of *absolute* current account deficits and surpluses. In 2021–22 fiscal expansion is more concentrated among current account deficit economies, with surplus economies withdrawing fiscal support to a greater extent, resulting in wider global balances.

[5]The analysis focuses on changes in taxes and government spending. The relationship between such fiscal measures and trade and currency movements is conceptually more direct than for other types of public sector support, including debt guarantees, which several country authorities have also implemented during the crisis (see the April 2021 *Fiscal Monitor*).

- Over the medium term, current account deficit economies are currently expected to implement more fiscal consolidation, resulting in a gradual reduction in global balances to below pre–COVID-19 levels. However, additional fiscal expansions by current account deficit economies, or a faster-than-expected pace of fiscal consolidation among current account surplus economies, could forestall this reduction. A synchronized global investment push in support of the recovery would have minimal implications for global balances.

The Impact of Fiscal Policy Changes on External Balances: Historical Evidence

This section reports new evidence on the impact of fiscal policy changes on the external sector for 33 advanced and emerging market and developing economies over the past 40 years. It starts by presenting results for the effect of fiscal consolidation on the current account and real exchange rate and then explores how the effects have evolved over time, comparing the experience of the past decade, which followed the global financial crisis, with that of earlier decades. The analysis also explores adjustment channels, including the effects on exports, imports, and overall economic activity.

Estimation Approach

To estimate the effect of fiscal policy changes, the analysis uses a Romer and Romer (2010) type narrative approach, extending the results of recent studies that also use this approach for a range of countries.[6] It examines contemporaneous policy documents and identifies tax and government spending changes not motivated by a response to the near-term economic outlook but, instead, by a desire to reduce budget deficits and ensure long-term public financial sustainability. As Romer and Romer (2010) and subsequent studies explain, such fiscal actions represent a response to past decisions and economic conditions rather than to prospective conditions.[7] They are thus unlikely to be systematically correlated with other developments affecting the economy in the short term, and are therefore valid for estimating the short-term effects of fiscal policy changes on the current account, exchange rate, and other macroeconomic variables.[8] As discussed in Online Annex 2.1, to address potential remaining sources of endogeneity, the analysis conducts several robustness checks.

To implement the narrative approach, the analysis merges existing multi-country narrative databases, includes additional economies, and identifies additional fiscal policy changes up to 2019.[9] The historical documents examined are IMF *Staff Reports;* IMF *Recent Economic Developments* reports; Stability and Convergence Programmes submitted by the authorities to the European Commission; Organisation for Economic Co-operation and Development Economic Surveys; and, for the United States, Congressional Budget Office reports.[10]

Figure 2.1 shows the 342 fiscal policy changes included in the chapter's data set, which average 1.04 percent of GDP a year, with a standard deviation of 0.98 percentage point of GDP and range from –0.9 percent of GDP

[6]See, for example, Devries and others (2011); Alesina and others (2018); and Carriere-Swallow, David, and Leigh (2021).

[7]The narrative approach to identifying fiscal policy shocks is preferred to the more traditional approach based on changes in the cyclically adjusted primary balance, given that the latter typically includes nonpolicy factors that may reflect other developments affecting the current account, such as asset price fluctuations, as well as discretionary policy changes motivated by responding to macroeconomic conditions.

[8]Applications of the Romer and Romer (2010) narrative approach include, among others, Bluedorn and Leigh (2011); Cloyne (2013); Mertens and Ravn (2013); Hayo and Uhl (2014); Guajardo, Leigh, and Pescatori (2014); Jordà and Taylor (2016); Alesina and others (2018); and Cloyne, Jordà, and Taylor (2020). As in these studies, when the historical record indicates that a change in fiscal policy is motivated primarily by restraining domestic demand or in response to a contracting economy, it is not used to estimate causal effects. A potential caveat regarding this approach is that in countries embarking on fiscal consolidation, narrative fiscal shocks might not be entirely orthogonal to prospective conditions if they are predictable based on past developments. To examine and address this possibility, the analysis implements, as a robustness check, the augmented inverse propensity score weighting estimator proposed for this purpose in Jordà and Taylor (2016), with the results suggesting similar or stronger effects to the baseline approach (see Online Annex 2.1, available at www.imf.org/en/Publications/ESR). As in these studies, the analysis assumes that the effects of positive and negative fiscal policy shocks are similar.

[9]The economies included are Argentina, Australia, Austria, Belgium, Bolivia, Brazil, Canada, Chile, China, Colombia, Costa Rica, Denmark, the Dominican Republic, Ecuador, Finland, France, Germany, Guatemala, India, Ireland, Italy, Jamaica, Japan, Mexico, The Netherlands, Paraguay, Peru, Portugal, Spain, Sweden, the United Kingdom, the United States, and Uruguay.

[10]These documents provide the estimated budgetary impact of fiscal consolidation measures. Following Romer and Romer (2010), the contemporaneous estimates contained in these sources are used, given that retrospective estimates are rarely available. The budgetary effects of the fiscal consolidation measures are recorded in the year in which they go into effect. To facilitate empirical work using the series, the budgetary impact of the measures is scaled in percent of GDP. If measures were announced, but subsequent editions of the historical documents suggest that they were not implemented, they are not included in the analysis.

Figure 2.1. Fiscal Consolidation over Time

The number of fiscal policy changes was highest in the early 2010s in the aftermath of the global financial crisis.

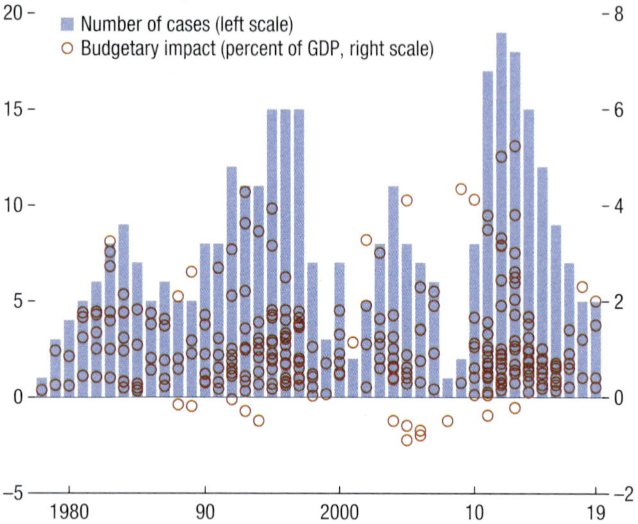

Sources: IMF, *World Economic Outlook*; and IMF staff calculations.

Figure 2.2. Effects of a 1 Percent of GDP Fiscal Consolidation

For a sample of 33 advanced and emerging market and developing economies spanning 1978–2019, changes in fiscal policy have strong and persistent effects on the current account and real effective exchange rate.

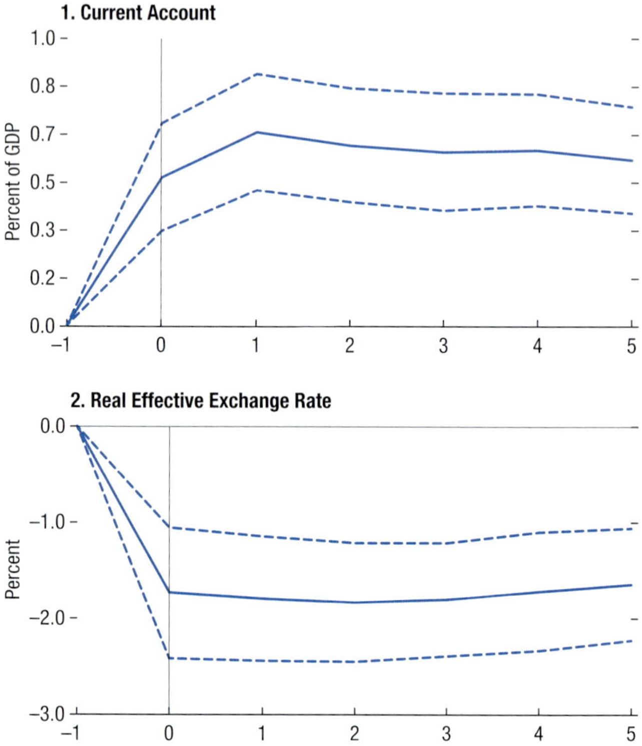

Source: IMF staff estimates.
Note: *X*-axis units are years, where $t = 0$ denotes the year of consolidation. Dashed lines indicate 90 percent confidence intervals.

(Uruguay, 2005) to 5.23 percent of GDP (Portugal, 2013). Negative values in the measure of policy changes reflect the expiration of temporary fiscal consolidation measures. Based on the narrative fiscal shocks, the analysis estimates the effects of fiscal policy changes using Jordà (2005) local projections.[11]

Baseline Results

The estimation results suggest that the effects of fiscal policy changes on the current account and on the real effective exchange rate are strong and long-lasting. As Figure 2.2 shows, a 1 percent of GDP fiscal consolidation raises the current account balance by 0.63 percent of GDP within two years, with a 90 percent confidence interval of 0.43 to 0.82 percent of GDP. It also comes with a real effective exchange rate depreciation of 1.80 percent within a year, with a 90 percent confidence interval of 1.15 to 2.45 percent. The effects persist over five years. These results suggest more powerful effects than typically found in existing studies based on more conventional approaches.[12]

[11]The main equation estimated takes the following form:

$$\Delta y_{i,t:t+h} = \alpha_i^h + \alpha_t^h + \beta^h \Delta F_{i,t:t+h} + \gamma^h X_{i,t} + e_{i,t}^h, \qquad (2.1)$$

where $\Delta y_{i,t:t+h}$ denotes the change in the variable of interest, such as the current-account-balance-to-GDP ratio, from year t to year $t + h$ in economy i; $\Delta F_{i,t:t+h}$ denotes the sum of narrative fiscal shocks from year t to year $t + h$; and $X_{i,t}$ denotes a set of control variables, which are two lags of both the external sector variable and the narrative fiscal shock. The sequence of estimated β^h coefficients indicates the effects of a 1 percent of GDP fiscal adjustment over h years. Following Ramey and Zubairy (2018) and Carriere-Swallow, David, and Leigh (2021), the effect of the cumulative narrative fiscal shock over h years is estimated. The specification also includes time fixed effects (α_t^h) to account for various common shocks and economy-specific fixed effects (α_i^h) to account for differences in economies' normal external dynamics. The inclusion of time fixed effects controls for common shocks, such as the world fiscal policy changes, shocks to oil and hydrocarbon prices, and other global supply shocks. Inference is based on Driscoll-Kraay standard errors to account for potential serial correlation and spatial dependence.

[12]See the literature survey in Abbas and others (2011). The smaller estimated effects of fiscal policy on the current account in the IMF staff External Balance Assessment model (see Cubeddu and others 2019) and in other studies in part reflect these studies' focus on the role of fiscal policy while holding constant the response of economic activity (as measured by the output gap, per capita income, economic growth, and other variables)—and are thus not directly comparable with the results presented here, which focus on the *overall* current account effect, including the impact via changes in economic activity.

The results hold up to a number of robustness checks, as reported in Online Annex 2.1.[13] The results are also similar when examining advanced and emerging market and developing economies separately (the point estimates are larger for the latter group but not statistically distinguishable) and when differentiating between spending-based and tax-based fiscal adjustments.

Adjustment Channels over Time

To investigate the channels through which fiscal policy affects external adjustment, the analysis reestimates the baseline equation (2.1) with real exports, real imports, as well as real investment and real GDP as the dependent variable. As Figure 2.3 shows, the main channel of adjustment is import compression stemming from the fall in output following fiscal consolidation. Both GDP and investment fall substantially and persistently following the fiscal consolidation. The response of exports is, on average, small and not statistically distinguishable from zero.[14]

Results for the past decade (2010–19), which followed the global financial crisis, suggest a strengthening of the effects of fiscal policy on external adjustment, with the current account balance rising by 0.82 percent of GDP within two years (Figure 2.3). This stronger effect mainly reflects a more pronounced reduction in aggregate demand, with real GDP falling by 1.64 percent within three years (compared with 0.51 before the global financial crisis) and larger associated declines in investment and imports. These results are consistent with those of studies that find evidence of larger fiscal multipliers in the years following the global financial crisis, reflecting substantial economic slack, a weaker financial system, and constrained monetary policy.[15] The real effective exchange rate depreciation following fiscal consolidation remains substantial and comparable to that estimated for earlier decades. As reported in Online Annex 2.1, the difference in estimation results for this decade compared with earlier decades is statistically significant for all variables except exports and the real effective exchange rate. Overall, the historical evidence suggests that fiscal policy has had strong and persistent effects both on macroeconomic variables and on external adjustment.

Figure 2.3. Channels of Adjustment: Focus on Recent Years

The increase in the current account following a fiscal consolidation of 1 percent of GDP mainly reflects import compression and the fall in GDP and investment. This channel became especially pronounced in the past decade, following the global financial crisis.

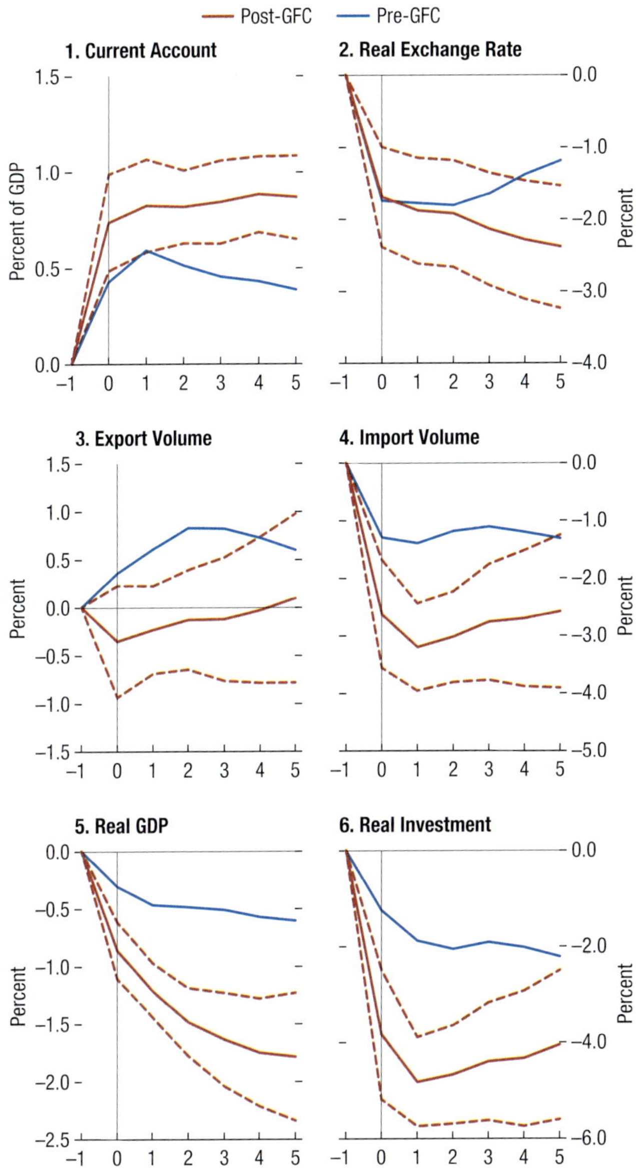

Source: IMF staff estimates.
Note: *X*-axis units are years, where $t = 0$ denotes the year of consolidation. Dashed lines indicate the 90 percent confidence interval around the point estimate. Post-global financial crisis (GFC) denotes 2010–19.

[13]All online annexes are available at www.imf.org/en/Publications/ESR.

[14]The lack of an increase in exports, on average, across the horizon considered is less consistent with conventional theoretical models but consistent with models featuring dominant currency pricing (Gopinath and others 2020).

[15]See, for example, Auerbach and Gorodnichenko (2012) and Blanchard and Leigh (2013).

What Shapes the Impact? Composition, Synchronization, and Economic Characteristics: Model-Based Insights

To complement the empirical analysis and shed light on the impact of additional aspects relevant today, such as the high degree of synchronization of fiscal policy changes across countries in response to the COVID-19 shock, as well as the composition of the fiscal response and the role of countries' economic characteristics, this section examines the nexus between fiscal policy and external accounts using IMF G20 Model simulations.

The G20 Model is an annual, general equilibrium model of the global economy combining both micro-founded and reduced-form formulations of various economic sectors. It includes all Group of Twenty (G20) countries, plus five regional blocks to model the rest of the world. Ricardian equivalence is broken in the model due to the assumption of finite lifetimes, liquidity-constrained consumers, and distortionary fiscal instruments. Each country and regional block is calibrated to reflect differences in size, macroeconomic steady-state ratios, and behavioral parameters.[16] The model allows an analysis of the impact of globally synchronized policy actions, which is relevant in the context of the COVID-19 shock, during which many countries have expanded fiscal policy at the same time.

Role of Composition

To investigate how the impact of fiscal policy changes on the current account depends on the type of fiscal instrument, the analysis simulates the impact of fiscal consolidation on the current account, based on seven policy tools available in the G20 Model: consumption taxes, capital income taxes, labor taxes, government consumption, general transfers, targeted transfers, and government investment.[17] For illustrative purposes, the simulations are conducted for the Canada block of the G20 Model.

Reassuringly, the model simulation results are broadly comparable with those found in the aforementioned empirical analysis for most fiscal policy instruments. A 1 percent of GDP fiscal consolidation raises the current account balance by 0.4 percent of GDP within three years and 0.5 to 0.6 percent within five years for all fiscal instruments except capital income taxation and government investment. When the entire fiscal consolidation package falls on either of those two fiscal tools, the impact on the current-account-to-GDP ratio is larger, reaching above 1 percent of GDP for capital income taxation. At the same time, in most cases, these two tools are not driving the unprecedented expansion in fiscal policy during 2020–21 or its expected withdrawal in the coming years.[18] In most cases, the budgetary fiscal expansion has focused on transfers and other support for firms and households, as well as on government consumption in the form of health spending (see the April 2021 *Fiscal Monitor* for a summary of the principal fiscal tools deployed as part of the 2020–21 fiscal expansion).[19]

Role of Synchronization

In the case of globally synchronized action, the results can be different from individual cases. Panel 2 of Figure 2.4 shows the response of the current account in the case of all economies in the model consolidating together by 1 percent of GDP. In this case, Canada's current account declines modestly in response to a global fiscal consolidation. This finding of no rise in the current account following fiscal consolidation should not be surprising. Because the sum of all current accounts in the world must be zero, it is impossible for all economies to increase their current account balance at the same time. What matters for the impact on the current account is the fiscal policy change relative to other countries, as well as individual economic characteristics, such as the degree of openness and the share of liquidity-constrained households.[20] In addition, as

[16]For a description of the structure of the G20 Model, see Andrle and others (2015).

[17]The capital income tax included in the G20 Model is different from corporate income tax. As Carton, Corugedo, and Hunt (2017) explain, a capital income tax "… falls exclusively on the return to capital (which severely distorts the capital accumulation process) rather than on the return to capital as well as the rents made by corporates (which is less distortionary)."

[18]A notable exception is China, for which investment played a substantial role in the fiscal expansion in 2020.

[19]Detailed data are available in the Database of Fiscal Policy Responses to COVID-19 at https://www.imf.org/en/Topics/imf-and-covid19/Fiscal-Policies-Database-in-Response-to-COVID-19.

[20]In the case of Canada, the current-account-to-GDP ratio declines modestly in response to the global fiscal consolidation. This result reflects the fact that in Canada the share of liquidity-constrained households is lower compared with the rest of the world. Given that liquidity-constrained households cannot borrow, fiscal consolidation results in a larger fall in consumption and domestic prices—and, hence, a real depreciation—on average, in the rest of the world or, equivalently, real appreciation for Canada. With this appreciation, Canada's current account declines. The global fiscal consolidation also leads to a fall in the world real interest rate (see Online Annex Figure 2.1.2).

Figure 2.4. Impact on the Current Account Model, by Fiscal Instrument

(Percent of GDP; G20 Model simulations)

For most fiscal instruments, the effect of a fiscal consolidation of 1 percent of GDP on the current account based on the IMF's G20 Model simulations is close to the average empirical estimate. It is larger for cuts in government investment or based on increases in taxes on capital income. The current account does not increase following a global fiscal consolidation synchronized across all economies.

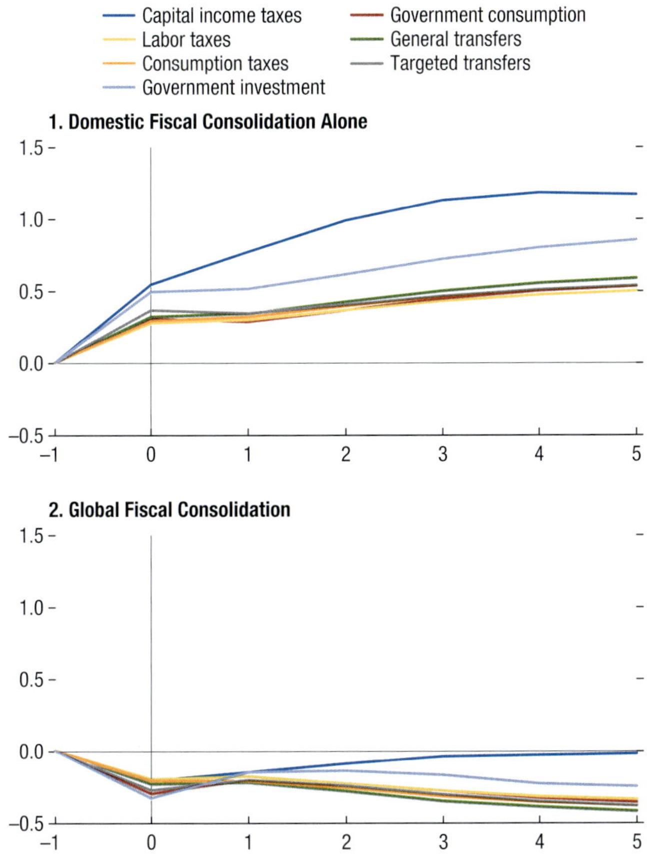

Source: IMF, G20 Model simulations.
Note: *X*-axis units are years, where $t = 0$ denotes the year of consolidation.

shown in Online Annex Figure 2.1.2, the impact of the global consolidation is partially absorbed by a fall in the world interest rate, which reduces the need for individual countries' private saving and investment to adjust.

Role of Economic Characteristics

To shed light on how country characteristics shape the impact, Figure 2.5 shows how the response of the current account to fiscal policy changes depends on such country characteristics as openness, the share of liquidity-constrained economic agents, and the

Figure 2.5. Effects on the Current Account, by Economic Characteristic

(Percent of GDP; years on x-axis; G20 Model simulations)

Fiscal consolidation has larger effects on the current account balance in economies that are more open to trade, have a greater share of liquidity-constrained households, and have fixed exchange rate regimes.

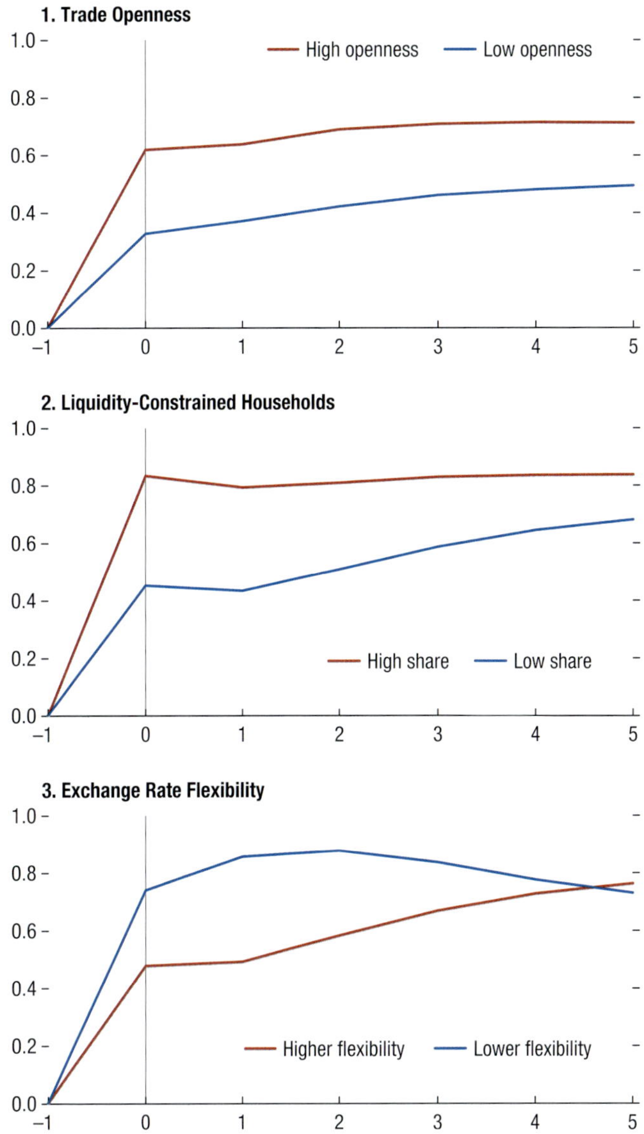

Source: IMF, G20 Model simulations.
Note: *X*-axis units are years, where $t = 0$ denotes the year of consolidation. The responses in the figure are model simulations based on the IMF's G20 Model for selected economies differentiated by each of the three highlighted characteristics (trade openness in terms of the ratio of imports and exports to GDP, share of liquidity-constrained households, and exchange rate flexibility) that are broadly comparable along the other two characteristics. Based on the calibration in Andrle and others (2015), it compares the following economies: for trade openness in terms of exports and imports as a share of GDP, United States (lower) and Korea (higher); for household liquidity constraints, Canada (lower) and emerging market oil exporters (higher); and for exchange rate flexibility, it compares an economy in a currency union (Germany) with other (non-euro-area) EU economies.

exchange rate regime. Fiscal consolidation has larger effects on the current account balance in economies that are more open to trade, have a greater share of liquidity-constrained households, and have fixed exchange rate regimes. Larger effects in the case of relatively open economies reflect the greater effect of the fiscal consolidation on imported than on domestically produced products. Figure 2.5 illustrates this aspect (panel 1) by comparing simulated responses for a relatively closed economy (United States) with those for one that is relatively open (Korea). In the case of economies with tighter liquidity constraints, the larger impact reflects a larger share of households that cannot smooth their consumption, which then respond more forcefully to the fiscal shock than in the case in which more households can borrow. This aspect is illustrated in panel 2 of Figure 2.5, which compares Canada, an economy with a smaller share of liquidity-constrained households, with emerging market oil exporters, which have a larger share of liquidity-constrained households. The larger impact in the case of economies with less flexible exchange rate regimes reflects the relative lack of a country-specific monetary policy response. This is illustrated in panel 3 of Figure 2.5, which compares Germany, an economy in a currency union without a country-specific monetary policy response, with non-euro-area EU economies.

Additional special factors beyond those reflected in these model simulations may have shaped the impact of fiscal policy on the current account during the COVID-19 crisis. Such factors include, notably, government-imposed lockdown measures that may have tempered the impact of fiscal policy changes on economic activity, exports, and imports. Government lockdowns, voluntary reduced mobility due to pandemic concerns, and uncertainty regarding future economic prospects related to the crisis may have limited both the ability and the willingness of households that received fiscal support to spend it. Those factors may have limited the impact on aggregate demand and imports of the recent fiscal expansions, as also suggested by increases in precautionary savings in major economies, which resulted in exceptionally high saving compared with other recessions (see the discussion in Chapter 1). In this regard, the impact of fiscal policy changes in 2020–21 may be smaller than in normal times. At the same time, as the pandemic is brought under control and lockdown measures ease, the associated influence on the transmission of fiscal policy should fade accordingly.

Implications of Fiscal Policies during 2020–26 for External Balances

The analysis now assesses how fiscal policy changes implemented and currently expected to be implemented have affected current account balances so far and how they are expected to affect them up to 2026.[21] The analysis examines the impacts both of individual economies' policy changes in isolation and the combined effects of policy changes taken globally. The focus is on changes in taxes and government spending. The relationship between such fiscal measures and trade and currency movements is conceptually more direct than for other types of public sector support, including debt guarantees, which several country authorities also implemented during the crisis. Figure 2.6 shows a summary measure of the fiscal policy changes implemented and expected under the baseline path—the cumulative change in the cyclically adjusted fiscal balance compared with 2019—for current account surplus and current account deficit economies.[22] The expected path of fiscal policy is based on the July 2021 WEO *Update* forecast, which incorporates the IMF staff's fiscal projections regarding the American Jobs Plan and the American Families Plan under discussion in the United States. As Figure 2.6 suggests, the budgetary fiscal response to the COVID-19 shock was greater for current account deficit economies in the immediate aftermath of the COVID-19 shock. For those economies, the GDP-weighted average of the change in the cyclically adjusted fiscal balance is close to 5 percent in 2020 and 2021. This reflects especially fiscal action by

[21]Forecasts of fiscal policy changes are based on the July 2021 WEO *Update*. Projections are formulated on a "current policy" basis. In the case of European Union (EU) countries, the WEO projections reflect the expected withdrawal of extraordinary fiscal support as well as increases in government investments financed with the EU Next Generation grants.

[22]Among advanced economies included in the model, those with current account deficits (based on 2019 data) comprise Canada, France, the United Kingdom, and the United States; current account surplus economies comprise Australia, Belgium, Germany, Italy, Japan, Korea, The Netherlands, Spain, Sweden, and Switzerland. An overwhelming majority of economies in the world have maintained an expansionary fiscal stance in 2020–21 (see also Figures 2.7 and 2.8).

Figure 2.6. Fiscal Policy Changes, 2020–26

Economies with current account deficits had, on average, larger fiscal expansions based on the change in the cyclically adjusted general government budget balance during 2020–21 and a larger fiscal withdrawal over the medium term.

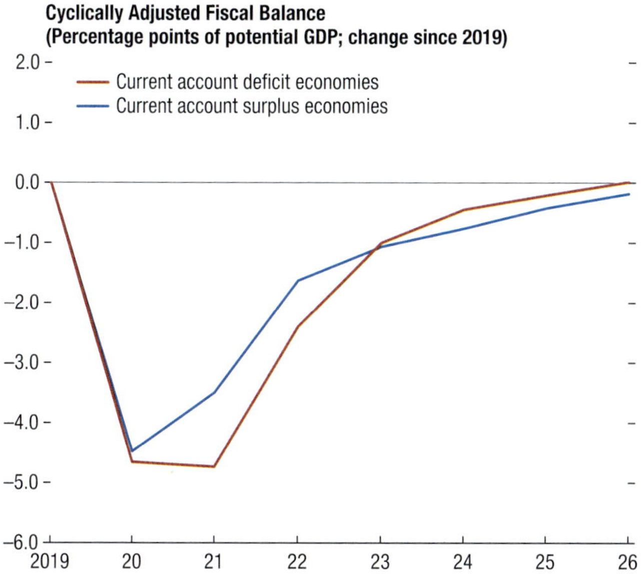

Sources: IMF, *World Economic Outlook* (WEO); and IMF staff calculations.
Note: Fiscal policy changes in 2020–26 are based on July 2021 WEO *Update* forecasts. Current account deficits and surpluses are based on 2019 data. Average is weighted by GDP.

Figure 2.7. Individual Direct Impact of Fiscal Policy Changes on the Current Account, 2020–26

The direct effect of fiscal policy actions in 2020–21 on current accounts is generally negative. Over the medium term, some economies' medium-term fiscal consolidations are larger than the fiscal expansion of 2020–21, resulting in a positive direct effect on the current account.

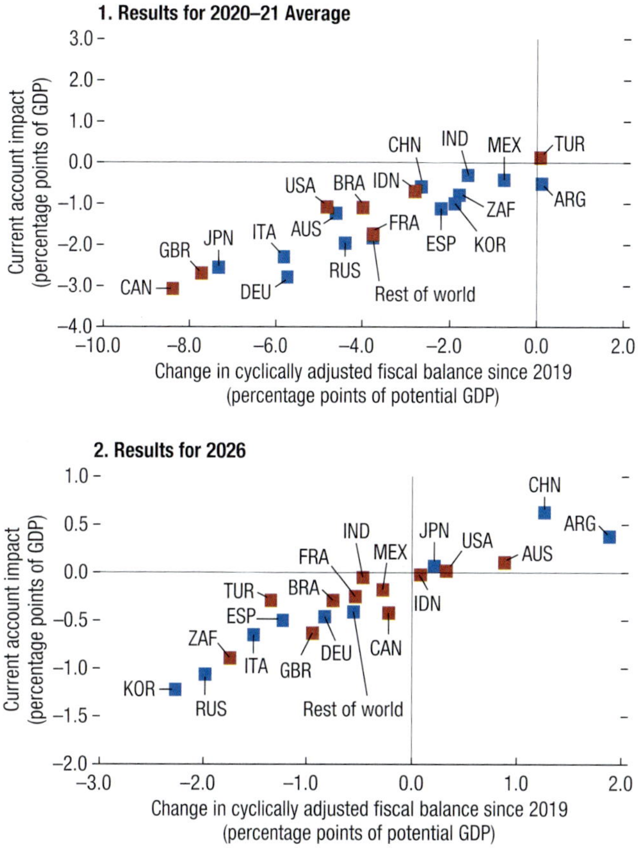

Sources: IMF, *World Economic Outlook* (WEO); and IMF staff estimates.
Note: The figure reports IMF G20 Model simulations. Red (blue) squares indicate economies with a current account deficit (surplus). Fiscal policy changes in 2020–26 are based on July 2021 WEO *Update* forecasts. The figure uses International Organization for Standardization (ISO) country codes.

advanced economies—the United States in particular. The opposite is true in the medium term, with current account deficit economies undertaking relatively greater withdrawal of the temporary fiscal support under current forecasts.

Individual Impact

Simulations based on the G20 Model indicate that the *direct* effect of fiscal expansions during 2020–21 on current account balances was to reduce them by an average of about 1.5 percent of GDP. Figure 2.7 shows those effects for 2020–21, as well as the medium-term impact of the currently expected fiscal path, for the case of individual fiscal action by each economy. The results highlight the importance of trade openness. For example, in 2020–21 the negative impact on Germany's current account is larger than for Italy, despite a broadly similar change in the cyclically adjusted fiscal balance in the two economies. Given that Germany's trade openness is greater than that of Italy, this result is in line with the larger impact of fiscal shocks on the current account in more open economies, also shown in Figure 2.5.

Global Impact

The case of global action captures the total effects stemming from changes in fiscal policy both domestically and in the rest of the world. A comparison of the global action simulations (Figure 2.8) with the individual action simulations (Figure 2.7) illustrates how *relative* fiscal policy changes matter for the ultimate impact. The case of Mexico is instructive. The impact on Mexico's current account in 2020–21 is about 1.5 percent of GDP for the

Figure 2.8. Global Impact of Fiscal Policy Changes on the Current Account, 2020–26

The effect of fiscal policy actions taken globally on current accounts depends on the relative size of the fiscal policy change as well as economies' structural features, both during 2020–21 and over the medium term.

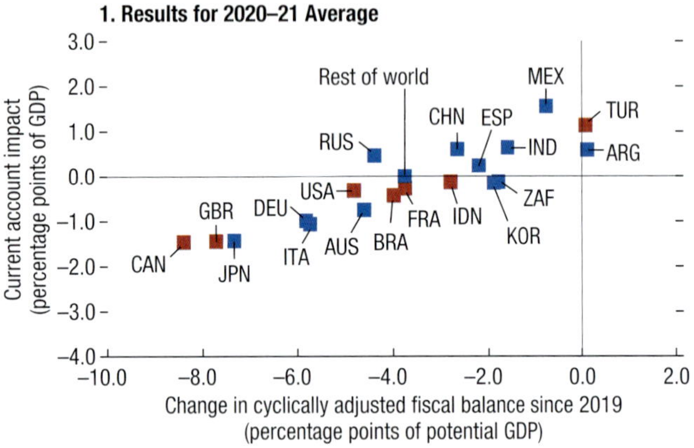

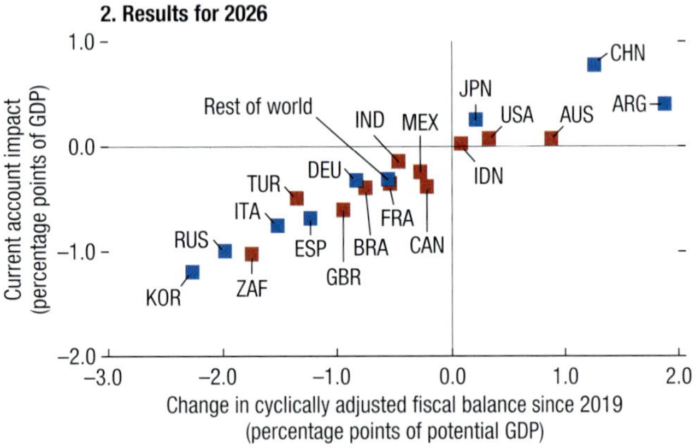

Sources: IMF, *World Economic Outlook* (WEO); and IMF staff estimates.
Note: The figure reports IMF G20 Model simulations. Red (blue) squares indicate economies with a current account deficit (surplus). Fiscal policy changes in 2020–26 are based on July 2021 WEO *Update* forecasts. The figure uses International Organization for Standardization (ISO) country codes.

Figure 2.9. Impact of Fiscal Policy on Global Absolute Current Account Balances, 2020–26
(Percent of world GDP)

Fiscal policy contributes to a widening of global current account balances for most of the projection period under the baseline, largely driven by the US fiscal expansion, but this widening effect dissipates by 2026.

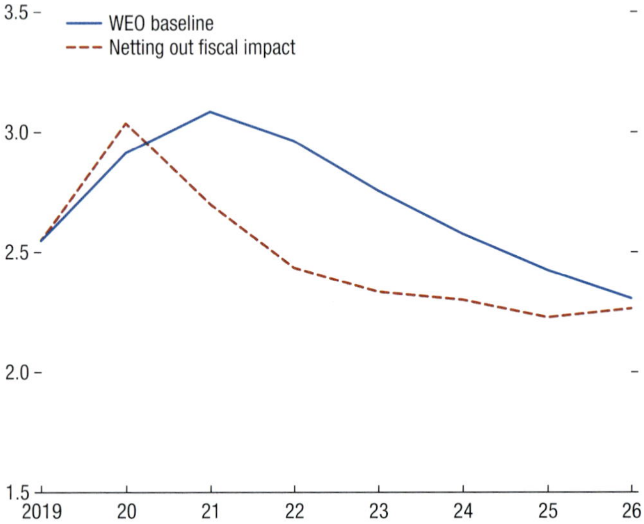

Sources: IMF, *World Economic Outlook* (WEO); and IMF staff estimates (G20 Model simulations).
Note: The figure reports IMF G20 Model simulations. Fiscal policy changes in 2020–26 are based on July 2021 WEO *Update* forecasts.

global fiscal action simulation, compared with –0.4 percent of GDP in the individual case. Given that Mexico is a relatively open economy, its current account benefits from the larger fiscal support carried out in the rest of the world.[23] As shown in Figure 2.9, fiscal policy contributes to a widening of global current account balances for most of the projection period under the baseline, largely driven by the US fiscal expansion, although this widening effect dissipates by 2026. The widening effect is particularly marked in 2021. In the absence of the fiscal policy response to COVID-19, global balances would have already been on a steep narrowing path beginning in 2021, instead of widening as in the baseline.[24]

Alternative Fiscal Policy Paths and Global Current Account Balances

Additional Fiscal Consolidation or Fiscal Expansion

In Figure 2.10, global current account balances under the current baseline (solid blue line) are compared with two alternative scenarios. The dashed blue line shows how global current account balances would evolve if current account surplus economies implemented an additional gradual 3 percent of GDP fiscal consolidation, starting in 2022, compared with the baseline.

[23]Both exports and imports are parameterized close to 40 percent of GDP for Mexico in the G20 Model, based on 2020 data.

[24]Figure 2.9 also shows that fiscal policy slightly narrowed current account imbalances in 2020. This result is driven by the fact that, given that major current account surplus economies tend to be more open (the GDP-weighted average of imports to GDP is 34.6 percent for current account surplus countries and 23.2 percent for current account deficit countries in the model calibration), the negative impact of fiscal support on their current account balance in 2020 was greater than for current account deficit economies.

Figure 2.10. Scenario with Additional Fiscal Consolidation: Impact on Global Absolute Current Account Balances, 2020–26
(Percent of world GDP)

Additional fiscal consolidation by economies with current account surpluses would substantially widen global balances over the medium term, while more fiscal consolidation by current account deficit economies would contribute to a further narrowing in global balances.

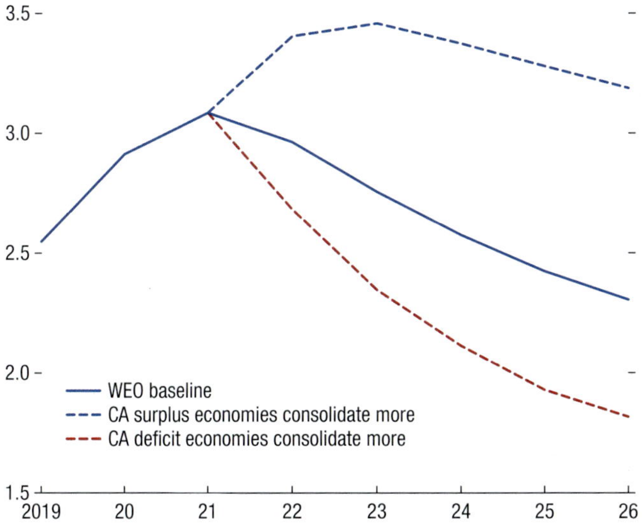

Sources: IMF, *World Economic Outlook* (WEO); and IMF staff estimates (G20 Model simulations).
Note: The figure reports the absolute sum of global current account deficits and surpluses under different fiscal policy scenarios, including an additional 3 percent of GDP in fiscal consolidation starting in 2022. The WEO baseline scenario is based on July 2021 WEO *Update* forecasts. CA = current account.

Figure 2.11. Scenario with Additional Fiscal Expansion: Impact on Global Absolute Current Account Balances, 2020–26
(Percent of world GDP)

Additional fiscal expansion by economies with current account deficits would substantially widen global balances over the medium term, while additional fiscal expansion by current account surplus economies would contribute to a further narrowing in global balances.

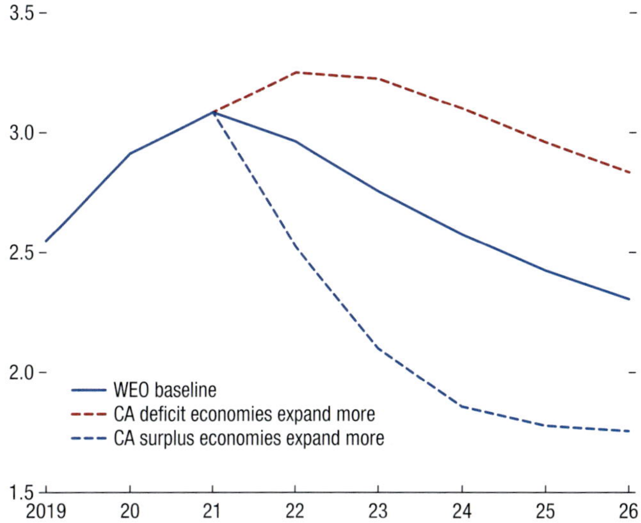

Sources: IMF, *World Economic Outlook* (WEO); and IMF staff estimates (G20 Model simulations).
Note: The figure reports the absolute sum of global current account deficits and surpluses under different fiscal policy scenarios, including an additional 3 percent of GDP in fiscal expansion starting in 2022. The WEO baseline scenario is based on July 2021 WEO *Update* forecasts. CA = current account.

The dashed red line shows how global current balances would evolve if current account deficit economies implemented the same additional consolidation.

The impact of the additional consolidation is larger for current account surplus economies than for deficit economies because surplus economies are currently, on average, more open than deficit economies. As a result, the same amount of fiscal consolidation reduces imports more in current account surplus economies than in current account deficit economies, thus increasing surpluses in current account surplus economies more than it reduces deficits in current account deficit economies undertaking additional fiscal consolidation. Importantly, Figure 2.10 also shows how, if current account surplus economies implement more fiscal consolidation (or less persistent fiscal support) than currently expected, global current account balances could widen substantially compared with the baseline scenario.

The case of additional fiscal expansion compared with the baseline—or, equivalently, a more persistent fiscal expansion than currently expected—is also worth considering. Figure 2.11 shows that in an alternative scenario under which current account deficit economies expand fiscal policy by an additional 3 percent of GDP, global current account balances widen substantially compared with the baseline. By the same token, under a scenario in which current account surplus economies provide more fiscal support compared with the baseline, global current account balances would be substantially reduced. The simulation is based on an illustrative 3 percent of GDP gradual additional fiscal support starting in 2022.

Synchronized Public Investment Push

In Figure 2.12, the evolution of global current account balances under the baseline is compared with an alternative scenario of a synchronized global

Figure 2.12. Scenario with Synchronized Public Investment Push: Impact on Global Absolute Current Account Balances, 2020–26
(Percent of world GDP)

A synchronized public investment expansion to support the recovery would have modest effects on global current account deficits and surpluses.

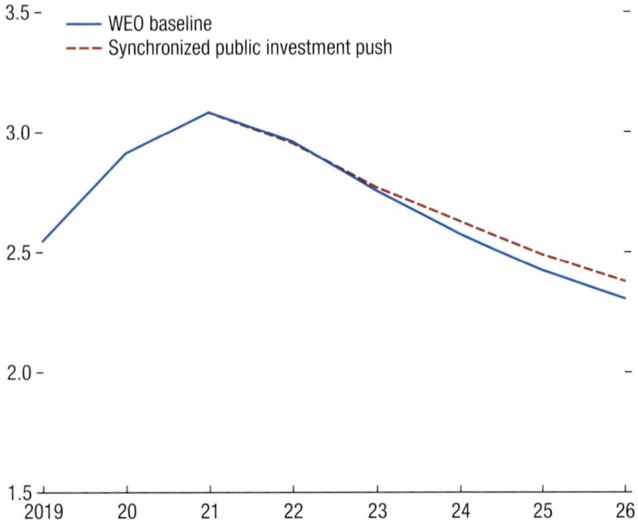

Sources: IMF, *World Economic Outlook* (WEO); and IMF staff estimates (G20 Model simulations).
Note: The figure reports the absolute sum of global current account deficits and surpluses under different fiscal policy scenarios. The WEO baseline scenario is based on April 2021 WEO forecasts.

investment push. Under this alternative scenario, it is assumed that G20 economies that have fiscal space increase public investment. The simulation assumes—following IMF (2020a), which focuses on the impact on real GDP—that in G20 economies with ample or some fiscal space, public infrastructure investment increases by ½ percent of GDP in 2021, rises to 1 percent of GDP in 2022, and stays at that elevated level until 2025. In G20 economies deemed at risk with respect to fiscal space, public infrastructure spending increases by one-third of the amount in countries with ample or some fiscal space. There is no increase in public infrastructure spending in countries with no fiscal space.[25]

Figure 2.12 suggests that the synchronized investment increases global current account balances only marginally (the deviation of the red dashed line from the blue line is very small). This is because the increase in investment is *synchronized* across various current account surplus and current account deficit economies. A synchronized global investment push, or a synchronized health spending push to end the pandemic and support the recovery, could have large effects on GDP, with limited effects on global balances (the sum of absolute current account deficits and surpluses).[26] The result that synchronized fiscal policy changes imply limited effects on global balances suggests that some of the global reforms currently being considered, such as a global synchronized increase in capital taxation and an international agreement for taxation of multinationals, could also have limited implications for overall global imbalances.

Implications for the External Outlook

After declining over the past several years, global current account deficits and surpluses increased during 2020–21, as discussed in Chapter 1. The analysis in this chapter suggests that the evolution of global balances over the medium term will depend crucially on the conduct of fiscal policy and on the progression of the COVID-19 virus, which remains highly uncertain. Policies should remain focused on ending the pandemic, as discussed in Chapter 1.

In the medium term, under currently expected policies, current account deficit economies implement more fiscal consolidation than current account surplus economies, contributing to a gradual reduction in global balances to below pre–COVID-19 levels. However, additional deficit-financed fiscal expansions by current account deficit economies, beyond what is currently expected, or a faster-than-expected pace of fiscal consolidation among current account surplus economies, could forestall this reduction and even widen current account balances, potentially fueling trade tensions and protectionist measures and increasing the likelihood of disruptive currency and asset price adjustments down the road.

For individual economies, what happens to the current account and real exchange rate will also depend critically on their relative fiscal policy stance compared with that of their trading partners. For economies that implemented less fiscal support than their trading partners during the COVID-19 crisis, even if the policy

[25]Fiscal space is defined as in IMF (2020b) and is based on pre-pandemic assessments during Article IV consultations.

[26]According to IMF (2020a), the level of global real GDP would increase by almost 2 percent by 2025 under a global synchronized investment push.

support was calibrated to their domestic economic needs, implications include rising current account balances and currency depreciation. This result highlights the importance of spillovers from the policy actions of advanced economies—where, as Chapter 1 highlights, fiscal expansions have been especially large—to emerging market and developing economies. The case of Mexico provides an example: the external current account increased sharply in 2020, in part reflecting the impact of fiscal expansions in major trading partners that were larger compared with Mexico's relatively muted fiscal response to the pandemic, as well as other factors (see Chapter 3). Similar consequences may apply for economies considering withdrawing fiscal support more rapidly than their trading partners. By the same token, for economies introducing greater fiscal expansions than their trading partners, a possible consequence is a widening trade deficit and a strengthening currency. At the same time, fiscal policies synchronized across many economies, such as a global push to upgrade public infrastructure and end the pandemic, support for the recovery, and enhanced resilience to climate change, are likely to have limited implications for individual economies' current account balances.

Given uncertainties and risks surrounding the baseline external sector outlook discussed in Chapter 1, ensuring a narrowing of excessive surpluses and deficits will also require a broader set of measures beyond fiscal policy. As discussed in Chapter 3, these include policies and structural reforms that promote the recovery in the near term and external rebalancing over the medium term in a manner supportive of growth. Specific policies discussed in Chapter 3 include medium-term fiscal consolidation in economies with excessive current account deficit balances, such as the United States, as well as policies aimed at promoting investment and diminishing excess saving in economies with excessive current account surpluses, such as Germany. Such policies will be critical to support external rebalancing over the medium term.

References

Abbas, S. M. Ali, Jacques Bouhga-Hagbe, Antonio Fatás, Paolo Mauro, and Ricardo C. Velloso. 2011. "Fiscal Policy and the Current Account." *IMF Economic Review* 59 (4): 603–29.

Alesina, Alberto, Gualtiero Azzalini, Carlo Favero, Francesco Giavazzi, and Armando Miano. 2018. "Is It the 'How or the When' That Matters in Fiscal Adjustment?" *IMF Economic Review* 66:144–88.

Andrle, Michal, Patrick Blagrave, Pedro Espaillat, Keiko Honjo, Benjamin Hunt, Mika Kortelainen, René Lalonde, Douglas Laxton, Eleonora Mavroeidi, Dirk Muir, Susanna Mursula, and Stephen Snuddenand. 2015. "The Flexible System of Global Models—FSGM." IMF Working Paper 15/64, International Monetary Fund, Washington, DC.

Auerbach, Alan J., and Y. Gorodnichenko. 2012. "Measuring the Output Responses to Fiscal Policy." *American Economic Journal: Economic Policy* 4 (2): 1–27.

Blanchard, Olivier, and Daniel Leigh. 2013. "Growth Forecast Errors and Fiscal Multipliers." IMF Working Paper 13/1, International Monetary Fund, Washington, DC.

Bluedorn, John, and Daniel Leigh. 2011. "The Effect of Fiscal Consolidation on the Current Account." *IMF Economic Review* 59 (4): 582–602.

Carriere-Swallow, Yan, Antonio David, and Daniel Leigh. 2021. "Macroeconomic Effects of Fiscal Consolidation in Emerging Economies: New Narrative Evidence from Latin America and the Caribbean." *Journal of Money, Credit and Banking.*

Carton, Benjamin, Emilio Fernandez Corugedo, and Benjamin L. Hunt. 2017. "No Business Taxation without Model Representation: Adding Corporate Income and Cash Flow Taxes to GIMF." IMF Working Paper 17/259, International Monetary Fund, Washington, DC.

Cloyne, James. 2013. "Discretionary Tax Changes and the Macroeconomy: New Narrative Evidence from the United Kingdom." *American Economic Review* 103:1507–28.

Cloyne, James, Òscar Jordà, and Alan M. Taylor. 2020. "Decomposing the Fiscal Multiplier." NBER Working Paper 26939, National Bureau of Economic Research, Cambridge, MA.

Cubeddu, Luis, Signe Krogstrup, Gustavo Adler, Pau Rabanal, Mai Chi Dao, Swarnali Ahmed Hannan, Luciana Juvenal, Nan Li, Carolina Osorio Buitron, Cyril Rebillard, Daniel Garcia-Macia, Callum Jones, Jair Rodriguez, Kyun Suk Chang, Deepali Gautam, and Zijiao Wang. 2019. "The External Balance Assessment Methodology: 2018 Update." IMF Working Paper 19/65, International Monetary Fund, Washington, DC.

Devries, Pete, Jaime Guajardo, Daniel Leigh, and Andrea Pescatori. 2011. "A New Action-Based Dataset of Fiscal Consolidation in OECD Countries." IMF Working Paper 11/128, International Monetary Fund, Washington, DC.

Gopinath, Gita, Emine Boz, Camila Casas, Federico Diez, Pierre-Olivier Gourinchas, and Mikkel Plagborg-Møller. 2020. "Dominant Currency Paradigm." *American Economic Review* 110 (3): 677–719.

Guajardo, Jaime, Daniel Leigh, and Andrea Pescatori. 2014. "Expansionary Austerity? International Evidence." *Journal of the European Economic Association* 12:949–68.

Hayo, Bernd, and Matthias Uhl. 2014. "The Macroeconomic Effects of Legislated Tax Changes in Germany." *Oxford Economic Papers* 66 (2): 397–418.

International Monetary Fund (IMF). 2020a. G20 Surveillance Note. Washington, DC. https://www.imf.org/external/np/g20/111920.htm.

International Monetary Fund (IMF). 2020b. Group of Twenty IMF Report—IMF Annual Meetings G20. "2020 Report on Strong, Sustainable, Balanced, and Inclusive Growth." Washington, DC. https://www.imf.org/external/np/g20/pdf/2020/110220.pdf.

Jordà, Òscar. 2005. "Estimation and Inference of Impulse Responses by Local Projections." *American Economic Review* 95 (1): 161–82.

Jordà, Òscar, and Alan M. Taylor. 2016. "The Time for Austerity: Estimating the Average Treatment Effect of Fiscal Policy." *Economic Journal* 126 (590): 219–55.

Kim, Soyoung, and Nouriel Roubini. 2008. "Twin Deficit or Twin Divergence? Fiscal Policy, Current Account, and Real Exchange Rate in the U.S." *Journal of International Economics* 74 (2): 362–83.

Mertens, Karel, and Morton O. Ravn. 2013. "The Dynamic Effects of Personal and Corporate Income Taxes in the United States." *American Economic Review* 103:1212–47.

Obstfeld, Maurice, and Kenneth Rogoff. 1996. *Foundations of International Macroeconomics.* Cambridge, MA: MIT Press.

Ramey, Valerie, and Sarah Zubairy. 2018. "Government Spending Multipliers in Good Times and in Bad: Evidence from US Historical Data." *Journal of Political Economy* 126 (2): 850–901.

Romer, Christina D., and David H. Romer. 2010. "The Macroeconomic Effects of Tax Changes: Estimates Based on a New Measure of Fiscal Shocks." *American Economic Review* 100 (3): 763–801.

CHAPTER 3

2020 INDIVIDUAL ECONOMY ASSESSMENTS

Methodology and Process

The individual economy assessments use a wide range of methods to form an integrated and multilaterally consistent view of economies' external sector positions. These methods are grounded in the latest vintage of the External Balance Assessment (EBA), developed by the IMF's Research Department to estimate desired current account balances and real exchange rates.[1] Model estimates and associated discussions on policy distortions (see Box 3.1 for an example) are accompanied by a holistic view of other external indicators, including capital and financial account flows and measures, foreign exchange intervention and reserves adequacy, and foreign asset or liability positions.[2] The policy discussion in the individual economy assessments highlights policies and reforms that contribute to supporting convergence toward (or maintenance of) external balance, in the context of a summary of the overall policy advice.

The EBA models provide numerical inputs for the identification of external imbalances but, in some cases, may not sufficiently capture all relevant economic characteristics and potential policy distortions. In such cases, the individual economy assessments may need to be complemented by analytically grounded judgment and economy-specific insights in the form of adjustors. IMF staff members estimate an economy's current account gap by combining the EBA model's current account gap estimate with adjustors. For the 2020 assessments, additional adjustors to account for the effects of the COVID-19 crisis on external positions were introduced (see Online Annex 1.1 in Chapter 1). The IMF staff estimates the real effective exchange rate (REER) gap consistent with the staff current account gap by applying a country-specific elasticity, although in some cases additional information is used, such as the EBA REER regression models, unit-labor-cost-based measures, and metrics, to arrive at the staff REER gap estimate. To integrate country-specific judgment in an objective, rigorous, and evenhanded manner, a process was developed for multilaterally consistent external assessments for the 30 largest economies, representing about 90 percent of global GDP. These assessments are also discussed with the respective authorities as part of bilateral surveillance.

External assessments are presented in ranges, in recognition of inherent uncertainties, and in different categories generally reflecting deviations of the overall external position from fundamentals and desired policies. As reported in Annex Table 1.1.2 (Chapter 1), the ranges of uncertainty for IMF staff–assessed current account gaps are generally about ±1 percent of GDP. For the REER, the ranges of uncertainty vary by country, reflecting country-specific factors, including different exchange rate semi-elasticities applied to the staff-assessed current account gaps. Overall external positions are labeled as either "broadly in line," "moderately weaker (stronger)," "weaker (stronger)," or "substantially weaker (stronger)" (see Table 3.A and Box 1.4). The criteria for applying the labels to overall external positions are multidimensional. Regarding the wording to describe the current account and REER gaps, (1) when comparing the cyclically adjusted current account with the current account norm, the wording "higher" or "lower" is used, corresponding to positive or negative current account gaps, respectively; (2) a quantitative estimate of the IMF staff's view of the REER gap is generally reported as (–) percent "over-" or "under" valued. External positions that are labeled as being "broadly in line" are consistent with current account gaps in the range of ±1 percent of GDP as well as REER gaps in the range that reflects the country-specific exchange rate semi-elasticity (for example, ±5 percent based on an elasticity of –0.2).

Selection of Economies

The 30 systemic economies analyzed in detail in this report and included in the individual economy assessments are listed in Table 3.B. They were generally chosen on the basis of a set of criteria, including each economy's global rank in terms of purchasing power GDP, as reported in the IMF's *World Economic Outlook*, and in terms of the level of nominal gross trade and degree of financial integration.

[1]See Cubeddu and others (2019) for a complete description of the EBA methodology and for a description of the most recent refinements.

[2]The individual economy assessments for 2020 are based on data and IMF staff projections as of June 30, 2021.

Table 3.A. Description in *External Sector Report* Overall Assessment

CA Gap	REER Gap (Using Elasticity of –0.2)	Description in Overall Assessment
>4%	<–20%	. . . substantially stronger . . .
[2%, 4%]	[–20%, –10%]	. . . stronger . . .
[1%, 2%]	[–10%, –5%]	. . . moderately stronger . . .
[–1%, 1%]	[–5%, 5%]	The external position is broadly in line with fundamentals and desirable policies.
[–2%, –1%]	[5%, 10%]	. . . moderately weaker . . .
[–4%, –2%]	[10%, 20%]	. . . weaker . . .
<–4%	>20%	. . . substantially weaker . . .

Table 3.B. Economies Covered in the *External Sector Report*

Argentina	Euro area	Italy	Poland	Sweden
Australia	France	Japan	Russia	Switzerland
Belgium	Germany	Korea	Saudi Arabia	Thailand
Brazil	Hong Kong SAR	Malaysia	Singapore	Turkey
Canada	India	Mexico	South Africa	United Kingdom
China	Indonesia	The Netherlands	Spain	United States

Box 3.1. Assessing Imbalances: The Role of Policies—An Example

A two-country example: To clarify how to analyze policy distortions in a multilateral setting and how to distinguish between domestic policy distortions, which may require a country to take action to reduce its external imbalance, and foreign policy distortions, which require no action by the home country (but for which action by the other would help reduce the external imbalance), consider a stylized example of a two-country world.

- Country A has a large *current account deficit* and a large fiscal deficit, as well as high public and external debt.
- Country B has a *current account surplus* (matching the deficit in Country A) and a large creditor position but has no policy distortions.

Overall external assessment: The analysis would show that Country A has an external imbalance reflecting its large fiscal deficit. Country B would have an equal and opposite surplus imbalance. Country A's exchange rate would look overvalued and Country B's undervalued.

Policy gaps: The analysis of policy gaps would show that Country A has a domestic policy distortion that needs adjustment. The analysis would also show that there are no domestic policy gaps in Country B—instead, adjustment by Country A would automatically eliminate the imbalance in Country B.

Individual economy write-ups: While the estimates of the needed *current account adjustment* and associated *real exchange rate change* would be equal and opposite in both cases (given there are only two economies in the world), the individual economy assessments would identify the different issues and risks facing the two economies.

- In the case of Country A, the *capital flows and foreign asset and liability position* sections would note the vulnerabilities arising from international liabilities, and the potential policy response section would focus on the need to rein in the *fiscal deficit* and limit *financial excesses*.
- For Country B, however, as there were no domestic policy distortions, the write-up would find no fault with policies and would note that adjustment among other economies would help reduce the imbalance.

Implications: It remains critical to distinguish between domestic and foreign fiscal policy gaps. The elimination of the fiscal policy gap in a systemic deficit economy would help reduce excess surpluses in other systemic economies. More generally, policy actions that contribute to addressing external imbalances relate to the determinants of current account balances, namely the private and public saving-investment balances. Structural or policy distortions can contribute to excessive or inadequate saving and investment, and the policy advice in the individual economy assessments highlights reforms and policy changes that can contribute to addressing these gaps. Policy advice also seeks to address vulnerabilities associated with external stock positions, including reserves, as well as foreign exchange intervention policies.

Abbreviations and Acronyms

Adj.	adjusted
ARA	assessing reserve adequacy
BOP	balance of payments
CA	current account
CFM	capital flow management
COVID-19	coronavirus disease 2019
CPI	consumer price index
Cycl.	cyclically
EBA	External Balance Assessment
ECB	European Central Bank
ESR	*External Sector Report*
EU	European Union
FDI	foreign direct investment
FX	foreign exchange
GDP	gross domestic product
IIP	international investment position
Liab.	liabilities
NEER	nominal effective exchange rate
NIIP	net international investment position
PIF	Public Investment Fund
QFII	qualified institutional investors
REER	real effective exchange rate
Res.	residual
RQFII	Renminbi qualified institutional investors
SDR	special drawing right
TARGET2	Trans-European Automated Real-time Gross Settlement Express Transfer System
ULC	unit labor cost

Table 3.1. Argentina: Economy Assessment

Overall Assessment: *The external position in 2020 was weaker than the level implied by medium-term fundamentals and desirable policies.* The recent successful sovereign FX debt restructuring agreements with private creditors have provided important short-term cash flow relief, yet a credible and strong macroeconomic and structural plan that can be supported by the international community is needed to improve Argentina's external position over the medium term.

Potential Policy Responses: Policies should carefully balance the need to support the recovery and strengthen domestic and external stability. Growth-friendly fiscal consolidation, combined with prudent monetary policies, is essential to maintain a strong trade surplus, rebuild international reserves, regain market access, and ensure debt sustainability, although this path will depend on the evolution of the global pandemic. In addition, structural reforms to boost Argentina's export capacity and encourage FDI are required. As stability is established, and the pandemic wanes, a gradual conditions-based unwinding of CFM measures and export taxes will need to be considered.

Foreign Asset and Liability Position and Trajectory

Background. Argentina's external gross liabilities rose to 72.6 percent of GDP in 2020, continuing the upward trend from 34 percent of GDP at the end of 2015, when Argentina regained access to international markets. Still, the NIIP increased to 32 percent of GDP (up 5.8 and 23.1 percentage points since the end of 2019 and the end of 2015, respectively), driven by continued private capital outflows and deleveraging by firms, despite strong capital controls.

Assessment. In 2020 Argentina successfully restructured about 99 percent of eligible domestic and foreign law sovereign FX debt held by the private sector (US$82 billion, or 21.4 percent of GDP) with cash flow relief of US$34 billion during 2020–30, yet limited up-front principal reduction. Meanwhile, several provinces and private firms have also reached restructuring agreements, while negotiations are ongoing in others. CFM measures introduced in 2019 remain necessary in the near term to mitigate capital outflow risks. Prospects of market access over the medium term will depend on implementation of a strong macroeconomic and structural reform plan.

2020 (% GDP)	NIIP: 32.0	Gross Assets: 104.6	Res. Assets: 10.3	Gross Liab.: 72.6	Debt Liab.: 57.4

Current Account

Background. The CA reached a surplus of 0.8 percent of GDP in 2020, compared with –0.9 percent of GDP in 2019. The improvement reflects a higher trade surplus (0.3 percent of GDP)—as the COVID-19–related import contraction outweighed the fall in exports—as well as an improvement in the income balance (1.3 percent of GDP), largely on account of lower interest payments related to the debt restructuring operations. The trade surplus narrowed during the latter part of 2020 as FX pressures (reflected in the gap between the official and parallel rates) encouraged imports and discouraged exports. Record-high export prices could support a further improvement in the trade and CA balance in 2021, partially offset by a strong recovery in imports.

Assessment. The EBA CA cyclically adjusted balance reached a deficit of 0.5 percent of GDP, compared with an EBA CA norm equivalent to a deficit of 1.3 percent of GDP. Factoring in the transitory impacts of the COVID-19 crisis in relation to the oil and travel services (including tourism) sectors (–0.2 and –0.3 percent of GDP, respectively) implies a –0.5 percent of GDP adjustment to the deficit. Furthermore, consistent with the need to bring down external debt service to more manageable levels and pave the way for market access, the IMF staff judges the near- to medium-term CA norm to be closer to 1.0 percent of GDP, implying an adjustment of 2.4 percent of GDP. As such, the IMF staff assesses the CA gap to be –2.1 ±1 percent of GDP, the bulk of which reflects a more expansionary fiscal policy stance than warranted as well as FX sales.

2020 (% GDP)	CA: 0.8	Cycl. Adj. CA: –0.5	EBA Norm: –1.3	EBA Gap: 0.8	COVID-19 Adj.: –0.5	Other Adj.: –2.4	Staff Gap: –2.1

Real Exchange Rate

Background. The official REER appreciated by 2.3 percent, on average, in 2020 relative to 2019 and depreciated 1 percent in end-of-period terms. This mostly reflects regained FX market stability, following the 2018–19 crisis (during which the REER depreciated by a combined 35 percent), supported in part by strict CFM measures and central bank interventions targeting a broadly unchanged REER. As of the end of May 2021, reflecting a slowdown in the rate of crawl, the REER had appreciated by 0.9 percent compared to the 2020 average and by about 5.9 percent since the end of 2020.

Assessment. The IMF staff CA gap implies a REER overvaluation of 15.3 percent in 2020 (applying an estimated elasticity of 0.14). However, the REER index model suggests an undervaluation of 2.9 percent. Overall, given realized and expected trade balance improvements and continued compression of wages in 2020, the IMF staff assesses the 2020 REER gap to be in the range of –2.5 to 12.5 percent, with a midpoint of 5 percent, also reflecting significant uncertainty about the equilibrium REER.

Capital and Financial Accounts: Flows and Policy Measures

Background. The CFM measures adopted in August 2019, when Argentina lost access to international markets, were further strengthened in late 2020 in response to FX pressures arising from the monetary financing of the budget and uncertainties over the direction of policies. Current CFM measures include (1) a surrender requirement for FX export proceeds, (2) central bank authorization for payment of dividends and profits, (3) limits on FX purchases by firms and individuals (when purchasing FX, individuals pay a 30 percent tax and a 35 percent fee that can be credited toward income tax payments), and (4) limits on external amortization payments (firms may service up to 40 percent of amortizations falling due between October 2020 and December 2021). There are no restrictions on FX deposit withdrawals for either individuals or firms.

Assessment. The CFM measures significantly reduced the size of the official FX market and slowed the rate of capital outflows. While the tightening of CFM measures may have helped reduce FX pressures (the gap fell from a peak of over 100 percent in October 2020 to about 75 percent in May), they are not a substitute for macroeconomic policies to address underlying imbalances. While CFM measures are needed in the near term, a conditions-based unwinding will be necessary, especially to encourage FDI.

FX Intervention and Reserves Level

Background. Gross international reserves fell to US$39.4 billion (about 10 percent of GDP) by the end of 2020 down US$5.5 billion and US$26 billion relative to the end of 2019 and 2018, respectively. The decline in reserves in 2020 reflects a combination of factors, including debt service payments (public and private) and FX sales (US$4.9 billion). As of the end of May 2021 gross international reserves stood at about US$42 billion, although, after excluding swap lines with other central banks and reserve requirements on domestic US dollar deposits, reserves (and related deposit insurance) reached close to US$8.5 billion.

Assessment. Gross international reserves represented about 60 percent of the IMF's composite metric as of end-2020 after smoothing of temporary effects, and 72 percent without the adjustment.[1] In the context of the projected trade surpluses and reduced debt service payments following external debt restructuring agreements, rebuilding of reserve coverage is necessary to pave the way for market access and the easing of CFM measures over the medium term. Given reserves scarcity, FX intervention (in the official or parallel market) should be limited to addressing disorderly conditions.

Table 3.2. Australia: Economy Assessment

Overall Assessment: *The external position in 2020 was broadly in line with the level implied by medium-term fundamentals and desirable policies.* The increase in the CA surplus recorded in 2020 reflects in large part temporary factors associated with the COVID-19 shock. While considerable uncertainty remains, the CA is expected to return to a deficit in the medium term as domestic demand picks up and temporary factors unwind.

Potential Policy Responses: Policies that promote domestic demand can contribute to maintaining the CA balance close to its norm. The substantial monetary policy easing and fiscal stimulus implemented in response to the COVID-19 shock were appropriate to support the economy and protect vulnerable households and firms. The policy priority in the period ahead should be to maintain adequate policy support, including by scaling up public investment, until the recovery is firmly entrenched. The continued accommodative fiscal and monetary policy stance will support domestic demand and contribute to the narrowing of the CA surplus while keeping the external position in line with fundamentals.

Foreign Asset and Liability Position and Trajectory

Background. Australia's NIIP declined to –52.6 percent of GDP in 2020 from –46.2 percent of GDP in 2019 as valuation changes from the Australian dollar's appreciation offset the effect of the CA surplus. The NIIP-to-GDP ratio is expected to stabilize at about –36 percent of GDP over the medium term. Although nearly one-half of Australia's gross liabilities are debt obligations, more than one-half of the liabilities are denominated in domestic currency, while assets are in foreign currency. Foreign liabilities are composed of about one-quarter FDI, one-half portfolio investment (principally banks' borrowing abroad and foreign holdings of government bonds), and one-quarter other investments and derivatives.

Assessment. The NIIP level and trajectory are sustainable. The structure of Australia's external balance sheet reduces the vulnerability associated with its high negative NIIP. With a positive net foreign currency asset position, a nominal depreciation tends to strengthen the external balance sheet, all else equal. The banking sector's net foreign currency liability position is mostly hedged, the maturity of banks' external funding has lengthened since the global financial crisis, and the Term Funding Facility implemented after the COVID-19 shock has reduced banks' dependence on foreign funding. Despite the recent increase in debt, the government's balance sheet remains strong and can provide credible support in a tail risk event in which domestic banks suffer a major loss.

2020 (% GDP)	NIIP: –52.6	Gross Assets: 171.3	Debt Assets: 47.5	Gross Liab.: 223.9	Debt Liab.: 104.4

Current Account

Background. While Australia has historically run CA deficits, averaging about 3 percent of GDP between 2014 and 2018, the CA balance switched to a surplus of 0.7 percent of GDP in 2019 and rose further to 2.5 percent of GDP in 2020. The increase in surplus in 2020 largely reflects temporary factors related to the COVID-19 shock, including a sharp increase in the primary income balance (an improvement of 1.6 percent of GDP relative to 2019 and the highest-recorded balance as a percent of GDP since the mid-1970s); a collapse in travel services imports, including tourism, while (especially education-related) travel services exports declined by less; relatively strong demand for Australian commodities; and an increase in commodity prices of Australia's main exports late in the year. While there is considerable uncertainty, the CA is expected to gradually return to a deficit over the medium term, albeit at a level lower than the historical average.

Assessment. The EBA model estimates a cyclically adjusted CA surplus of 2.4 percent of GDP compared with a CA norm of –0.1 percent of GDP, suggesting a model-based CA gap of 2.6 percent of GDP. However, in the IMF staff's view, two adjustments are warranted to the cyclically adjusted CA balance: (1) an adjustment of –0.5 percent of GDP to reflect temporary factors related to the COVID-19 shock, mostly due to an increase in the travel services balance; and (2) an adjustment of –1.2 percent of GDP to reflect temporarily lower dividend payments on FDI and portfolio liabilities. Taking these adjustments into consideration, the IMF staff–adjusted CA gap is in the range of –0.1 to 1.9 percent of GDP, with a midpoint of 0.9 percent of GDP.

2020 (% GDP)	CA: 2.5	Cycl. Adj. CA: 2.4	EBA Norm: –0.1	EBA Gap: 2.6	COVID-19 Adj.: –1.7	Other Adj.: 0.0	Staff Gap: 0.9

Real Exchange Rate

Background. Australia's REER depreciated by 0.8 percent in 2020 compared with the 2019 average and is about 5 percent lower than its 2015 level. However, the average depreciation in 2020 masks substantial volatility over the course of the year. The REER depreciated in the first half of the year amid the rise in global risk aversion. The second half of the year saw a significant appreciation, with the fourth quarter of 2020 average REER close to 4 percent higher than that of the fourth quarter of 2019 due to a rise in commodity prices of Australia's main exports and a relatively quicker recovery in economic activity in Australia compared with the rest of the world. As of May 2021 the REER had appreciated by about 8.2 percent relative to the 2020 average.

Assessment. The IMF staff CA gap implies a REER gap of –4.5 percent (applying an estimated elasticity of 0.2). The EBA REER level model points to an overvaluation of 9.8 percent, while the REER index model points to a slight undervaluation of 2.1 percent. Overall, the IMF staff assesses the REER gap to be in the range of –8 to 2 percent, with a midpoint of –3 percent.

Capital and Financial Accounts: Flows and Policy Measures

Background. The financial account recorded net outflows in 2020, reflecting the sizable CA surplus. While net FDI inflows continued (though at lower levels on account on lower inflows amid the COVID-19 shock), these were offset by net portfolio outflows, other net outflows (mainly reflecting outflows from the financial sector as banks were able to replace foreign borrowing with funding from the central bank using the Term Funding Facility), and derivatives outflows (where both inflows and outflows increased significantly, with net outflows of about 1.1 percent of GDP).

Assessment. Vulnerabilities related to the financial account remain contained, supported by a credible commitment to a floating exchange rate.

FX Intervention and Reserves Level

Background. The currency has been free floating since 1983. The central bank has not intervened in the FX market since the global financial crisis.

Assessment. The authorities are strongly committed to a floating regime, which reduces the need for reserve holdings. Although domestic banks' external liabilities remain sizable, they are either in local currency or hedged, so reserve needs for prudential reasons are also limited.

Table 3.3. Belgium: Economy Assessment

Overall Assessment: *The external position in 2020 was moderately weaker than the level implied by medium-term fundamentals and desirable policies.*

Potential Policy Responses: In the near term, the overarching policy priority remains mitigation of the health and economic impact of the COVID-19 pandemic, avoiding a premature unwinding of policy support. However, narrowing policy space will require measures to be increasingly targeted as the recovery firms up, balancing protection of vulnerable households and viable firms with facilitating resource reallocation to mitigate scarring. In light of imbalances that existed before the COVID-19 outbreak, in the medium term, policies should refocus on strengthening competitiveness by addressing structural challenges—including labor and product market reforms and other reforms to foster green, digital, and inclusive growth that will support competitiveness through investment in infrastructure, education, and training—as well as on rebuilding fiscal space. These steps could contribute to bringing the external position more in line with medium-term fundamentals and desirable policy settings.

Foreign Asset and Liability Position and Trajectory

Background. The NIIP declined from 51 percent of GDP at the end of 2019 to 45 percent at the end of 2020, driven by valuation changes, to just below its five-year average of 48 percent. Belgium's large creditor position is underpinned by sizable net household financial wealth. While household savings increased thanks to income support measures and precautionary savings during the pandemic, the impact on the NIIP was offset by external borrowing by the government. Gross foreign assets reached 467 percent of GDP in 2020 (up 22 percentage points from 2019 despite a modest decline in nominal terms), inflated by intragroup corporate treasury activities. Gross foreign assets of the banking sector stood at 81 percent of GDP at the end of 2020, well below the pre-global-financial-crisis peak of more than 200 percent, following a decade of consolidation and deleveraging. External public debt increased to 75 percent of GDP in 2020, up from 64 percent in 2019, reflecting a sharp increase in financing needs and demand from international investors, and is predominantly denominated in euros. Though declining as support measures are unwound, public sector financing needs are projected to remain high over the medium term as deficits remain well above precrisis levels and large redemptions come due. TARGET2 balances averaged –€49.6 billion (–11 percent of GDP) in 2020, up from –€27.4 billion in 2019.

Assessment. Belgium's large gross international asset and liability positions are inflated by the presence of corporate treasury units, which do not appear to create macro-relevant mismatches. Looking ahead, based on the projected CA and growth paths, the NIIP-to-GDP ratio is expected to decline. The large and positive NIIP and its trajectory do not raise sustainability concerns.

2020 (% GDP)	NIIP: 45.1	Gross Assets: 466.7	Debt Assets: 172.8	Gross Liab.: 421.6	Debt Liab.: 195.0

Current Account

Background. The CA averaged 0.4 percent of GDP over 2015–19 and has been on a downward but volatile path since its post-global-financial-crisis peak of 1.4 percent in 2015. Volatility in the trade and primary income balances is driven by sizable operations of multinationals and large revisions.[1] In 2020 the CA turned into a deficit of 0.2 percent of GDP from a surplus of 0.3 percent of GDP in 2019, driven by a deterioration in net current transfers (0.3 percent of GDP) linked to a higher EU contribution and a modest decline in the trade balance (0.2 percent of GDP). The latter reflects a decline in net exports of goods in volume terms that was only partially offset by improvements in the terms of trade (energy prices) and in the services balance driven by travel and transportation (especially tourism, where Belgium is a net importer and spending abroad declined more than receipts). For 2021 the CA deficit is projected to widen further, as import growth is expected to outpace export growth, due to the recovery in domestic and external demand—given the large foreign content of exports—and gradual reversal of temporary factors that supported the CA in 2020. The income balance is expected to remain broadly unchanged.

Assessment. EBA model estimates yield a CA gap of –1.5 percent of GDP for 2020, based on a cyclically adjusted CA balance of –0.1 percent of GDP. Adjustment for transitory COVID-19 effects on the CA of –0.3 percent of GDP (driven by –0.4 percent of GDP for travel services, including tourism) and 0.1 and –0.1 percent of GDP for the shift in household consumption from services to consumer goods and the impact on medical goods trade, respectively, brings the gap to –1.8 percent of GDP (relative to an estimated norm of 1.4 percent of GDP). This is within a range estimated by the IMF staff for the CA gap of between –2.8 and –0.8 percent of GDP, applying a standard range for the CA gap of ±1 percent of GDP.

2020 (% GDP)	CA: –0.2	Cycl. Adj. CA: –0.1	EBA Norm: 1.4	EBA Gap: –1.5	COVID-19 Adj.: –0.3	Other Adj.: —	Staff Gap: –1.8

Real Exchange Rate

Background. After depreciating in 2019 by about 2 percent, in excess of euro depreciation (NEER depreciated by 1.1 percent), the ULC- and CPI-based REER appreciated by 3 and 1.4 percent, respectively, relative to the 2019 average. This brings the cumulative appreciation of the ULC- and CPI-based REER, respectively, to 6 and 7 percent over the past five years, thus reversing the sharp depreciation in 2014–15 brought about by wage moderation. The ULC- and CPI-based REER further appreciated by 4.7 and 0.3 percent, respectively, by the end of May 2021 relative to the 2020 average.

Assessment. The IMF staff CA gap implies a REER gap of 4.3 percent in 2020 (applying an estimated elasticity of 0.42). EBA model estimates point to a REER overvaluation of between 9.6 and 18.2 percent, based on the CPI-based REER index and level models. Consistent with the IMF staff CA gap, the IMF staff assesses the REER to be overvalued in the range of 1.8 to 6.8 percent, with a midpoint of 4.3 percent.[2]

Capital and Financial Accounts: Flows and Policy Measures

Background. Gross financial outflows and inflows were on an upward trend prior to the global financial crisis as banks expanded their cross-border operations. These flows have shrunk considerably and have become more volatile as banks have deleveraged. Short-term external debt accounted for 25 percent of gross external debt in 2020. The capital account is open.

Assessment. Belgium remains exposed to financial market risks, but the structure of financial flows does not point to specific vulnerabilities. The large and positive NIIP reduces the vulnerabilities associated with high external public debt.

FX Intervention and Reserves Level

Background. The euro has the status of a global reserve currency.

Assessment. Reserves held by the euro area are typically low relative to standard metrics, but the currency is free floating.

Table 3.4. Brazil: Economy Assessment

Overall Assessment: *The external position in 2020 was broadly in line with the level implied by medium-term fundamentals and desirable policies.* In the wake of the COVID-19 shock, the CA deficit contracted due to the large currency depreciation and improvements in the service and income balances. The trend is expected to persist in 2021.

Potential Policy Responses: Policies that would help keep the CA in line with its norm include desirable fiscal consolidation, accompanied by measures to support public and private investment, including structural reforms to improve efficiency and reduce the cost of doing business. FX intervention, including using derivatives, may be appropriate to alleviate disorderly market conditions in the FX market.

Foreign Asset and Liability Position and Trajectory

Background. Brazil's NIIP was –38 percent of GDP at the end of 2020, moderately stronger than at the end of 2019 (–42 percent of GDP) mainly due to valuation effects associated with the currency depreciation (assets are predominantly denominated in FX while liabilities are more concentrated in local currency). At the end of 2020 external debt declined by about 5 percent in nominal terms compared with 2019, accounting for about 44 percent of GDP and 303 percent of exports, against a value of 36 percent of GDP and 299 percent of exports in 2019, with the large increase in the external-debt-to-GDP ratio in 2020 driven by the significant output contraction when measured in US dollars.

Assessment. Brazil's NIIP has been negative since 2001. Short-term gross external financing needs are significant, at about 11 percent of projected 2021 GDP, with capital flows and the exchange rate particularly sensitive to global financing conditions.

2020 (% GDP)	NIIP: –38.3	Gross Assets: 63.5	Res. Assets: 24.8	Gross Liab.: 102.0	Debt Liab.: 44.3

Current Account

Background. The CA deficit contracted from –3.5 percent of GDP in 2019 to –1.7 in 2020 due to improvements in the trade, service, and income balances, supported, respectively, by the currency depreciation, the contraction in tourism and transportation service imports, and lower distribution of profits and dividends. In 2021 the trade balance is expected to continue to improve on the back of a recovery in economic activity in trading partners that would boost exports, more than offsetting the rebound in imports. Overall, the IMF staff projects a CA balance of about –0.4 percent of GDP for 2021.

Assessment. In 2020 the cyclically adjusted CA balance was –1.6 percent of GDP. EBA estimates suggest a CA norm in 2020 of –2.4 percent of GDP. The IMF staff assesses a CA norm between –1.9 percent of GDP and –2.9 percent of GDP. Thus, after adjusting for the transitory impacts of the COVID-19 crisis on the oil; travel services, including tourism; and medical goods sectors (resulting in an impact on the CA balance of 0.3 percent, –0.3 percent, and 0.1 percent of GDP, respectively), the IMF staff CA gap is assessed at 0.9 percent of GDP. The medium-term outlook for the CA is still difficult to assess, given the unfolding COVID-19 crisis and related policy response.

2020 (% GDP)	CA: –1.7	Cycl. Adj. CA: –1.6	EBA Norm: –2.4	EBA Gap: 0.8	COVID-19 Adj.: 0.1	Other Adj.: 0.0	Staff Gap: 0.9

Real Exchange Rate

Background. After remaining broadly stable in 2019 (–1.9 percent), the REER depreciated sharply in 2020 (–20.6 percent), driven by large capital outflows in the first half of the year. Depreciation pressures have subsided since mid-May 2020. As of end-May 2021, the REER had depreciated by 3.5 percent compared with the 2020 average.

Assessment. The IMF staff CA gap implies a REER gap of –7.1 percent in 2020 (applying an estimated elasticity of 0.13). The REER index (–36.6 percent) and level (–21.3 percent) methodologies point to some possible overshooting of the nominal exchange rate. Overall, the IMF staff assesses the REER gap at the end of 2020 to be closer to the REER gap implied by the IMF staff CA gap. Therefore, considering the CA norm standard error of 0.8 percent, the IMF staff assesses the REER gap to be in the range of –14.6 to 0.4 percent, with a midpoint of –7.1 percent (undervaluation).

Capital and Financial Accounts: Flows and Policy Measures

Background. Net FDI has fully financed CA deficits since 2015 (averaging 3.2 percent of GDP during 2015–20, while CA deficits averaged –2.2 percent), despite net portfolio outflows (0.6 percent of GDP, on average, during 2015–20). In 2020 net FDI stood at 3.5 percent of GDP against a CA deficit of 1.7 percent. Net portfolio outflows accelerated sharply in the first half of the year before easing in the third quarter and then partly recovering in the fourth quarter, recording a balance of –0.9 percent of GDP over the year (–1 percent of GDP in 2019). Net FDI was stronger than in 2019 due to divestment abroad that more than compensated for lower FDI inflows.

Assessment. The composition of capital flows is expected to remain favorable over the medium term, with positive net FDI inflows outweighing negative portfolio outflows that started in 2016 following the sovereign's downgrade to below investment grade. Nevertheless, the high degree of uncertainty about the scarring effects of COVID-19 on the global economy make it challenging to assess the medium-term prospects for capital flows. A renewed spike in international risk aversion, linked to a potential second wave of COVID-19, or a sudden tightening of global financing conditions could trigger a new bout of capital market volatility.

FX Intervention and Reserves Level

Background. Brazil has a floating exchange rate. In 2020 the central bank sold FX in the spot, repo, and FX swap markets in the amount of US$44.5 billion to dampen excess exchange rate volatility associated with the COVID-19 shock. Nevertheless, reserves remained high at US$356 billion at the end of 2020.

Assessment. The flexible exchange rate has been an important shock absorber. Reserves are adequate relative to various criteria, including the IMF's reserve adequacy metric (161 percent as of the end of 2020) and serve as insurance against external shocks. The authorities should retain strong external buffers, with intervention limited to addressing disorderly market conditions.

Table 3.5. Canada: Economy Assessment

Overall Assessment: *The external position in 2020 was moderately weaker than the level implied by medium-term fundamentals and desirable policies.* It will take time for the economy to adjust to structural shifts in the allocation of resources, restore lost production capacity, and address productivity underperformance. The CA deficit narrowed in 2020 due to the contraction of demand-induced imports but will moderately widen in the medium term as domestic demand rebounds.

Potential Policy Responses: If imbalances persist, policies should aim to boost Canada's nonenergy exports. These policies include measures geared toward improving labor productivity, investing in research and development and physical capital, promoting FDI, developing services exports, and diversifying Canada's export markets. The planned increase in public infrastructure investment should boost competitiveness and improve the external position in the medium term. The recent sharp increase in government debt that resulted from the government's response to COVID-19 underscores the importance of developing a credible medium-term fiscal consolidation plan to support external rebalancing.

Foreign Asset and Liability Position and Trajectory

Background. Despite running a CA deficit, Canada's NIIP has improved since 2010, reaching 61.3 percent of GDP in 2020, up from 22.5 percent in 2015 and –18.1 percent in 2010. This largely reflects valuation gains on external assets. At the same time, gross external debt increased to 142.8 percent of GDP at the end of 2020, of which about one-third is short term.

Assessment. Canada's foreign assets have a higher foreign currency component than its liabilities, which provides a hedge against currency depreciation. The NIIP level and trajectory are sustainable.

2020 (% GDP)	NIIP: 61.3	Gross Assets: 299.4	Debt. Assets: 88.0	Gross Liab.: 238.1	Debt Liab.: 142.8

Current Account

Background. The CA deficit stood at 1.8 percent of GDP in 2020, down from 2.1 percent of GDP in 2019, reflecting improvements in primary income balance and in services. The CA deficit has been financed by non-FDI net financial inflows, which have more than offset net outflows of FDI.

Assessment. The EBA estimates a CA norm of 2.5 percent of GDP and a cyclically adjusted CA of –1.3 percent of GDP for 2020. The IMF staff assesses the CA gap to be narrower after considering (1) CA measurement issues;[1] (2) the authorities' demographic projections and current immigration targets;[2] and (3) the temporary impact of the COVID-19 crisis on oil (0.6 percent of GDP); travel services, including tourism (–0.3 percent of GDP); and the global shift in household consumption from services to consumer goods and the impact on medical goods trade (0.3 percent of GDP each). Taking these factors into consideration, the IMF staff CA gap is in the range of –2.6 to 0.4 percent of GDP.

2020 (% GDP)	CA: –1.8	Cycl. Adj. CA: –1.3	EBA Norm: 2.5	EBA Gap: –3.8	COVID-19 Adj.: 0.8	Other Adj.: 1.9	Staff Gap: –1.1

Real Exchange Rate

Background. Relative to the 2019 average, the REER depreciated by 1.1 percent through December 2020. As of end-May, the REER had appreciated by 7.5 percent compared to the 2020 average.

Assessment. The IMF staff CA gap implies a REER gap of 3.9 percent in 2020 (applying an estimated elasticity of 0.28). The EBA REER index model points to an overvaluation of 2.6 percent in 2020, while the REER level model points to an undervaluation of about 6.5 percent. In the IMF staff's view, the REER level model could overstate the extent of undervaluation. Consistent with the IMF staff CA gap, the IMF staff assesses the REER to be overvalued in the range of –1.6 to 9.4 percent, with a midpoint of 3.9 percent.[3]

Capital and Financial Accounts: Flows and Policy Measures

Background. The CA deficit in 2020 was financed by non-FDI net financial flows: portfolio (3.7 percent of GDP) and other investment (–0.7 percent of GDP). FDI recorded net outflows of 1.4 percent of GDP (lower than the net outflows in 2019). In 2020 estimated errors and omissions recorded an outflow of 0.1 percent of GDP.

Assessment. Canada has an open capital account. Vulnerabilities are limited by a credible commitment to a floating exchange rate.

FX Intervention and Reserves Level

Background. Canada has a free-floating exchange rate regime and has not intervened in the FX market since September 1998 (with the exception of participating in internationally concerted interventions). Canada has limited reserves, but its central bank has standing swap arrangements with the Federal Reserve and four other major central banks (it has not drawn on these swap lines).

Assessment. Policies in this area are appropriate to the circumstances of Canada. The authorities are strongly committed to a floating regime, which, together with the swap arrangement, reduces the need for reserve holdings.

Table 3.6. China: Economy Assessment

Overall Assessment: *The external position in 2020 was in line with the level implied by medium-term fundamentals and desirable policies.* The CA surplus widened in 2020, driven by transitory factors linked to the global pandemic crisis, including falling commodity prices; the halt to outbound travel, including tourism; and a surge in pandemic-related exports. When these temporary factors dissipate, the CA surplus is expected to return to its medium-term downward trend as China's economy rebalances toward higher-quality, more-consumption-driven growth.

Potential Policy Responses: Policies that will ensure that the external position remains broadly in line with fundamentals include (1) accelerating structural reforms—further opening domestic markets, reforming state-owned enterprises, and ensuring competitive neutrality with private firms while promoting green investment and strengthening social safety nets—to boost potential growth; (2) shifting policy support toward strengthening social safety nets to reduce high household saving; and (3) further increasing exchange rate flexibility to help the economy adjust to the changing external environment. China has room to provide more fiscal support if needed, preferably through household support and green investment, with monetary policy broadly supportive of economic activity.

Foreign Asset and Liability Position and Trajectory

Background. The NIIP, which declined from a peak of 30.4 percent of GDP in 2008 to 14.5 percent in 2019, further decreased to 14.5 percent in 2020. The drop reflects higher inward direct investment and securities investment received amid relatively robust GDP growth after the first quarter, despite a higher CA surplus and an increase in loans extended abroad.

Assessment. The NIIP-to-GDP ratio is expected to remain positive, with a modest decline over the medium term. The NIIP is not a major source of risk at this point, as assets remain high—reflecting large foreign reserves (US$3.4 trillion, 22.6 percent of GDP)—and liabilities are mostly FDI related.

2020 (% GDP)	NIIP: 14.5	Gross Assets: 58.5	Res. Assets: 22.6	Gross Liab.: 44.1	Debt Liab.: 15.9

Current Account

Background. The widening of the CA surplus to 1.8 percent of GDP in 2020 from 0.7 percent in 2019, underpinned by a higher savings-investment balance in the wake of the COVID-19 outbreak, mostly reflects the impact of the global pandemic, including (1) the sudden collapse in outbound travel spending, including tourism; (2) lower commodity prices amid weak global demand; and (3) a surge in exports related to the pandemic enabled by China's relatively early recovery from the initial lockdown. This export surge affected predominantly pandemic-related goods (such as medical equipment and health care products) and durable goods, driven by the global shift in household consumption composition from services to goods, amplified by a significant increase in export prices. The income balance turned more negative in 2020, driven by a higher investment income deficit. The impact of the pandemic is expected to be temporary, with the CA surplus projected to converge to about 0.5 percent of GDP over the medium term, in line with continued rebalancing toward higher-quality and more-consumption-driven growth.

Assessment. The EBA CA methodology estimates the CA gap in 2020 to be 1.9 percent of GDP. Considering that the pandemic-related temporary factors raised the CA surplus by 1.2 percent of GDP (with contributions of 0.1 percent of GDP from the oil balance, 0.5 from the travel services balance, and 0.2 and 0.4 from the shift in household consumption from services to consumer goods and the impact on medical goods trade, respectively), the IMF staff assesses the CA gap to range from –0.7 to 2.1 percent of GDP, with a midpoint of 0.7 percent. The range around the midpoint reflects a number of uncertainties, including about how temporary the impact of the pandemic will be. EBA-identified policy gaps are close to nil on balance as the impact of China's still-high credit growth offsets that of a relatively closed capital account (in a de jure sense), while the fiscal policy gap widened, reflecting more expansionary fiscal policy. The overall gap is largely accounted for by the residual, which reflects factors not directly captured by the underlying model, including distortions that encourage excessive saving.

2020 (% GDP)	CA: 1.8	Cycl. Adj. CA: 1.7	EBA Norm: –0.3	EBA Gap: 1.9	COVID-19 Adj.: –1.2	Other Adj.: 0.0	Staff Gap: 0.7

Real Exchange Rate

Background. After a depreciation of 11.7 percent during 2015–19, the REER appreciated by 2.1 percent in 2020 from the 2019 average, largely driven by the appreciation in the NEER (0.9 percent). In the context of declining depreciation pressure, the use of a countercyclical adjustment factor was phased out in October. As of end-May 2021, the REER had appreciated by 3.0 percent compared ot the 2020 average.

Assessment. The IMF staff CA gap implies a REER gap of –3.1 percent in 2020 (applying an estimated elasticity of 0.23). The EBA REER index regression estimates the REER gap in 2020 to be –0.3 percent, and the EBA REER level regression estimates the REER gap to be 13.0 percent. Overall, the IMF staff assesses the REER gap to be in the range of –10.5 to 9.5 percent, with a midpoint of –0.5 percent.

Capital and Financial Accounts: Flows and Policy Measures

Background. Capital outflows (including net errors and omissions) increased to US$246 billion (or 1.7 percent of GDP) in 2020, up from US$122 billion (or 0.8 percent of GDP) in 2019 but still below the average annual outflows of US$636 billion during 2015–16. In part, the increase reflects continued opening up. The reserve requirement on FX forwards, a CFM measure, was lowered from 20 percent to zero in October 2020. Two other CFM measures were adjusted: (1) the ceiling on cross-border financing under the macroprudential assessment framework for financial institutions and enterprises was raised by 25 percent in March 2020, but lowered to the original level for financial institutions in December 2020 and for enterprises in January 2021; and (2) restrictions on the investment quota of foreign institutional investors (QFII and RQFII) were removed, while a new quota ($12.7 billion) was introduced for domestic institutional investors.

Assessment. While currently absent, substantial net outflow pressures may resurface as the private sector seeks to accumulate foreign assets faster than nonresidents accumulate Chinese assets. Over the medium term, the sequence of further capital account opening consistent with exchange rate flexibility should carefully consider domestic financial stability. Specifically, further capital account opening is likely to create substantially larger two-way gross flows. Hence, the associated balance sheet adjustments and the shifts in market sentiment require prioritizing the shift to an effective float (while using FX intervention to counter disorderly market conditions) and strengthening domestic financial stability prior to substantial further opening. Efforts should be redoubled to encourage inward FDI, which would support growth, and to improve corporate governance. CFM measures should not be used to actively manage the capital flow cycle or substitute for warranted macroeconomic adjustment and exchange rate flexibility.

FX Intervention and Reserves Level

Background. FX reserves continued to increase (by US$134 billion in 2020) to US$3.4 trillion, mainly reflecting valuation effects and adjustments in net forward positions, with no sign of large FX intervention.

Assessment. The level of reserves—at 75 percent of the IMF's standard composite metric at the end of 2020 (85 percent in 2019) and 120 percent of the metric adjusted for capital controls (135 percent in 2019)—is assessed to be adequate. The decline in the ratios reflects higher exports, broad money, external debt, and other liabilities, all of which raised the metric.

Table 3.7. Euro Area: Economy Assessment

Overall Assessment: *The external position in 2020 was broadly in line with the level implied by medium-term fundamentals and desirable policies.* The pandemic has led to a collapse of the services and primary income balances, which was largely offset by an improvement in the goods balance, reducing the CA balance slightly to 2.2 percent of GDP in 2020. In the medium term, the CA surplus is projected to increase relative to the 2019 levels, reflecting in part higher private sector savings, although the range of uncertainty around this projection is exceptionally high given the nature of this crisis. Imbalances could remain sizable at the national level.

Potential Policy Responses: Short-term policies should continue focusing on containing the COVID-19 outbreak and its economic consequences and provide relief to households and firms to reduce scarring from the crisis. The recent COVID crisis initiatives—both at the national and EU levels—have supported these efforts and could potentially help reduce the CA surplus by supporting investment and consumption, thereby increasing imports. Looking ahead, monetary policy should remain accommodative until inflation has durably converged to the ECB's medium-term price stability objective, and fiscal support should remain in place until the recovery is firmly established, before gradually consolidating toward medium-term objectives. If imbalances in policy gaps persist at the national level, countries with excess CA surpluses should continue to strengthen investment and potential growth, whereas those with weak external positions should undertake reforms to raise productivity, reduce structural and youth unemployment, and enhance competitiveness as the acute phase of the pandemic recedes. Euro-area-wide initiatives to make the currency union more resilient (for example, banking and capital markets union and fiscal capacity for macroeconomic stabilization) could further reinvigorate investment and, hence, reduce the aggregate CA surplus.

Foreign Asset and Liability Position and Trajectory

Background. The NIIP of the euro area had fallen to about –23 percent of GDP by the end of 2009 but rose substantially to about 0.8 percent of GDP by the end of 2020. The rise was driven by stronger CA balances and modest nominal GDP growth. Relative to 2019 the NIIP increased by 1.1 percentage points of GDP, reflecting primarily the net increase in long-term portfolio securities, partially offset by a decline in net "other investment" assets. Gross foreign positions were about 268.3 percent of GDP for assets and 267.5 percent of GDP for liabilities in 2020. However, net external assets reached elevated levels in large net external creditors (for example, Germany and The Netherlands), whereas net external liabilities remained high in some countries, including Portugal and Spain.

Assessment. Projections of continued CA surpluses over the medium term suggest that the NIIP-to-GDP ratio will rise further, at a moderate pace. The region's overall NIIP financing vulnerabilities appear low. Despite rising CA balances over the medium term, large net external debtor countries still bear a greater risk of a sudden stop of gross inflows.

2020 (% GDP)	NIIP: 0.8	Gross Assets: 268.3	Debt Assets: 103.8	Gross Liab.: 267.5	Debt Liab.: 103.7

Current Account

Background. The CA balance for the euro area declined slightly to 2.2 percent of GDP in 2020. The collapse in the services and primary income balances was offset by an improvement in the goods balance. Both precautionary and forced savings of the private sector increased sharply in 2020, offsetting the decline in public sector savings, which was largely driven by expansionary policies. Bilateral CA surpluses declined the most vis-à-vis the United Kingdom and the United States, and deficits increased vis-à-vis China. Some large creditor countries, such as Germany and The Netherlands, continued to have sizable surpluses, reflecting high corporate and household saving and weak investment. At the end of the projection horizon, the CA balance will be above the 2019 level, mainly driven by higher private sector savings in Italy and some smaller countries, including Ireland.

Assessment. The EBA model estimates a CA norm of 1.0 percent of GDP, against a cyclically adjusted CA of 1.8 percent of GDP. This implies a gap of 0.8 percent of GDP. IMF staff analysis indicates a slightly higher CA norm than estimated by the EBA model, consistent with the assessed external positions of euro area member countries. The higher CA norm considers policy commitments to reduce the large net external liability positions in some countries (for example, Spain) and uncertainty about the demographic outlook and the impact of recent large-scale immigration (for example, Germany). In addition, adjustments to the underlying CA were made in Ireland and The Netherlands, given measurement issues. Adjustments for the transitory impact of the COVID-19 crisis on the composition of household consumption, as well as on the medical goods, travel services (including tourism), and oil balance sum to 0.2 percent of GDP. Considering these factors and uncertainties in the estimates, including the cyclical adjustment, the IMF staff CA gap is 0.6 percent of GDP for 2020, with a range of –0.2 to 1.4 percent of GDP.

2020 (% GDP)	CA: 2.2	Cycl. Adj. CA: 1.8	EBA Norm: 1.0	EBA Gap: 0.8	COVID-19 Adj.: 0.2	Other Adj.: –0.3	Staff Gap: 0.6

Real Exchange Rate

Background. The CPI-based REER appreciated by 2.1 percent in 2020, reversing the depreciation in 2019. This reflects a nominal appreciation of 4.1 percent in 2020, which was partially offset by weaker euro area inflation relative to its trading partners. The ULC-based REER appreciated by 2.0 percent. Other published REERs, based on extra-euro-area trading partners, appreciated by 0.8 percent, on average. As of end-May 2021, the REER had appreciated by 1.7 percent compared to the 2020 average.

Assessment. The IMF staff CA gap implies a REER gap of –1.8 percent in 2020, applying an estimated elasticity of 0.35.[1] The EBA REER index model suggests an overvaluation of 5.5 percent, and the EBA REER level model implies an undervaluation of 0.6 percent. Consistent with the IMF staff CA gap, the IMF staff assesses the REER gap to be in the range of –3.8 to 0.2 percent, with a midpoint of –1.8 percent. As with the CA, the aggregate REER gap masks a large degree of heterogeneity in REER gaps across euro area member states, ranging from an undervaluation of 9.2 percent in Germany to overvaluations of 0 to 10 percent in several small to large euro area member states. The substantial differences in REER gaps within the euro area highlight the continued need for net external debtor countries to improve their external competitiveness and for net external creditor countries to boost domestic demand.

Capital and Financial Accounts: Flows and Policy Measures

Background. Mirroring the CA surplus in 2020, the euro area experienced net capital outflows, largely driven by portfolio investment, which more than offset the net inflow of direct and other investment into the euro area.

Assessment. Gross external indebtedness of euro area residents increased by 8 percentage points of GDP due to increases in both short-term debt securities and government and Eurosystem liabilities.

FX Intervention and Reserves Level

Background. The euro has the status of a global reserve currency.

Assessment. Reserves held by euro area economies are typically low relative to standard metrics, but the currency is free floating.

Table 3.8. France: Economy Assessment

Overall Assessment: *The external position in 2020 was weaker than the level implied by medium-term fundamentals and desirable policies.*

Potential Policy Responses: In response to the COVID-19 pandemic, France deployed significant fiscal resources to bolster the health care system and provide targeted support to affected firms and individuals. In the near term, efforts should continue to focus on saving lives and supporting those most affected by the crisis. Uncertainty surrounding the medium-term outlook is unusually large. If imbalances persist, policies would need to continue focusing on further improving competitiveness by reinvigorating structural reforms and on rebuilding fiscal space once the recovery is secured. These policies would bring the external position more in line with medium-term fundamentals and desirable policies.

Foreign Asset and Liability Position and Trajectory

Background. The NIIP stood at –26 percent of GDP in the fourth quarter of 2020, below the range observed during 2014–19 (between –16 and –23 percent of GDP). The NIIP fell by about 3½ percent of GDP since the end of 2019, largely driven by an increase in banks' and public sector gross debt (about 17 and 9 percent of GDP, respectively). While the net position is moderately negative, gross positions are large. Gross assets stood at 352 percent of GDP in the fourth quarter of 2020, of which banks' non-FDI-related assets accounted for about 42 percent, reflecting their global activities. Gross liabilities reached 378.4 percent of GDP in the fourth quarter of 2020, of which external debt was about 242 percent of GDP (53 percent accounted for by banks and 27 percent by the public sector). About three-quarters of France's external debt liabilities are denominated in domestic currency. The average TARGET2 balance in 2020 was about –€2.2 billion.

Assessment. The NIIP is negative, but its size and projected stable trajectory do not raise sustainability concerns. However, there are vulnerabilities coming from large public external debt (65 percent of GDP in the fourth quarter of 2020) and banks' gross financing needs—the stock of banks' short-term debt securities was €76 billion in the fourth quarter of 2020 (3.3 percent of GDP), and financial derivatives stood at about 46 percent of GDP.

2020 (% GDP)	NIIP: –26.4	Gross Assets: 352.0	Debt Assets: 199.7	Gross Liab.: 378.4	Debt Liab.: 242.0

Current Account

Background. The CA deficit widened to 2.3 percent of GDP (from 0.7 percent in 2019), driven by a contraction in non-oil goods and services exports. While the deterioration in the CA balance is partly explained by one-off factors (for example, imports of health-care-sector equipment) and temporary factors that are expected to gradually normalize (for example, services balance, including business and tourism travel), it also reflects factors likely to weigh more lastingly on the external position (for example, aeronautics net exports, which contracted by about ½ percent of GDP). Lower investment income also reduced the contribution of the income account (by about 0.2 percent of GDP). Over the medium term, the IMF staff projects the CA deficit will narrow to about 0.7 percent of GDP by 2026 as temporary factors dissipate and selected reforms to improve France's competitiveness start to pay off.

Assessment. The 2020 cyclically adjusted CA deficit is estimated at –2.3 percent of GDP compared with an EBA-estimated norm of a 0.2 percent surplus. The model residual accounts for the bulk of the estimated gap (–2.5 percent of GDP) and its increase since 2019. The IMF staff estimates CA net adjustments related to COVID-19 at 0.4 percent of GDP, driven by travel-services-related transitory factors (0.2 percent of GDP) and exports of medical goods (0.3 percent), which were partially offset by fluctuations in the oil balance (–0.1 percent of GDP). On this basis, the IMF staff assesses that the CA gap in 2020 was between –2.7 and –1.7 percent of GDP (compared with –1.6 to –0.6 percent of GDP in 2019), with a midpoint of –2.2. The CA gap is expected to narrow over the medium term as the effect of the crisis fades.

2020 (% GDP)	CA: –1.9	Cycl. Adj. CA: –2.3	EBA Norm: 0.2	EBA CA Gap: –2.5	COVID-19 Adj.: 0.4	Other Adj.: 0.0	Staff CA Gap: –2.2

Real Exchange Rate

Background. Following a depreciation of the ULC-based REER and the CPI-based REER of 2.6 and 1.7 percent, respectively, in 2019, largely exceeding the depreciation of the euro (the NEER depreciated by only about 1 percent in 2019), both REER measures appreciated strongly in 2020. The ULC-based REER appreciated by 6.1 percent with respect to the 2019 average, while the CPI-based REER appreciated by 1.0 percent. From a longer-term perspective, although both REER measures depreciated by about 10 percent between 2008 and 2019, France has not managed to regain the loss of about one-third of its export market share registered in the early 2000s (while the export market share of the euro area remained broadly stable between 2000 and 2018). As of end-May 2021, the REER had appreciated by 1.3 percent compared to the 2020 average.

Assessment. The IMF staff CA gap implies a REER gap of 8.0 percent in 2020 (applying an estimated elasticity of 0.27).[1] The EBA REER index model points to a REER gap of –1.9 percent, while the EBA REER level model points to a REER gap of 2.9 percent. Consistent with the IMF staff CA gap, the IMF staff assesses the REER to be overvalued in the range of 6.0 to 10.0 percent, with a midpoint of 8.0 percent.

Capital and Financial Accounts: Flows and Policy Measures

Background. The CA deficit in 2020 was financed mostly by net portfolio debt inflows (0.4 percent of GDP), other investment flows (2 percent of GDP), and financial derivative flows (1 percent of GDP). Both outward and inward direct investment flows decreased significantly between 2019 and 2020, by 1.2 and 1.8 percent of GDP, respectively. The capital account is open.

Assessment. France remains exposed to financial market risks owing to the large refinancing needs of the sovereign and banking sectors.

FX Intervention and Reserves Level

Background. The euro has the status of a global reserve currency.

Assessment. Reserves held by the euro area are typically low relative to standard metrics, but the currency is free floating.

Table 3.9. Germany: Economy Assessment

Overall Assessment: *The external position in 2020 was stronger than the level implied by medium-term fundamentals and desirable policies.* The assessment accounts for certain transitory factors owing to the COVID-19 crisis impact on global trade flows. The CA surplus is projected to return to pre-pandemic levels as the current shock recedes—with the recovery in the goods trade surplus more than offsetting the lower services balance—and to resume its modest gradual narrowing over the medium term, supported by a gradual realignment of price competitiveness and solid domestic demand. As Germany is part of the euro area, the nominal exchange rate does not flexibly adjust to the country's external position, but stronger wage growth relative to euro area trading partners is expected to contribute to realigning price competitiveness within the monetary union. However, the projected adjustment is partial, and additional policy actions will be necessary for external rebalancing.

Potential Policy Responses: Policies aimed at promoting investment and diminishing excess saving would support external rebalancing and a further reduction of the CA balance toward its norm. In particular, the sizable fiscal stimulus in response to the COVID-19 crisis is a welcome use of Germany's substantial fiscal space. In the near term, policies should continue mitigating the outbreak while supporting households and businesses in a way that minimizes economic scarring and facilitates a swift recovery. If imbalances and policy distortions persist, growth-oriented fiscal policy, with greater public sector investment in such areas as digitalization, infrastructure, and climate change mitigation, would help crowd in private investment, promote potential growth, and make the economy more resilient. Structural reforms to foster entrepreneurship (for example, by expanding access to venture capital and stronger tax incentives for research and development) would also stimulate investment and reduce external imbalances. Additional tax relief for lower-income households, boosting their purchasing power, and pension reforms prolonging working lives would help reduce excess saving and ameliorate external imbalances.

Foreign Asset and Liability Position and Trajectory	**Background.** Germany's positive NIIP reached 76 percent of GDP by end-2020, more than doubling its level over the last five years. The net rise in foreign assets over this period has, however, still fallen short of the accumulation of CA surpluses. The NIIP of financial corporations other than monetary financial institutions is large and positive (65 percent of GDP), whereas that of the general government is large and negative (26 percent of GDP), partly reflecting Germany's safe haven status. The NIIP is expected to exceed 80 percent of German GDP by 2022, as the projected CA surplus remains large through the medium term but is expected to be partly offset by valuation changes. Foreign assets are well diversified by instrument. The stock of Germany's TARGET2 claims on the Eurosystem has increased during the pandemic and associated quantitative easing (QE) operations of the ECB, exceeding €1.1 trillion at the end of 2020 (32 percent of GDP). **Assessment.** With continued implementation of QE measures by the ECB, Germany's exposure to the Eurosystem remains large.
2020 (% GDP)	NIIP: 76.3 | Gross Assets: 308.3 | Debt Assets: 183.4 | Gross Liab.: 232.0 | Debt Liab.: 165.2
Current Account	**Background.** The CA surplus has widened significantly since 2001, peaking at 8.6 percent of GDP in 2015 and falling gradually since then. At 7.0 percent of GDP in 2020, the CA surplus narrowed slightly from 2019, despite an improved balance on oil and gas as well as services (driven in turn by a sharp fall in global oil prices and outbound tourism). The bulk of the CA surplus reflects the large saving-investment surplus of households. The saving-investment balance of the government is expected to turn strongly negative due to the unprecedented fiscal stimulus, and the nonfinancial corporate balance is also projected to be negative due to lower profits. **Assessment.** The cyclically adjusted CA balance is estimated by the EBA model to reach 6.9 percent of GDP. The IMF staff assesses the CA norm at 2 to 4 percent of GDP, with a midpoint 0.35 percent of GDP above the 2.6 percent CA norm implied by the EBA model. This upward adjustment reflects uncertainty over the demographic outlook and the impact of recent large-scale immigration on national savings. Staff also assesses the cyclically adjusted CA balance to be 0.6 percent of GDP lower than estimated by the model to account for the temporary sharp drop in outbound travel (–0.7 percent of GDP) and in the volume of oil trade associated with the pandemic (–0.1 percent of GDP), partially offset by larger net imports of medical goods (0.2 percent of GDP). Taking these factors into account, staff assesses the 2020 CA gap to be in the range of 2.4 to 4.4 percent of GDP, with a midpoint of 3.4 percent of GDP.[1]
2020 (% GDP)	Actual CA: 7.0 | Cycl. Adj. CA: 6.9 | EBA Norm: 2.6 | EBA Gap: 4.3 | COVID-19 Adj.: –0.6 | Other Adj.: –0.35 | Staff CA Gap: 3.4
Real Exchange Rate	**Background.** The yearly average CPI-based REER appreciated by 1.3 percent in 2020 relative to 2019, reflecting primarily the appreciation of the euro against the currencies of key trading partners—notably the US dollar. As of end-May 2021, the REER had appreciated by 1.8 percent compared to the 2020 average. **Assessment.** The IMF staff CA gap implies a REER gap of –9.2 percent in 2020 (applying an estimated elasticity of about 0.4). The EBA REER level and index models suggest an undervaluation of 15.4 percent and an overvaluation of 5.6 percent, respectively.[2] Consistent with the IMF staff CA gap, the IMF staff assesses the REER to be undervalued in the range of 4.2 to 14.2 percent, with a midpoint of 9.2 percent.
Capital and Financial Accounts: Flows and Policy Measures	**Background.** In 2020 net derivatives and other investment outflows comprised the bulk of the capital and financial accounts balance. Reversing a long-standing trend, net portfolio investment outflows shrank due to increased foreign purchases of domestic debt. Net FDI outflows remained positive but declined due to higher inflows. **Assessment.** Safe haven status and the strength of Germany's current external position limit risks.
FX Intervention and Reserves Level	**Background.** The euro has the status of a global reserve currency. **Assessment.** Reserves held by euro area countries are typically low relative to standard metrics. The currency floats freely.

Table 3.10. Hong Kong SAR: Economy Assessment

Overall Assessment: *The external position in 2020 was broadly in line with the level implied by medium-term fundamentals and desirable policies.* The CA surplus (in percent of GDP) widened in 2020 mostly due to the sharp decline in economic activity amid the COVID-19 pandemic and stronger income balance. From a longer-term perspective, the CA surplus remained below its pre-2010 level on account of structural factors, including the opening of mainland China's capital account and changes in offshore merchandise trade activities. As a result of Hong Kong SAR's Linked Exchange Rate System, short-term movements in the REER largely reflect US dollar developments. The credibility of the currency board arrangement has been ensured by a transparent set of rules governing the arrangement, large fiscal and FX reserves, strong financial regulation and supervision, the flexible economy, and a prudent fiscal framework.

Potential Policy Responses: In the near term, accommodative policies, particularly fiscal policy, are still needed to support the economic recovery from the COVID-19 pandemic. In the medium to long term, measures should be taken to ensure fiscal sustainability, given the rapidly aging population. Maintaining policies that support wage and price flexibility is crucial to preserving competitiveness under the currency board arrangement. Robust and proactive financial supervision and regulation, prudent fiscal management, flexible markets, and the Linked Exchange Rate System have worked well, and continuation of these policies will help keep the external position broadly in line with fundamentals.

Foreign Asset and Liability Position and Trajectory

Background. The NIIP increased significantly to 621 percent of GDP in 2020, from 432 percent in 2019. This was mainly due to a large increase in gross assets by 269 percentage points of GDP, in particular equity investments. Both gross assets and liabilities are high, reflecting Hong Kong SAR's status as a global financial center. Valuation changes have been sizable, as the increase in NIIP during 2016–20 (297 percent of GDP) far exceeded the cumulative financial account balances (31 percent of GDP).

Assessment. Vulnerabilities are low, given the positive and sizable NIIP and its favorable composition. FX reserves are large and stable (142 percent of GDP), and direct investments account for a large share of gross assets and liabilities (33 and 49 percent, respectively); only 13 percent of gross liabilities are portfolio investments.

2020 (% GDP)	NIIP: 621	Gross Assets: 1,814	Debt Assets: 609	Gross Liab.: 1,193	Debt Liab.: 437

Current Account

Background. The CA surplus widened to 6.5 percent of GDP in 2020 amid the pandemic, from 5.8 percent in 2019, driven by a further weakening of domestic demand and a stronger income balance. The trade surplus widened as a large decline in the service surplus—particularly in transportation-related services due to the sharp fall in tourist arrivals (–94 percent year over year)—was more than offset by the narrower goods deficit arising from weaker domestic demand. The income balance improved further, mostly driven by a smaller direct investment deficit in equity and fund shares. From a longer-term perspective, the gradual decline in private saving, driven by robust consumption growth, a tight labor market, and wealth effects related to the strong housing market, accounted for most of the drop in the CA surplus from its peak of 15 percent of GDP in 2008. The CA balance is projected to gradually decline to about 4.0 percent of GDP over the medium term.

Assessment. After adjusting for cyclical factors and for the transitory impact of the COVID-19 crisis on the oil, travel services (including tourism), and medical sectors (adjustments of –0.4, 1, and 0.1 percent of GDP, respectively), the CA surplus is estimated to be 5.8 percent of GDP in 2020, within the IMF staff–assessed CA norm range of 3.8 to 6.8 percent of GDP. The IMF staff–assessed CA gap range is hence about –1 to 2 percent of GDP, with a midpoint of 0.5 percent. Given that Hong Kong SAR is not in the EBA sample, the CA norm is estimated by applying EBA-estimated coefficients to Hong Kong SAR and adjusted for measurement issues related to the large valuation effects in the NIIP and the discrepancies between stocks and flows.[1]

2020 (% GDP)	CA: 6.5	Cycl. Adj. CA: 5.2	EBA Norm: —	EBA Gap: —	COVID-19 Adj.: 0.6	Other Adj.: —	Staff Gap: 0.5

Real Exchange Rate

Background. Under the currency board arrangement, REER dynamics are largely determined by US dollar developments and inflation differentials between the United States and Hong Kong SAR. In line with the US dollar, after appreciating by about 20 percent between 2012–19, the average REER depreciated by about 0.6 percent in 2020. As of end-May 2021, the REER had depreciated by 5.0 percent compared to the 2020 average.

Assessment. The IMF staff assesses the REER gap, based on the IMF staff CA gap range, to be in the range of –5.3 to 2.7 percent, with a midpoint of –1.3 percent (based on the average CA-REER elasticity of about 0.4).[2]

Capital and Financial Accounts: Flows and Policy Measures

Background. As a global financial center, Hong Kong SAR has an open capital account. Nonreserve financial flows turned into net inflows of US$3.0 billion in 2020, from net outflows of US$31.3 billion in 2019, largely driven by other investment flows. The financial account is typically very volatile, reflecting financial conditions in Hong Kong SAR and mainland China (transmitted through growing cross-border financial linkages),[3] shifting expectations of US monetary policy and related arbitrage in the FX and rate markets.

Assessment. Large financial resources, proactive financial supervision and regulation, and deep and liquid markets should help limit the risks from potentially volatile capital flows. The greater financial exposure to mainland China could also pose risks to the financial sector through real sector linkages, particularly in trade and tourism; credit exposures of the banking sector; and fundraising by mainland firms in local financial markets. Financial stress could emerge amid elevated tensions between the United States and China, including potential sanctions on financial institutions in Hong Kong SAR. However, Hong Kong SAR's banking system is assessed to be broadly resilient to macro-financial shocks, given its high capital buffers and profitability.

FX Intervention and Reserves Level

Background. The Hong Kong dollar has appreciated and remained close to the strong side of the convertibility undertaking since April 2020. The strong side of the convertibility undertaking was triggered several times from April to October 2020, mainly driven by increased carry trade activities and equity-related demand for the Hong Kong dollar. This prompted the Hong Kong Monetary Authority to sell HK$383.5 billion in 2020 as part of the currency board arrangement. Total reserve assets increased to about 142 percent of GDP at the end of 2020 (or 1.8 times the monetary base), up from 121 percent in 2019.

Assessment. FX reserves are currently adequate for precautionary purposes and should continue to evolve in line with the automatic adjustment inherent in the currency board system. Despite a large fiscal deficit in 2020, Hong Kong SAR still holds significant fiscal reserves (about 33 percent of GDP at the end of 2020) built up through a track record of strong fiscal discipline in previous years.

Table 3.11. India: Economy Assessment

Overall Assessment: *The external position in 2020 was broadly in line with the level implied by medium-term fundamentals and desirable policies.* India's low per capita income, favorable growth prospects, demographic trends, and development needs justify running CA deficits. External vulnerabilities remain, stemming from volatility in global financial conditions and an oil price surge, as well as a retreat from cross-border integration. Progress has been made on FDI and portfolio flow liberalization, but trade barriers remain significant.

Potential Policy Responses: Policy responses to the ongoing pandemic have appropriately prioritized support to vulnerable households and firms, through fiscal, monetary, and financial sector policies and structural reforms. Fiscal policy should remain accommodative in the near term, but a concrete medium-term fiscal consolidation is critical to ensure credibility and continued market confidence. Fiscal policy should be accompanied by efforts to further strengthen the financial sector. Improving the business climate, easing domestic supply bottlenecks, and liberalizing trade and investment will be important to help attract FDI, improve the CA financing mix, and contain external vulnerabilities. Exchange rate flexibility should act as the main shock absorber, with intervention limited to addressing disorderly market conditions.

Foreign Asset and Liability Position and Trajectory	**Background.** As of the end of 2020 India's NIIP improved to –13.1 percent of GDP from –15.0 percent of GDP at the end of 2019 on the back of a temporarily positive CA balance and reserve asset accumulation. Gross foreign assets and liabilities were 32.7 and 45.7 percent of GDP, respectively. The bulk of assets are in the form of official reserves and FDI, whereas liabilities include mostly other investments and FDI. External debt amounted to some 21.6 percent of GDP, of which about 51.9 percent was denominated in US dollars and another 33.1 percent in Indian rupees. Short-term external debt on a residual maturity basis stood at 44.8 percent of total external debt and 43.1 percent of FX reserves. **Assessment.** With CA deficits projected to widen in the medium term, the NIIP-to-GDP ratio is expected to weaken marginally. India's external debt is moderate compared with that of other emerging market economies, and rollover risks are limited in the short term. The moderate level of foreign liabilities reflects India's gradual approach to capital account liberalization, which has focused primarily on attracting FDI.
2020 (% GDP)	NIIP: –13.1 | Gross Assets: 32.7 | Res. Assets: 22.5 | Gross Liab.: 45.7 | Debt Liab.: 21.6
Current Account	**Background.** The CA balance is estimated to have improved to 1.0 percent of GDP surplus in fiscal year 2020/21 from a 0.9 percent deficit in the previous year. The improvement in the CA balance was largely driven by a sharp decline in imports caused by the negative domestic demand shock amid the COVID-19 pandemic and lower oil prices in the first half of fiscal year. Exports of both goods and services decelerated less than imports owing to a relatively smaller decline in key trading partners' demand. From a saving-investment perspective, the change in the CA reflects a sharp increase in private savings and a decline in private investment, which outweighed the drop in the public sector saving-investment balance. The CA balance is projected to return toward a deficit over the 2021/22 fiscal year due to recovery in domestic demand and higher oil prices, in the context of unusually high uncertainty over the cyclical position of the economy and the outlook for the pandemic. **Assessment.** The EBA cyclically adjusted CA balance stood at –0.8 percent of GDP in fiscal year 2020/21. The EBA CA regression estimates a norm of –2.4 percent of GDP, with a standard error of 1.3 percent, thus implying a CA gap of 1.7 percent. In the IMF staff's judgment, a CA deficit of 2½ percent of GDP is financeable over time. FDI flows are not yet sufficient to cover protracted and large CA deficits; portfolio flows are volatile and susceptible to changes in global risk appetite. Additional cyclical considerations factor in the transitory impacts of the COVID-19 crisis on oil (–0.6 percent of GDP) and travel services, including tourism (0.2 percent of GDP) balances, and on trade in medical products (–0.1 percent of GDP). Thus, with the IMF staff–assessed CA norm and additional cyclical considerations, the IMF staff–assessed CA gap is assessed to be 1.0 percent of GDP, with a range of 0 to 2 percent of GDP. Positive policy contributions to the CA gap stem mostly from an increase in FX reserves, the credit gap, and capital controls and are partly offset by a larger-than-desirable domestic fiscal deficit (although it is narrower than the world average).
2020 (% GDP)	CA: 1.0 | Cycl. Adj. CA: –0.8 | EBA Norm: –2.4 | EBA Gap: 1.7 | COVID-19 Adj.: –0.6 | Other Adj.: 0.0 | Staff Gap: 1.0
Real Exchange Rate	**Background.** The average REER in 2020 appreciated by about 0.4 percent from its 2019 average. As of end-May 2021, the REER had depreciated by 1.8 percent compared to the 2020 average. **Assessment.** The IMF staff CA gap implies a REER gap of –6.3 percent (applying an estimated elasticity of 0.17). The EBA REER index and REER level models suggest an overvaluation of 10.9 and 6.6 percent, respectively. Consistent with the IMF staff CA gap, the IMF staff assesses the REER to be in the range of –12.8 to 0.2 percent, with a midpoint of –6.3 percent for fiscal year 2020/21.
Capital and Financial Accounts: Flows and Policy Measures	**Background.** The sum of FDI, portfolio, and financial derivative flows, on a net basis, is estimated at 2.7 percent of GDP in 2020, remaining at a similar level as in 2019. Capital inflows have been supported by investor-friendly reforms in recent years. After a sharp decline in the first half of 2020, net FDI inflows recovered significantly from the third quarter onward and are estimated at 2.0 percent of GDP in 2020 as a whole. Similarly, India faced significant portfolio outflows (0.5 percent of GDP) in the first quarter of 2020 amid the COVID-19 shock. However, portfolio inflows returned after the second quarter, aided by loose global financial conditions and policy measures to ease debt inflows. **Assessment.** Yearly capital inflows are relatively small, but, given the modest scale of FDI, flows of portfolio and other investments are critical to finance the CA in the medium term. As evidenced by the episodes of external pressure, portfolio debt flows have been volatile, and the exchange rate has been sensitive to these flows and changes in global risk aversion. Attracting more stable sources of financing is needed to reduce vulnerabilities.
FX Intervention and Reserves Level	**Background.** With the CA surplus and renewed FDI and portfolio flows, in the context of mostly one-sided interventions, foreign reserves reached a record high (US$585.8 billion) in 2020, which has improved the external position. The precautionary accumulation of reserves is aimed at building buffers to mitigate risks due to external vulnerabilities and an associated adverse feedback loop with corporate and financial sectors. Net spot FX purchases were US$88 billion (3.3 percent of GDP), and net forwards purchases were US$43 billion (1.6 percent of GDP) in 2020. Reserve coverage currently is about 22.5 percent of GDP and about 12 months of prospective imports of goods and services. **Assessment.** Reserve levels are adequate for precautionary purposes, relative to various criteria, and represent about 236 percent of short-term debt on residual maturity and 197 percent of the IMF's composite metric as of the end of 2020. In this context, further accumulation of reserves is less warranted, and FX intervention should be limited to addressing disorderly market conditions.

Table 3.12. Indonesia: Economy Assessment

Overall Assessment: *The external position in 2020 was broadly in line with the level implied by medium-term fundamentals and desirable policies.* Exchange rate flexibility and structural policies should help contain the CA deficit over the medium term. External financing needs appear sustainable. However, they are sizable, and with a large share of foreign portfolio investment, they expose the economy to fluctuations in global financial conditions.

Potential Policy Responses: The projected effect of fiscal consolidation on the CA would be more than offset by the projected pickup in economic activity as the negative effects of the pandemic unwind. Therefore, maintaining external balance will require structural reforms to boost competitiveness and facilitate post–COVID-19 sectoral adjustment. Reforms should include higher infrastructure and social spending aimed at fostering human capital development (while maintaining fiscal sustainability through revenue mobilization), fewer restrictions on FDI and external trade (nontariff trade barriers), and labor market flexibility (for example, streamlining stringent job protection, improving job placement services). Flexibility of the exchange rate should continue to support external stability in a context of increased market volatility associated with the COVID-19 pandemic.

Foreign Asset and Liability Position and Trajectory

Background. At the end of 2020 Indonesia's NIIP was –26.5 percent of GDP, improving from –30 percent of GDP at the end of 2019. The improvement in the NIIP is mainly explained by an increase of 4.8 percentage points of GDP in assets (that is, reserves, FDI, and deposits). In 2020 gross external assets reached 38 percent of GDP (of which 34 percent were reserve assets), and gross external liabilities stood at 65 percent of GDP. Indonesia's gross external debt was moderate at 39 percent of GDP at the end of 2020 and 89 percent maturing after one year.

Assessment. The level and composition of the NIIP and gross external debt indicate that Indonesia's external position is sustainable and subject to limited rollover risk. The share of nonresident holdings of rupiah-denominated government bonds declined from 39 percent of the total stock at the end of 2019 to 25 percent (or 6.3 percent of GDP) at the end of 2020 but remains sizable, making Indonesia vulnerable to global financial volatility, higher US interest rates, and a stronger US dollar. The NIIP, as a percent of GDP, will continue to strengthen over the medium term, reflecting small CA deficits and relatively strong nominal GDP growth.

2020 (% GDP)	NIIP: –26.5	Gross Assets: 38.2	Res. Assets: 12.8	Gross Liab.: 64.7	Debt Liab.: 39.4

Current Account

Background. Indonesia's CA deficit narrowed to 2.7 percent of GDP in 2019 from a 2.9 percent deficit in 2018, driven mainly by weak import growth. In 2020 the CA deficit narrowed to –0.4 percent of GDP as the softening in domestic demand led to import contraction that more than compensated for the decline in exports that was associated with low commodity prices and weak external demand. The negative impact on national savings of the fiscal expansion in response to the crisis was more than offset by an increase in private savings, in a context of subdued private consumption. Structural policies are expected to help limit the CA deficit in the medium term.

Assessment. The IMF staff estimates a CA gap of 0.7 percent for 2020, consistent with an estimated cyclically adjusted CA deficit of –0.8 percent of GDP, an IMF staff–assessed norm of –0.5 percent of GDP, and an IMF staff adjustor of 0.9 for demographics. The estimated effects of the COVID-19 crisis are 0 percent.[1] Considering uncertainties in the estimation of the norm, the CA gap for 2020 is in the range of –0.8 to 2.2 percent of GDP.[2] Maintaining external balance will require structural reforms, including strengthening revenue mobilization, and increasing public expenditure on health care, education, and infrastructure.

2020 (% GDP)	CA: –0.4	Cycl. Adj. CA: –0.8	EBA Norm: –0.5	EBA Gap: –0.3	COVID-19 Adj.: 0.0	Other Adj.: 0.9	Staff Gap: 0.7

Real Exchange Rate

Background. In 2019 the average REER appreciated by 4.3 percent relative to the 2018 average following an easing of global financial conditions and an inflow of capital. With the COVID-19 shock, the REER depreciated by about 10 percent between February and April before recovering toward the middle of the year. In 2020 the REER depreciated by 1.3 percent compared with the 2019 average. As of end-May 2021, the REER had depreciated by 2.1 percent compared to the 2020 average.

Assessment. The IMF staff CA gap estimate of 0.7 percent of GDP implies a REER gap of –3.9 percent with standard elasticities.[3] The REER index and level REER models point to 2020 REER gaps of about 2.1 percent to –11.6 percent, respectively, with an upward shift in the range of the estimated gaps compared with 2019. In the IMF staff's assessment, the EBA index and CA models are most relevant for Indonesia. Considering all inputs, as well as the moderate REER depreciation in 2020, the IMF staff assesses the REER gap in the –6 to 4 percent range, with a midpoint of –1 percent.[4]

Capital and Financial Accounts: Flows and Policy Measures

Background. In 2019 net capital and financial account inflows (3.3 percent of GDP) were sustained by net FDI inflows (1.8 percent of GDP), net portfolio inflows (1.9 percent of GDP), and net other investment inflows of –0.5 percent of GDP. Starting in March 2020 Indonesia faced large capital outflows from sales of rupiah-denominated securities by nonresident investors, although these outflows were largely offset by inflows from the subsequent issuance of foreign-currency-denominated government bonds.

Assessment. Net and gross financial flows continue to be prone to periods of volatility. The broadly contained CA deficit and strengthened policy frameworks, including exchange rate flexibility since mid-2013, have helped reduce capital flow volatility. Continued strong policies, focused on safeguarding the fiscal position, keeping inflation in check, advancing financial deepening, and easing supply bottlenecks, would help sustain capital inflows in the medium term.

FX Intervention and Reserves Level

Background. Since mid-2013 Indonesia has had a more flexible exchange rate policy framework. At the end of 2019 reserves were US$129.2 billion compared with US$120.7 billion at the end of 2018. The reserve accumulation reflects mainly the net capital inflows and FX receipts from the oil and gas and other sectors. In addition, contingencies and swap lines amounting to about US$95 billion are in place. In a context of increased market volatility associated with the COVID-19 pandemic, the Bank of Indonesia intervened in the spot and forward FX markets in March and April 2020 and introduced daily FX swap auctions to ensure adequate market liquidity. International reserves recovered from April 2020 onward and reached US$136 billion in December 2020.

Assessment. The current level of reserves (equal to 12.8 percent of GDP, about 121 percent of the IMF's reserve adequacy metric and about eight months of prospective imports of goods and services) should provide a sufficient buffer against a wide range of possible external shocks, with predetermined drains also manageable. Exchange rate flexibility should continue to play its role as a shock absorber. If external pressures result in disorderly market conditions in the exchange rate market, the use of FX intervention may be appropriate to mitigate the negative impact on balance sheet exposures.

Table 3.13. Italy: Economy Assessment

Overall Assessment: *The external position in 2020 was broadly in line with the level implied by medium-term fundamentals and desirable policies.* Nonetheless, chronic weak productivity and uncertainty about medium-term growth prospects continue to dampen investment and consumption. During 2020 there was large public support for income losses caused by the pandemic, while the household saving rate increased sharply, offsetting government dissaving and keeping the CA broadly unchanged.

Potential Policy Responses: Raising productivity and improving the business climate through structural reforms, and increasing investment under the National Recovery and Resilience Plan, would allow the CA balance to remain near its norm, even as household saving declines and the underlying primary fiscal surplus returns to its pre–COVID-19 level over the medium term, with the external position remaining broadly in line with medium-term fundamentals and desirable policies. In particular, upskilling the workforce and increasing the quality of infrastructure and the effectiveness of the judiciary and public administration would boost productivity, reduce high unemployment, and raise output and domestic absorption. Improving budget efficiency by curtailing wasteful spending and removing extensive tax loopholes would reduce vulnerabilities associated with the rollover of external debt.

Foreign Asset and Liability Position and Trajectory

Background. Italy's NIIP was close to balance (1.8 percent of GDP) at the end of 2020, having trended gradually upward from a strongly negative position since 2013 owing to sustained CA surpluses. Gross assets and liabilities, however, jumped sharply during 2020 to 187 and 185 percent of GDP, respectively. This includes an increase in TARGET2 liabilities (to a record high of 31 percent of GDP) following a moderate decrease in 2019, which offset reduced foreign holdings of Italian sovereign bonds. About one-half of the gross external liabilities is attributable to the general government and the Bank of Italy.

Assessment. Further strengthening public balance sheets and undertaking reforms would lessen vulnerabilities associated with the high public debt and reduce the potential for negative feedback loops between the debt stock and debt servicing costs, as well as between sovereign debt and the financial system.

2020 (% GDP)	NIIP: 1.8	Gross Assets: 186.9	Res. Assets: 10.4	Gross Liab.: 185.1	Debt Liab.: 118.0

Current Account

Background. Italy's CA averaged –1¼ percent of GDP during the decade following euro adoption. In 2013 it moved to balance and in 2019 it registered a multiyear high of 3.0 percent of GDP, which was surpassed marginally in 2020 as weak domestic demand weighed on imports. The COVID-19 shock negatively affected exports, imports, and travel services (including tourism), but the estimated net impact on the trade balance is small. The rising CA in the past decade mirrors the increase in private sector net savings. More than one-half of the increase since 2013 is due to the trade surplus, with the rest reflecting a higher income balance as the nonfinancial private sector's net holdings of foreign assets increased and interest payments on external liabilities declined owing to the ECB's accommodative monetary stance in the context of subdued growth and inflation. The positive primary income balance also reflects the larger share of equity in foreign assets than in liabilities. In terms of saving and investment, the increase in the CA since 2010 is due to higher gross national savings and lower gross domestic investment, particularly private investment.

Assessment. The cyclically adjusted CA is estimated at 2.5 percent of GDP in 2020, 0.3 percentage point below the EBA-estimated CA norm of 2.8 percent of GDP. Given that the pandemic-specific impact on the travel services (including tourism) and oil sectors, as well as the household consumption shift from services to consumer goods and the impact on medical goods trade, is not captured by the usual cyclical adjustment, an adjustor of 0.4 percent of GDP (mostly reflecting the impact on travel services) has been applied, indicating that the CA gap is about 0.1 percent of GDP. Taking into account estimation error, the IMF staff assesses the CA gap to be in the range of –0.9 to 1.1 percent of GDP.

2020 (% GDP)	CA: 3.5	Cycl. Adj. CA: 2.5	EBA Norm: 2.8	EBA Gap: –0.3	COVID-19 Adj.: 0.4	Other Adj.:0.0	Staff Gap: 0.1

Real Exchange Rate

Background. During 2010–19 the CPI-based and ULC-based REER depreciated by 10 and 20 percent, respectively, and both indicators lie below their 1999 levels. Because of a stronger euro, the CPI-based REER appreciated in 2020 (by 0.5 percent relative to the 2019 average), although official statistics may not fully capture actual price and wage dynamics during the pandemic period. As of end-May 2021, the REER had appreciated by 0.6 percent compared to the 2020 average.

Assessment. The IMF staff CA gap implies a REER gap of –0.3 percent in 2020 (applying an estimated elasticity of 0.25). The level and index CPI-based REER models suggest an overvaluation in 2020 of 2.5 percent and 7.7 percent, respectively, with an average of about 5 percent. Consistent with the IMF staff CA gap, the IMF staff assesses the REER to be in the range of –4.3 to 3.7 percent, with a midpoint of –0.3 percent.

Capital and Financial Accounts: Flows and Policy Measures

Background. The financial account posted net outflows of 3.0 percent of GDP in 2020, reflecting residents' net purchases of foreign assets. However, portfolio investment shifted from inflows to outflows as foreign investors reduced their holdings of Italian sovereign debt securities at the beginning of the COVID-19 pandemic.

Assessment. The current low-global-interest-rate environment is conducive to the smooth functioning of the sovereign debt market. However, large refinancing needs of the sovereign and the banking sector, as well as COVID-19–related balance sheet weakness in some banks, suggest that Italy remains vulnerable to market volatility.

FX Intervention and Reserves Level

Background. The euro has the status of a global reserve currency.

Assessment. Reserves held by the euro area are typically low relative to standard metrics, but the currency is free floating.

Table 3.14. Japan: Economy Assessment

Overall Assessment: *The external position in 2020 was broadly in line with the level implied by medium-term fundamentals and desirable policies.* Japan's CA surplus is mainly driven by its income surplus arising from a large positive NIIP and high net returns, which are expected to continue over the medium term.

Potential Policy Responses: The policy response to the ongoing COVID-19 shock has appropriately prioritized support to affected households, workers, and firms while maintaining the smooth functioning of financial markets. A coordinated policy package will be needed to ensure that the external position remains in line with fundamentals. As the recovery strengthens, extraordinary policy support should gradually be withdrawn. In particular, post-pandemic policies should shift toward structural reforms and fiscal sustainability, and fiscal consolidation should proceed in a gradual manner. A well-specified medium-term fiscal framework, accommodative monetary policy, and structural reforms are needed to mobilize investment, reduce debt, and support reflation and growth. Priority should be given to reforms to increase labor supply, boost productivity and wages, reduce barriers to entry in some industries, and accelerate agricultural and professional services sector deregulation.

Foreign Asset and Liability Position and Trajectory

Background. The NIIP has grown since 2016, largely driven by an increase in foreign assets related to outward FDI and portfolio outflows. Due to a decline in foreign liabilities and the GDP contraction, the NIIP-to-GDP ratio at the end of 2020 rose to 66.3 percent from 63.8 percent at the end of 2019. On the back of CA surpluses, the NIIP is projected to rise to about 70 percent of GDP in the medium term. Japan holds the world's largest stock of net foreign assets, valued at US$3.3 trillion at the end of 2020.

Assessment. Japan's foreign asset holdings are well diversified, both by geography and risk classes. Portfolio investment accounts for nearly one-half of gross foreign assets. By currency, 21 percent of portfolio investment is yen-denominated and about one-half is denominated in US dollars. In the event of yen appreciation against the US dollar, the risk of negative valuation effects could materialize. Liabilities' vulnerabilities are limited, with equity and direct investment accounting for 33 percent of gross foreign liabilities. The NIIP generated net annual investment income of 3.6 percent of GDP in 2020. The large positive NIIP, in part, is driven by asset accumulation for old-age consumption, which is expected to be gradually unwound over the long term.

2020 (% GDP)	NIIP: 66.3	Gross Assets: 212.8	Debt. Assets: 84.4	Gross Liab.: 146.5	Debt Liab.: 90.5

Current Account

Background. Japan's CA surplus reflects a high private sector saving-investment balance that more than compensates for the low government saving-investment balance. It also reflects a sizable income balance, owing to its large net foreign asset position. The CA surplus narrowed to 3.3 percent of GDP in 2020 compared with an average of 3.8 percent of GDP during 2016–19. The narrowing in the 2020 CA surplus was largely driven by a decline in the services trade balance amid international travel restrictions. In contrast, the goods trade balance remained in surplus, as a decline in imports caused by the negative domestic demand shock and lower energy prices outweighed a fall in exports. From the saving-investment perspective, the narrowing in the CA reflects a larger fall in saving, particularly for the public sector, relative to the investment-to-GDP ratio. The income balance continued to contribute the most to the CA surplus, at 3.6 percent of GDP in 2020. After the COVID-19 shock dissipates, the CA balance is projected to stabilize at a level slightly above 3 percent of GDP.

Assessment. The 2020 CA assessment uses the EBA model, in which the estimated cyclically adjusted CA is 3.2 percent of GDP and the cyclically adjusted CA norm is estimated at 3.6 percent of GDP, with a standard error of 1.2 percent of GDP. The IMF staff estimates a 2020 CA norm range between 2.4 and 4.8 percent of GDP. After factoring in the transitory impacts of the COVID-19 crisis on the CA in relation to the oil, travel services (including tourism), and medical goods sectors (–0.1, 0.3, and 0.1 percent of GDP, respectively), the 2020 CA gap midpoint is assessed at –0.1 percent of GDP, with the CA gap range between –1.3 and 1.1 percent of GDP. The EBA-identified policy gaps reflect relatively greater medium-term fiscal consolidation needs, as well as a positive credit gap, in relation to medium-term desired policy. The overall gap is accounted for by the residual, potentially reflecting structural impediments and country-specific factors not included in the model, such as investment bottlenecks, including entrepreneurship entry barriers and corporate savings distortions.

2020 (% GDP)	CA: 3.3	Cycl. Adj. CA: 3.2	EBA Norm: 3.6	EBA Gap: –0.4	COVID-19 Adj.: 0.3	Other Adj.: 0.0	Staff Gap: –0.1

Real Exchange Rate

Background. The REER appreciated by 0.9 percent in 2020, relative to the 2019 average. This reflects changes in global risk aversion and the monetary policy stances of key central banks in response to the pandemic. As of end-May 2021, the REER had depreciated by 8.7 percent compared to the 2020 average.

Assessment. The IMF staff CA gap implies a REER gap of 0.7 percent in 2020 (applying an estimated elasticity of 0.13). The EBA REER level and index models deliver REER gaps of –12 and –20 percent, respectively, for the 2020 average REER. However, the EBA REER level and index models are not used for the assessment because they do not capture Japan-specific factors well. Consistent with the IMF staff CA gap, the IMF staff assesses the REER to be in the range of –8.3 to 9.7 percent, with a midpoint of 0.7 percent.

Capital and Financial Accounts: Flows and Policy Measures

Background. Amid increased global financial volatility, portfolio and FDI outflows decreased sharply in 2020: portfolio outflows to Central and South America and outward FDI flows to Europe and Asia recorded the largest declines. Net FDI and portfolio flows comprise the bulk of the 2020 financial account (2.1 and 0.7 percent of GDP, respectively). Other investments (net) recorded outflows of 0.1 percent of GDP in 2020 compared with inflows of 2 percent of GDP in 2019. At the onset of the pandemic, net short yen positions increased. Nevertheless, this reversed beginning in mid-March, helped by a coordinated policy response by major central banks to enhance the provision of US dollar liquidity.

Assessment. Vulnerabilities are limited. Inward investment tends to be equity-based, and the home bias of Japanese investors remains strong. So far, outward spillovers from Japan's policies to financial conditions in other economies (interest rates, credit growth) are contained.

FX Intervention and Reserves Level

Background. Reserves are about 28 percent of GDP, reflecting legacy accumulation. There has been no FX intervention in recent years.

Assessment. The exchange rate is free floating. Interventions are isolated (last occurring in 2011), intended to reduce short-term volatility and disorderly exchange rate movements.

Table 3.15. Korea: Economy Assessment

Overall Assessment: *The external position in 2020 was broadly in line with the level implied by medium-term fundamentals and desirable policies.* The CA surplus widened from the 2019 level on account of a recovery in exports, lower oil prices, and narrowing of the service sector deficit and is projected to narrow slightly over the medium term as domestic demand recovers and transitory factors related to the COVID-19 shock recede.

Potential Policy Responses: To support activity following the COVID-19 outbreak, the authorities have deployed fiscal and monetary stimulus, of which a substantial part is expected to be temporary. Ensuring that the external position remains in line with medium-term fundamentals will require continued accommodative fiscal and monetary policies as well as structural policies to stimulate investment and facilitate rebalancing of the economy toward services and other new growth drivers. Desirable reforms include reducing barriers to firm entry and investment, deregulating the nonmanufacturing sector, and strengthening the social safety net to lessen the need for precautionary saving across sectors. Reforms in some of these areas are contained in the authorities' Korean New Deal, to be implemented over the next five years. The exchange rate should remain market determined, with intervention limited to preventing disorderly market conditions.

Foreign Asset and Liability Position and Trajectory	**Background.** The NIIP has been positive since 2014. Data for 2020 imply that, in 2020, Korea's NIIP was 28.4 percent of GDP, with gross liabilities at 91.4 percent of GDP, of which about one-third was gross external debt. The NIIP declined by about 3 percent of GDP from the 2019 level, largely reflecting valuation effects resulting from a sharp rally in domestic equity prices in the second half of 2020. The NIIP is projected to rise to about 50 percent of GDP in the medium term on the back of CA surpluses and search-for-yield activity by financial institutions driven by asset accumulation for old-age consumption. **Assessment.** The positive NIIP is a source of external sustainability. Foreign asset holdings are diversified, with about 36 percent held in equity or debt securities. About 60 percent of foreign assets are denominated in US dollars, implying that depreciation of the won could have positive valuation effects. The structure of liabilities limits vulnerabilities, with equity and direct investment accounting for about 60 percent of total liabilities.
2020 (% GDP)	NIIP: 28.4 · Gross Assets: 119.8 · Debt Assets: 31.0 · Gross Liab.: 91.4 · Debt Liab.: 30.8
Current Account	**Background.** The CA surplus in 2020 widened to 4.6 percent of GDP from 3.6 percent in 2019, driven by a rebound in exports since the third quarter of 2020 and a narrowing of the services deficit due to COVID-19 travel restrictions. The CA surplus has been trending down from the peak of 7.2 percent of GDP in 2015, reflecting a fall in savings, particularly for the household sector, and an increase in the investment-to-GDP ratio. Over the medium term, the CA surplus is projected to narrow slightly to 4.3 percent of GDP as export demand and the service sector balance normalize. **Assessment.** The EBA model estimates the cyclically adjusted CA at 4.3 percent of GDP. The CA norm is estimated at 3.5 percent of GDP, with a standard error of 0.9 percent of GDP. After accounting for transitory factors arising from the COVID-19 shock (mainly in the travel services—including tourism—and oil sectors), the IMF staff estimates the 2020 CA gap midpoint at –0.1 percent of GDP. The relative policy gap contribution is estimated at 1.5 percent of GDP; however, this is driven mainly by large exceptional fiscal stimulus in the rest of the world relative to Korea and is not expected to persist over the medium term.
2020 (% GDP)	CA: 4.6 · Cycl. Adj. CA: 4.3 · EBA Norm: 3.5 · EBA Gap: 0.8 · COVID-19 Adj.: –0.9 · Other Adj.: 0.0 · Staff Gap: –0.1
Real Exchange Rate	**Background.** Following sustained appreciation during 2015–18, the REER depreciated in 2019 by about 4.5 percent, returning to its 2015 level. The REER depreciated further in the first half of 2020 before recovering somewhat more recently. Overall, the average REER for 2020 depreciated by about 2 percent relative to the 2019 average. As of end-May 2021, the REER had appreciated by 0.8 percent compared to the 2020 average. **Assessment.** The IMF staff CA gap implies a REER gap of 0.2 percent (applying an estimated elasticity of 0.36). The EBA REER index model estimates a REER undervaluation of 3.7 percent, while the REER level model estimates a 12 percent undervaluation. The IMF staff uses the estimated CA gap for its assessment, given the better fit of the EBA CA model. Consistent with the IMF staff CA gap, the IMF staff assesses the REER gap to be in the range of –2.3 to 2.7 percent, with a midpoint of 0.2 percent.
Capital and Financial Accounts: Flows and Policy Measures	**Background.** Net FDI and portfolio outflows have declined since 2017, when outflows peaked at 4.6 percent of GDP. Portfolio outflows were 3.6 percent of GDP in 2020, reflecting further portfolio diversification and institutional investors' continued search for yield. Net FDI and portfolio outflows comprised the bulk of the 2020 financial account (1.4 and 2.5 percent of GDP, respectively), whereas other investments (net) recorded inflows (0.6 percent of GDP). Despite nonresident equity outflows in the first half of the year, overall capital flows have remained relatively stable in 2020, supported by portfolio debt inflows and a slowdown in outward FDI. **Assessment.** The present configuration of net and gross capital flows appears sustainable over the medium term. In recent years, including in the context of the COVID-19 shock, Korea has demonstrated ample capacity to absorb short-term capital flow volatility.
FX Intervention and Reserves Level	**Background.** Korea has a floating exchange rate. As of the end of 2020, reserves stood at 27 percent of GDP, largely reflecting legacy accumulation. FX intervention data released by the Bank of Korea show net purchases of US$5.3 billion (0.3 percent of GDP) in 2020, with net sales of US$5.9 billion in the first quarter to dampen excess FX volatility amid the COVID-19 shock and net purchases of US$11.5 billion in the fourth quarter, when the won appreciated sharply in nominal effective terms. With valuation gains from non–US dollar-denominated assets, gross reserves rose by US$34.3 billion (2.1 percent of GDP) in 2020. During March–May 2020 the Bank of Korea temporarily drew US$20 billion from the US$60 billion swap line established with the Federal Reserve. **Assessment.** Intervention has continued to be two-sided and appears to have been limited to preventing disorderly market conditions. As of the end of 2020, FX reserves were about 99 percent of the IMF's composite reserve adequacy metric, which, together with access to the Federal Reserve swap facility, provides an adequate buffer against a wide range of possible external shocks.

Table 3.16. Malaysia: Economy Assessment

Overall Assessment: *Malaysia's external position in 2020 was substantially stronger than the level implied by medium-term fundamentals and desirable policies due to the large pandemic-related fiscal expansions worldwide compared with Malaysia.*

Potential Policy Responses: Near-term policies should continue to support the recovery through targeted lifelines to households and businesses in the context of accommodative monetary and financial policies. Over the medium term, policies that could support external rebalancing and bring the CA balance closer to its norm include strengthening the social safety net in Malaysia and continuing to encourage private investment and productivity growth, as well as the unwinding of pandemic-related policy support worldwide.

Foreign Asset and Liability Position and Trajectory	**Background.** Since 2010 Malaysia's NIIP has averaged about 1 percent of GDP. The NIIP was 4.8 percent of GDP in 2020 (compared with –3 percent of GDP at the end of 2019), reflecting higher reserve assets, an increase in net other investment, and a decline in net portfolio investment. Direct investment and portfolio investment abroad contribute the most to assets, whereas direct investment and portfolio liabilities contribute the most to liabilities. Total external debt, measured in US dollars, was about 69 percent of GDP in 2020 (compared with 63.4 percent at the end of 2019), of which about two-thirds was in foreign currency and 38 percent in short-term debt, by original maturity. **Assessment.** Malaysia's NIIP is projected to rise over the medium term, reflecting projected CA surpluses. Malaysia's balance sheet strength, exchange rate flexibility, and increased domestic investor participation should continue to help withstand shocks (as they have in the context of the COVID-19 crisis).
2020 (% GDP)	NIIP: 4.8 / Gross Assets: 134.6 / Res. Assets: 30.6 / Gross Liab.: 129.8 / Debt Liab.: 28.1
Current Account	**Background.** Between 2010 and 2019 Malaysia's CA surplus contracted by 7 percentage points, underpinned by lower national savings and robust domestic demand. In 2020 the CA surplus increased to 4.2 percent of GDP against a backdrop of transitory factors, including (1) the decline in travel income, given international travel restrictions; (2) the decline in the oil balance following the slump in fuel prices in 2020; (3) an increase in demand for pandemic-related exports, including rubber glove products and electronic and electrical equipment; (4) the decline in outward remittances as a result of the crisis; and (5) a one-off transaction in the third quarter of 2020, creating a surplus in the secondary income balance. **Assessment.** The EBA CA model estimates a cyclically adjusted CA of 4.6 percent of GDP and a CA norm at –0.6 percent of GDP for 2020. After factoring in the transitory effect on the CA of the net exports of pandemic-related medical goods, including rubber glove products (1 percent of GDP); the global household consumption composition shift (0.6 percent of GDP); a one-off transaction in the third quarter of 2020 (0.8 percent of GDP); lower net remittances (0.1 percent of GDP); the decline in receipts from travel services, including tourism (–1.2 percent); and the decline in the oil balance (–0.3 percent of GDP), the IMF staff estimate of the CA gap is about 4.1 percent of GDP (±1 percent of GDP). Relative policy gaps explain 2.0 percentage points of the CA gap. Low public health care expenditures compared with the rest of the world contribute 0.7 percentage point to the CA gap, while the looser fiscal policies adopted in 2020 in the rest of the world relative to Malaysia contribute 1.2 percentage points to the excess surplus. Unidentified residuals are large and likely reflect structural impediments and country-specific factors not included in the model.
2020 (% GDP)	CA: 4.2 / Cycl. Adj. CA: 4.6 / EBA Norm: –0.6 / EBA Gap: 5.2 / COVID-19 Adj.: –0.2 / Other Adj.: –0.8 / Staff Gap: 4.1
Real Exchange Rate	**Background.** In 2020 the REER depreciated by 3.6 percent relative to the 2019 average and was about 6 percent lower than in 2015. The depreciation in 2020 can be mainly explained by the impact of capital outflows and lower commodity prices on the NEER. As of end-May 2021, the REER had depreciated by 1.0 percent compared to the 2020 average. **Assessment.** The IMF staff CA gap implies a REER undervaluation of –9.0 percent in 2020, applying an estimated elasticity of 0.46. The EBA REER index and level models estimate Malaysia's REER to be undervalued by –32 percent and –42 percent, respectively. At the same time, considering the lack of underlying macroeconomic stresses, such as inflation or wage pressures, and the broad stability of FX reserves, the IMF staff assesses the REER to be undervalued in the range of –7.0 to –11.0 percent, with a midpoint of –9.0 percent, consistent with the IMF staff CA gap.
Capital and Financial Accounts: Flows and Policy Measures	**Background.** Since the global financial crisis, Malaysia has experienced periods of significant capital flow volatility, largely driven by portfolio flows in and out of the local-currency-debt market, in response to both the change in global financial conditions and domestic factors. In 2020 Malaysia saw capital outflows during the March 2020 global risk-off episode, but capital flows stabilized afterward. Since late 2016 the Financial Markets Committee has implemented measures to develop the onshore FX market and increase hedging opportunities.[1] **Assessment.** Continued exchange rate flexibility and macroeconomic policy adjustments are necessary to manage capital flow volatility. CFM measures should be gradually phased out, with due regard for market conditions.
FX Intervention and Reserves Level	**Background.** The risk-off episode caused by the COVID-19 pandemic reduced reserves by about US$1.9 billion by March 2020, to US$101.7 billion. Reserve levels rose thereafter and stood at US$107.6 billion as of December 2020 (compared with $103.6 billion at the end of December 2019). **Assessment.** Under the IMF's composite ARA metric, reserves remain broadly adequate. Gross official reserves were about 118 percent of the ARA metric at the end of December 2020. FX interventions should continue to be limited to preventing disorderly market conditions. In case of an inflow surge, some reserve accumulation would be appropriate to increase the reserve coverage ratio, while still allowing the exchange rate to adjust as a first line of defense.

Table 3.17. Mexico: Economy Assessment

Overall Assessment: *The external position in 2020 was stronger than the level implied by medium-term fundamentals and desirable policies.* Mexico's external position strengthened in 2020 owing to the impact of the large fiscal expansions in other major economies (whose actual fiscal balances are relatively further below their desirable medium-term levels) compared with Mexico's muted fiscal response to the pandemic and continued weakening of the domestic investment climate. The assessment remains subject to considerable uncertainty around how temporary the nature of COVID-19 is and its implications for imports and fiscal policies.

Potential Policy Responses: Further domestic fiscal support is needed in the near term to ease the strains of the pandemic, reduce scarring, and facilitate the recovery. Steadfast implementation of structural reforms to deliver stronger investment would help bring down the saving-investment balance and, hence, the external position closer to the level implied by medium-term fundamentals and desirable policies. Such policies should be part of a comprehensive package focused on pursuing strong, durable, and inclusive growth, which should also include credible medium-term tax reform when the recovery is well underway. The floating exchange rate should continue to serve as the main shock absorber, with FX interventions used only to prevent disorderly market conditions. The IMF's Flexible Credit Line continues to provide an added buffer against global tail risks.

Foreign Asset and Liability Position and Trajectory

Background. Mexico's NIIP is projected to improve from about –55 percent of GDP in 2020 to –40 percent of GDP over the medium term, driven mainly by the decline in foreign liabilities. Foreign assets are mostly direct investment (21 percent of GDP) and reserves (18 percent of GDP). Foreign liabilities are mostly FDI (60 percent of GDP) and portfolio investment (49 percent of GDP). Gross public external debt was 29 percent of GDP, of which about one-third was holdings of local currency government bonds.

Assessment. Whereas the NIIP is sustainable, and the local currency denomination of a large share of foreign public liabilities reduces FX risks, the large gross foreign portfolio liabilities could be a source of vulnerability in case of global financial volatility. Exchange rate vulnerabilities are moderate as most Mexican firms with FX debt have natural hedges and actively manage their FX exposures.

2020 (% GDP)	NIIP: –54.9	Gross Assets: 62.6	Res. Assets: 18.5	Gross Liab.: 117.5	Debt Liab.: 45.6

Current Account

Background. In 2020 the CA balance improved sharply to 2.5 percent of GDP from –0.3 percent in 2019, driven by a dramatic contraction in imports amid lower capital inflows (17 percent), a smaller export contraction owing to the relatively larger fiscal expansion in other major economies, the global household consumption composition shift, trade diversion related to the US–China trade dispute (12 percent), and soaring worker remittances (11 percent in US dollar terms). In terms of saving and investment, the increase in saving contributed one-third and the decline in investment contributed two-thirds of the improvement in the CA-to-GDP balance; the private sector saving-investment balance rose by 5.0 percentage points of GDP, more than offsetting the dissaving by the public sector of 2.2 percentage points. The 2021 CA surplus is projected at 1.8 percent of GDP and is subject to considerable uncertainty. Over the medium term, the CA balance is projected to deteriorate toward –1 percent of GDP as the temporary COVID-19 impact on US household consumption composition, remittances, and trade diversion effects dissipate.

Assessment. The EBA model estimates a cyclically adjusted CA norm of –1.9 percent of GDP in 2020. This implies a CA gap of 3.6 percent of GDP, with a range of 2.6 to 4.6 percent of GDP. The relative policy gap contribution is estimated at 2.6 percent of GDP, mainly led by COVID-19–driven accommodation of fiscal policy in the rest of the world. The IMF staff adjustments were made to account for the transitory impact of the COVID-19 pandemic on the travel services sector, including tourism; the global household consumption shift; and remittances (adjustments of 0.4 percent of GDP, –0.6 percent of GDP, and –0.3 percent of GDP, respectively) as well as trade diversion effects related to the US-China trade dispute (adjustment of about –0.3 percent of GDP). Including these adjustments, the IMF staff assesses the CA gap at 2.8 percent of GDP, with a range of 1.8 to 3.8 percent of GDP.

2020 (% GDP)	CA: 2.4	Cycl. Adj. CA: 1.7	EBA Norm: –1.9	EBA Gap: 3.6	COVID-19 Adj.: –0.5	Other Adj.: –0.3	Staff Gap: 2.8

Real Exchange Rate

Background. In 2020 the peso fluctuated considerably in a range of 18–25 percent vis-à-vis the US dollar. The average REER in 2020 was about 7.6 percent lower than the 2019 average, mostly driven by a nominal depreciation. As of end-May 2021, the REER had appreciated by 7.0 percent compared to the 2020 average.

Assessment. The IMF staff CA gap implies a REER gap of –21.8 percent of GDP (applying an elasticity of 0.13). The EBA REER level and index models estimate an undervaluation of 10.0 and 20.9 percent, respectively, in 2020. The IMF staff's overall assessment, based on the CA gap, is a REER gap in the range of –29.8 to –13.8 percent, with a midpoint of –21.8 percent.

Capital and Financial Accounts: Flows and Policy Measures

Background. In 2020 net portfolio and other investment flows were negative, driven by residents' increased acquisition of overseas assets and nonresidents' lower acquisition of Mexican assets. Meanwhile, net FDI inflows remained relatively strong despite the COVID-19 pandemic.

Assessment. While the long maturity of sovereign debt and the high share of local-currency-denominated debt reduce the exposure of government finances to depreciation risks, high foreign ownership of sovereign bonds could contribute to vulnerabilities. The banking sector is broadly resilient. Nonfinancial corporate debt is low, and FX risks are generally covered by natural and financial hedges. But the strong presence of foreign investors leaves Mexico exposed to capital flow reversals and risk premium increases.

FX Intervention and Reserves Level

Background. The central bank remains committed to a free-floating exchange rate, whereas discretionary intervention is used solely to prevent disorderly market conditions. At the end of 2020 gross international reserves amounted to US$199 billion (18.5 percent of GDP), up from US$183 billion at the end of 2019, mostly owing to the federal government's debt management operations and valuation changes. In 2020 two nondeliverable forward auctions were conducted, alongside further US dollar liquidity provision measures, in response to large external shocks.

Assessment. At 128 percent of the ARA metric and 281 percent of short-term debt (at remaining maturity), the end-of-2020 level of foreign reserves remains adequate. The IMF staff recommends that the authorities continue to maintain reserves at an adequate level over the medium term. The Flexible Credit Line arrangement continues to provide an additional buffer.

Table 3.18. The Netherlands: Economy Assessment

Overall Assessment: *The external position in 2020 was stronger than the level implied by medium-term fundamentals and desirable policies.* The Netherlands' status as a trade and financial center and natural gas exporter makes an external assessment particularly challenging.

Potential Policy Responses: The use of available fiscal buffers by the authorities to provide ongoing support to the health care sector and to households and businesses affected by the COVID-19 pandemic remains appropriate, also against the backdrop of the additional space provided by the sustained activation of the escape clause from the EU Stability and Growth Pact. Even after the pandemic subsides, it appears that the government will command room to pursue a growth-oriented fiscal policy. Therefore, policies should avoid a rush to consolidate, thereby promoting and safeguarding the recovery while also supporting public and private investment in physical and human capital to foster potential robust growth, which would also contribute to external rebalancing.

Foreign Asset and Liability Position and Trajectory

Background. The NIIP of The Netherlands reached 113.9 percent of GDP at the end of 2020, reflecting gross assets and liabilities of 1,165.5 and 1,051.6 percent of GDP, respectively, rising from a nearly balanced NIIP at the end of 2009. The largest component of the NIIP comes from the net FDI stock—about €1,111 billion (138.9 percent of GDP) at the end of 2020. According to the latest Coordinated Direct Investment Survey, the inward and outward FDI positions of The Netherlands were second only to those of the United States at the end of 2019, with the largest gross bilateral stocks accounted for by the United States (US$1.85 trillion), the United Kingdom (US$1.06 trillion), and Luxembourg (US$0.87 trillion). The central bank's net TARGET2 claims on the ECB amounted to €38 billion at the end of 2020. Reflecting a persistent CA surplus, the NIIP is expected to increase as a ratio to GDP in 2021, likely keeping it considerably above the 100 percent mark in the absence of large revaluation effects, despite a rising denominator on the back of a rebound in GDP.

Assessment. The Netherlands' safe haven status and its sizable foreign assets limit risks from its large foreign liabilities.

2020 (% GDP)					
	NIIP: 113.9	Gross Assets: 1,165.5	Debt Assets: 260.6	Gross Liab: 1,051.6	Debt Liab: 308.2

Current Account

Background. In 2020 the CA surplus, in place since 1981, declined to 7.0 percent of GDP (7.5 percent cyclically adjusted). The historically positive goods and services balance, primarily the result of surpluses vis-à-vis EU trading partners, improved at the margin. By contrast, the primary income balance turned into a 1.7 percent of GDP deficit in 2020, despite the positive NIIP, as lower net investment income on FDI was only partly compensated for by a reduction in payouts on net portfolio investment. Likewise, the secondary income balance deteriorated to –1.7 percent of GDP, mainly on the back of other current transfers by the nongovernment sector abroad. Substantial FDI outflows have been the key driver of the financial account since 2000, constituting the counterpart to high nonfinancial corporate net saving (gross saving minus domestic business investment), whereas household net saving (gross saving minus residential investment) has played a comparatively smaller role due to the offsetting impact of substantial mandatory contributions to second-pillar pension funds and high real estate investment. The Netherlands' status as a trade and financial center and natural gas exporter also contribute to a structurally strong external position. In 2021 the CA surplus is projected to rebound to 9.0 percent of GDP.

Assessment. The EBA CA model estimates a CA norm of 3.4 percent of GDP and a CA gap of 4.0 percent of GDP in 2020, with an unexplained residual of 1.1 percent of GDP that primarily reflects the high gross saving of multinationals based in The Netherlands. In addition, measurement errors or biases in official statistics may also contribute to an overstatement of the net accumulation of wealth that is attributed to Dutch residents, an issue of particular relevance for The Netherlands as the foreign ownership of publicly listed Dutch corporations has been consistently above 85 percent over the past 10 years. An IMF staff adjustment of –1.4 percent of GDP to offset this bias is approximated with the help of historical data about the foreign ownership structure of Dutch firms provided by the central bank. Moreover, another –0.2 percent of GDP adjustment is applied to account for the (temporary) effects of the COVID-19 pandemic, reflecting lower spending on travel services, including tourism, by Dutch residents abroad (–0.3 percent of GDP) and higher-than-usual trade in medical goods (0.1 percent of GDP). Taking these factors into consideration, and against a norm in a range of 1.4 to 5.4 percent of GDP, the IMF staff assesses a CA gap of 0.4 to 4.4 percent of GDP.[1]

2020 (% GDP)							
	CA: 7.0	Cycl. Adj. CA: 7.5	EBA Norm: 3.4	EBA Gap: 4.0	COVID-19 Adj.: –0.2	Other Adj.: –1.4	Staff Gap: 2.4

Real Exchange Rate

Background. The annual average CPI-based REER appreciated by 2.0 percent in 2020, with part of the rise in the euro NEER offset by inflation in The Netherlands staying below that of its trading partners, while the average ULC-based REER appreciated by 3.8 percent. However, drawing conclusions from both indicators about shifts in competitiveness in 2020 is hampered by the distortions the COVID-19 pandemic implied for the measurement of consumer prices and ULCs across different countries. As of May 2021 the CPI-based REER was 0.6 percent above its 2020 average.

Assessment. Assuming a semi-elasticity of 0.7, the IMF staff CA gap of 2.4 percent of GDP implies a REER undervaluation of about 3.5 percent. The EBA REER models indicate an overvaluation between 4.2 percent (level model) and 17.8 percent (index model) in 2020, predominantly reflecting unexplained residuals. Taking into account all estimates and the uncertainty surrounding the EBA REER results, the IMF staff views the REER as undervalued by about 0.5 to 6.5 percent, with a midpoint of 3.5 percent, based on its assessment of the CA gap and its range.

Capital and Financial Accounts: Flows and Policy Measures

Background. Net FDI and portfolio outflows dominate the financial account. FDI outflows are driven by the investment of corporate profits abroad, largely by multinationals. More than 40 percent of gross FDI assets and liabilities are attributable to subsidiaries of multinationals.

Assessment. The strong external position limits vulnerabilities from capital flows. The financial account is likely to remain in deficit as long as the corporate sector continues to invest substantially abroad.

FX Intervention and Reserves Level

Background. The euro has the status of a global reserve currency.

Assessment. Reserves held by euro area economies are typically low relative to standard metrics, but the currency is free floating.

Table 3.19. Poland: Economy Assessment

Overall Assessment: *The external position in 2020 was substantially stronger than the level implied by medium-term fundamentals and desirable policies.* The CA balance increased to 3.5 percent of GDP in 2020 from 0.5 percent in 2019, reflecting a large trade surplus in addition to a reduction in the primary income deficit arising from lower earnings of foreign companies in Poland during the pandemic. This comes after a decade-long transition from a large deficit to a small surplus in 2019. A CA surplus is deemed excessive, given that income convergence is incomplete. In 2021 the CA surplus is projected to decrease as the recovery in domestic demand supports import growth and foreign companies' profitability recovers. Uncertainty is high over the medium term due to the COVID-19 pandemic; however, as the economy recovers, the CA surplus is expected to gradually vanish as private net saving returns to a lower level, offsetting an anticipated improvement in government net saving. Next Generation EU grants are expected to boost investment, contributing to the moderation of the CA balance in the projection horizon. Reserves are adequate to insulate against external shocks and disorderly market conditions.

Potential Policy Responses: In the short term, fiscal policy should bolster the health care system, provide businesses with liquidity, and support incomes of vulnerable households, including through employment preservation. Monetary and financial policies should prevent a tightening of financial conditions and enable the financial sector to support firms' liquidity. The tapering of expansionary policies should be gradual once the recovery is in full swing. In the medium term, to help move the CA toward the norm, policies should aim to boost investment by (1) deploying the Next Generation EU funds to raise public investment, support the recovery, and help tackle infrastructure gaps, digitalization, and climate change; and (2) using public policies to foster corporate investment and productivity, while active labor market policies should facilitate sectoral transitions, with structural reforms focused on raising potential growth. Room should be made for priority fiscal spending by better targeting social benefits according to need.

Foreign Asset and Liability Position and Trajectory	**Background.** The NIIP is estimated to have improved to –46 percent of GDP in 2020 from –50 percent in 2019. Gross assets and liabilities reached 58 and 103 percent of GDP, respectively. The stock of net FDI (equity and debt), accounting for 36 percent of gross external liabilities, remains diversified across sectors and source countries. While gross external debt in 2020 was a sizable 62.4 percent of GDP, 28 percent of the debt is liabilities to direct investors via intercompany lending, and 74 percent of the debt is of long-term maturity. Short-term debt (excluding intercompany short-term debt), amounting to 16 percent of total debt (10 percent of GDP), is mainly owed by banks (currency and deposits) and the nonfinancial private sector (trade credit). Automatic debt dynamics, helped by Next Generation EU grants, are projected to continue to reduce the negative NIIP in the medium term. **Assessment.** While sizable external debt is a vulnerability, rollover risk is mitigated by the large share of long-term debt, as well as by intercompany lending that tends to be automatically rolled over. Adequate reserves reduce residual rollover risk from short-term debt (gross reserves stood at 161 percent of short-term debt in 2020).
2020 (% GDP)	NIIP: –45.9 | Gross Assets: 57.6 | Res. Assets: 25.9 | Gross Liab: 103.4 | Debt Liab.: 62.4
Current Account	**Background.** The CA has moved from large deficits toward surplus since the 2008 crisis. This reflects a larger trade surplus (mainly services), despite sustained high primary income deficits from reinvested earnings and dividend payments to direct investors and net earnings of foreign workers in Poland. Low investment and high saving by the corporate sector have been partially offset by net borrowing by households and the government. Poland's CA surplus increased from 0.5 percent of GDP in 2019 to 3.5 percent of GDP in 2020, driven by a larger trade surplus, reflecting resilience in exports, as well as import compression, and by a lower primary income deficit, reflecting foreign companies' lower earnings. In the medium term as the economy recovers from the pandemic, the CA surplus is expected to vanish as private net saving returns to a lower level, offsetting an increase in government net saving. **Assessment.** For 2020 the EBA CA model estimates a norm of –2.1 percent of GDP (with the standard error of the norm estimate 0.6 percent of GDP) against a cyclically adjusted CA of 3.9 percent of GDP. The resulting EBA gap of 6.0 percent of GDP includes identified policy gaps (2.2 percent of GDP) and an unexplained residual of 3.9 percent of GDP. However, in view of the pandemic-related decline in the primary income account, judged to be transitory, an adjustment of –0.7 percent of GDP to the cyclically adjusted CA balance has been made. Furthermore, an additional adjustment of –0.4 percentage point of GDP has been made, which consists of 0.3 percentage point of GDP to reflect the contraction in travel services (including tourism) net exports, 0.2 point of GDP to reflect increased global demand for medical goods, –0.1 percentage point of GDP to reflect changes in the oil balance, and –0.7 percentage point of GDP to reflect shifts in household consumption composition. In summary, the total adjustment of –1.1 results in a CA gap of 4.9 (±0.6) percent of GDP.
2020 (% GDP)	CA: 3.5 | Cycl. Adj. CA: 3.9 | EBA Norm: –2.1 | EBA Gap: 6.0 | COVID-19 Adj.: –1.1 | Other Adj.: 0.0 | Staff Gap: 4.9
Real Exchange Rate	**Background.** The annual average REER appreciated by 0.7 percent in 2020 compared with the 2019 average. During the pandemic, unlike during the global financial crisis, movements in the NEER and REER have been muted. In nominal terms, the zloty depreciated by 4.3 percent against the dollar but appreciated by 4.8 percent against the euro since the end of 2019. Over the same period, inflation in Poland has been only slightly higher than in its trading partners. The REER depreciated by 3.9 percent between January and April but appreciated by 4.3 percent between April and December. As of end-May 2021, the REER had appreciated by 1.0 percent compared to the 2020 average. **Assessment.** The IMF staff CA gap implies a REER gap of –11.1 percent in 2020 (applying an estimated elasticity of 0.44). EBA REER index and level model estimates point to an undervaluation of 2.9 and 19.3 percent, respectively. Consistent with the IMF staff CA gap, the IMF staff assesses the REER to be undervalued in the range of –12.6 to –9.6 percent, with a midpoint of –11.1 percent.
Capital and Financial Accounts: Flows and Policy Measures	**Background.** The capital account, dominated by inflows of EU funds for financing investment projects, has averaged about 2 percent of GDP over the past 10 years. The capital account surplus increased to 2.4 percent of GDP in 2020 and is expected to increase further, supported by Next Generation EU grants. Financial market volatility at the onset of the pandemic triggered sizable but short-lived outflows in bond and equity markets, which stabilized beginning in May. Financial account outflows in 2020 amounted to 1.3 percent of GDP. **Assessment.** Foreign holdings of domestic government securities have declined significantly since 2016 and, by the end of 2020, represented 17.1 percent of the total. Nevertheless, the overall stock remains sizable at 5.8 percent of GDP and could pose risks, although the diversified foreign investor base is a mitigating factor.
FX Intervention and Reserves Level	**Background.** Gross international reserves increased by 20 percent to US$154 billion by the end of 2020. Net reserves, which exclude the central bank's repo operations (part of its reserve management strategy) and government FX deposits, are estimated at US$131 billion at the end of 2020, reflecting in part the central bank's conversion to zloty of a portion of EU funds received by the government. This is consistent with the central bank's strategy of building an adequate precautionary reserve buffer. The zloty is free floating. The central bank intervened in the FX market in December 2020 by purchasing FX, the first intervention since 2013. **Assessment.** At about 141 percent of the IMF's reserve adequacy metric at the end of 2020, the level of gross reserves is adequate to guard against external shocks and disorderly market conditions.

Table 3.20. Russia: Economy Assessment

Overall Assessment: *The external position in 2020 is moderately stronger than the level implied by medium-term fundamentals and desirable policies.*

Potential Policy Responses: In view of large uncertainties surrounding near-term recovery prospects, the authorities should stand ready to extend targeted support to viable sectors and firms still under stress. Over the medium term, structural reforms to improve the business climate and address inefficiencies in the state-owned enterprise sector, together with investment in infrastructure, health, and education, could lift potential growth and diversify the economy away from oil and gas exports, helping to bring the external sector into balance.

Foreign Asset and Liability Position and Trajectory

Background. The NIIP increased to US$504.53 billion in 2020, which, at 34 percent of GDP, is well above the near balance position in 2010. Since 2018 gross assets rose from 81 percent of GDP to 105.2 percent of GDP as of the end of 2020, though liabilities also increased from 58 to 71 percent of GDP. External debt is about one-half of total gross liabilities, and about one-quarter of external debt is in domestic currency. There are no obvious maturity mismatches between the gross asset and liability positions, and the share of nonresidents' holdings of domestic government debt declined from 32.2 percent in December 2019 to 23.3 percent in December 2020.

Assessment. The projected CA surpluses suggest that Russia will be able to maintain its positive NIIP, lowering risks to external stability. Moreover, the accumulated official external assets, which have increased rapidly since the introduction of the new fiscal rule, provide an important buffer against the COVID-19 shock to oil production and prices.

2020 (% GDP)	NIIP: 34.2	Gross Assets: 105.2	Res. Assets: 40.3	Gross Liab.: 71.0	Debt Liab.: 31.6

Current Account

Background. In spite of the sharp fall in oil prices and oil demand, the CA balance registered a surplus of US$33.9 billion (2.3 percent of GDP) in 2020. This was in part because of less travel abroad due to the pandemic, with service imports declining by about US$34.4 billion relative to 2019.

Assessment. The EBA CA model estimates a norm of 3.2 percent of GDP for 2020 and a cyclically and terms-of-trade adjusted CA surplus of 4.0 percent of GDP. After an adjustment to the underlying CA of 1.1 percent of GDP, to reflect the exceptionally sharp shock to oil prices and oil demand (2.1 percent of GDP), as well as a temporary adjustment for travel service imports, including tourism (–0.9 percent of GDP), the staff CA gap was 1.9 percent of GDP in 2020, with a range of 0.4 to 3.4 percent of GDP. Identified policies contributed 1.5 percent of GDP to the gap. About one-fifth of the total policy gap is due to fiscal policy, reflecting larger consolidation needs in the rest of the world compared with Russia.

2020 (% GDP)	CA: 2.3	Cycl. Adj. CA: 4.0	EBA Norm: 3.2	EBA Gap: 0.8	COVID-19 Adj.: 1.1	Other Adj.: 0.0	Staff Gap: 1.9

Real Exchange Rate

Background. The average REER depreciated by 7.4 percent in 2020 and by 14.4 percent over 2017–20. As of end-May 2021, the REER had depreciated by 3.8 percent compared to the 2020 average.

Assessment. The IMF staff CA gap implies a REER undervaluation of 7.6 percent in 2020 (applying an estimated elasticity of 0.25). The EBA REER index and level model estimates point to a REER undervaluation of 12.3 and 20.8 percent, respectively. Consistent with the IMF staff CA gap, the IMF staff assesses the REER to be undervalued in the range of 1.6 to 13.6 percent, with a midpoint of 7.6 percent.

Capital and Financial Accounts: Flows and Policy Measures

Background. Following the decline in net private capital outflows in 2019, Russia experienced a period of high volatility accompanied by moderate outflows by both the banking and nonbanking private sectors in early 2020. This volatility abated somewhat, though external private sector deleveraging continued through December. Pressures on financial flows could stem from volatility in oil prices and demand as well as from geopolitical uncertainty.

Assessment. While Russia is exposed to risks of further outflows, the large FX reserves and the floating exchange rate regime provide substantial buffers to help absorb shocks. The substantial external deleveraging in recent years has also helped reduce susceptibility to external shocks.

FX Intervention and Reserves Level

Background. Since the floating of the ruble in November 2014, FX interventions have been limited, and reserve accumulation has been mostly driven by the fiscal rule and oil prices being above the fiscal reference level. In 2020, faced with declining oil prices and capital outflows, the central bank engaged in some reserve sales and halted previously ongoing scheduled FX purchases. Despite FX sales of US$13.7 billion, international reserves rose to US$595.8 billion at the end of 2020 from US$555.2 billion in 2019, thanks to valuation changes related to higher gold prices.

Assessment. International reserves in 2020 were equivalent to 360.7 percent of the IMF's reserve adequacy metric. Taking into account Russia's vulnerability to oil price shocks, an additional commodity buffer of US$75 billion is appropriate, translating to a ratio of reserves to the buffer-augmented ARA metric of 242.5 percent. While considerably above the adequacy range of 100 to 150 percent, the level of reserves remains appropriate, taking into account Russia's exposure to other external shocks as well as geopolitical tensions.

Table 3.21. Saudi Arabia: Economy Assessment

Overall Assessment: *The external position in 2020 was moderately weaker than the level implied by medium-term fundamentals and desirable policies.* The external balance sheet remains strong. Reserves remain adequate when judged against standard IMF metrics, although external savings are not sufficient from an intergenerational equity perspective. The pegged exchange rate provides Saudi Arabia with a credible policy anchor. Given the close link between the fiscal and external balance and the structure of the economy, external adjustment will be driven primarily by fiscal policy.

Potential Policy Responses: In the near term, withdrawal of remaining policy support should be carefully managed to ensure that the ongoing recovery continues. Over the medium term, fiscal consolidation could bring the CA balance closer to its norm. The increase in the value-added tax rate, the termination of the cost-of-living allowances, and the reduction in capital spending in 2020 have significantly strengthened the medium-term fiscal position. Other policies announced by the government—energy price reforms and restraint of current spending—if fully implemented, should deliver the additional needed fiscal adjustment at the central government level. Structural reforms that help diversify the economy and boost the non-oil tradables sector would enhance the resilience of the economy to external shocks and could also help bring the CA closer to its norm.

Foreign Asset and Liability Position and Trajectory

Background. Net external assets are estimated at 89 percent of GDP at the end of 2020, up from 85 percent of GDP in 2019 but down from 105 percent in 2015. Only broad categories are available on the composition of external assets. Portfolio and other investments, reserves, and FDI account for 50, 39, and 11 percent of total external assets, respectively.

Assessment. The external balance sheet remains very strong. Substantial accumulated assets represent both protection against vulnerabilities from oil price volatility and saving of exhaustible resource revenues for future generations.

2020 (% GDP)	NIIP: 88.8	Gross Assets: 164.5	Res. Assets: 64.8	Gross Liab.: 75.6	Debt Liab.: 34.1

Current Account

Background. The CA balance is estimated to have registered a deficit of 2.8 percent of GDP in 2020 compared with a surplus of 4.8 percent in 2019. The trade balance is estimated to have decreased by 8.5 percent of GDP as the price and volume of oil exports declined. The terms of trade are estimated to have deteriorated by 34.2 percent. The CA is expected to be in surplus in 2021 as oil revenues recover (the terms of trade are projected to improve by 40.7 percent).[1]

Assessment. Saudi Arabia's reliance on oil complicates the application of standard external assessment methodologies, given the wide swings of oil prices in 2020. The EBA-Lite methodology generally estimates a negative CA gap, although the size of the estimated gap varies by approach. The estimated CA gap in 2020 is –2.2 percent of GDP using the CA-regression approach. An upward adjustment of 5.6 percent of GDP is applied to the CA to account for the temporary impact of the COVID-19 crisis regarding oil trade (5.3 percent of GDP); travel services trade, including tourism (0.1 percent of GDP); and the shift of household consumption composition from services to consumer goods (0.2 percent of GDP). The Consumption Allocation Rules suggest a CA gap of 0.2 and –3.1 percent of GDP for the constant real annuity and constant real per capita annuity allocation rules, respectively. The Investment Needs model suggests a CA gap of –0.8 percent of GDP. The IMF staff assesses a CA gap of –1.5 percent of GDP, with a range of –2.7 to –0.3 percent of GDP in 2020.[2]

2020 (% GDP)	CA: –2.8	Cycl. Adj. CA: –1.3	EBA Norm: —	EBA Gap: —	COVID-19 Adj.: 5.6	Other Adj.: —	Staff Gap: –1.5

Real Exchange Rate

Background. The riyal has been pegged to the US dollar at a rate of 3.75 since 1986. On average, the REER appreciated by 2.5 percent in 2020 and was 7.5 percent above its 10-year average. However, the REER appreciation was mainly driven by the impact of the value-added tax increase on inflation (the NEER only appreciated by 0.6 percent, on average, in 2020 and depreciated by 6 percent from its peak in April). As exports are not subject to value-added taxes, the impact of the REER appreciation on competitiveness is limited unless there is a strong pass-through to costs of labor and intermediate inputs. As of end-May 2021, the REER had depreciated by 2.3 percent compared to the 2020 average.

Assessment. Exchange rate movements have a limited impact on competitiveness in the short term, as most exports are oil or oil-related products and there is limited substitutability between imports and domestically produced products, which in turn have significant imported labor and intermediate input content. Consistent with the IMF staff CA gap and based on an elasticity of 0.2, the IMF staff assesses the REER to be overvalued by about 7 percent, with a range of 1 to 13 percent.

Capital and Financial Accounts: Flows and Policy Measures

Background. Net financial outflows continued in 2020 as the PIF invested abroad, although net outflows were smaller than in 2019. The equity market saw large outflows in March 2020 as oil prices declined and COVID-19 struck global financial markets, but has rebounded since April. FX reserves decreased by US$45.9 billion mainly due to a Saudi Arabia Monetary Authority transfer of US$40 billion to the PIF. Reserves are expected to stabilize in 2021 as investments overseas by public sector institutions start to slow.

Assessment. Analysis of the financial account is complicated by the lack of detailed information on the nature of the financial flows. The strong reserves position limits risks and vulnerabilities to capital flows.

FX Intervention and Reserves Level

Background. The investments of the PIF are increasing, although most of the government's foreign assets are still held at the central bank within international reserves. Net FX reserves declined to US$449 billion (64 percent of GDP, 25.1 months of imports, and 333 percent of the IMF's reserve adequacy metric) at the end of 2020 from US$494 billion at the end of 2019 ($724 billion in 2014). This was mainly driven by transfers of foreign assets from the Saudi Arabia Monetary Authority to the PIF.

Assessment. Reserves play a dual role—savings for both precautionary motives and for future generations. Reserves are adequate for precautionary purposes (measured by the IMF's metrics). Nevertheless, fiscal adjustment is needed over the medium term to strengthen the CA and increase savings for future generations.

Table 3.22. Singapore: Economy Assessment

Overall Assessment: *The external position in 2020 was substantially stronger than is consistent with fundamentals and desirable policies.* The assessment is subject to a wide range of uncertainty, reflecting Singapore's very open economy and status as a global trading and financial center.

Potential Policy Responses: A sizable fiscal policy response to the COVID-19 pandemic helped reduce external imbalances in 2020, and expected execution of major infrastructure projects should contribute to further reduction of external imbalances in the near term. Over the medium term, Singapore's economy will be undergoing structural transformation, in light of a rapidly aging population and its transition to a new digital economy, while facing challenges linked to climate change. Higher public investment addressing these issues, including spending on health care and investments in physical infrastructure and human capital, would help keep CA imbalances moderate over the medium term by lowering net public saving. Structural reforms are also necessary to improve productivity.

Foreign Asset and Liability Position and Trajectory

Background. The NIIP stood at 308 percent of GDP in 2020, up from 208 percent of GDP in 2019 and the average level of 212 percent of GDP in 2015–19. Gross assets and liabilities are high, reflecting Singapore's status as a financial center. About half of foreign liabilities is in FDI, and about a quarter is in the form of currency and deposits. The CA surplus has been a main driver since the global financial crisis, but valuation effects were material in some years. CA and growth projections imply that the NIIP will rise over the medium term. The large positive NIIP in part reflects the accumulation of assets for old-age consumption, which is expected to be gradually unwound over the long term.

Assessment. Large gross non-FDI liabilities (508 percent of GDP in 2020)—predominantly cross-border deposit taking by foreign bank branches—present some risks, but these are mitigated by large gross asset positions, banks' large short-term external assets, and the authorities' close monitoring of banks' liquidity risk profiles. Singapore has large official reserves and other official liquid assets.

2020 (% GDP)	NIIP: 307.8	Gross Assets: 1,361.2	Debt Assets: 617.0	Gross Liab.: 1,053.4	Debt Liab.: 417.6

Current Account

Background. The CA surplus was 17.6 percent of GDP in 2020, up from 14.3 percent in 2019. This rise was led by a large decline in service imports, a narrower oil trade deficit, and a decrease in net payments of primary income related to the COVID-19 shock. The CA balance is slightly higher than the average of 16.6 percent since 2015 and significantly lower than the post-global-financial-crisis peak of 22.9 percent in 2010. Singapore's large CA balance reflects a strong goods balance and small surplus in the services balance that is partly offset by a deficit in the income account balance.[1] Structural factors and policies that boost savings, such as Singapore's status as a financial center, consecutive fiscal surpluses in most years, and the rapid pace of aging—combined with a mandatory defined-contribution pension program (whose assets were about 98.5 percent of GDP in 2020), as well as relatively high productivity—are the main drivers of Singapore's strong external position. The CA surplus is projected to narrow over the medium term on the back of increased infrastructure and social spending. In 2020 public saving decreased with a sizable fiscal expansion in response to the pandemic, while private saving increased.

Assessment. Guided by the EBA framework, the IMF staff assesses the 2020 CA gap to be in the range of 1.2 to 7.2 percent of GDP.[2] The identified policy gaps narrowed significantly to close to zero in 2020, reflecting the sizable fiscal package and an increase in health care expenditure.

2020 (% GDP)	CA: 17.6	Cycl. Adj. CA: 16.9	EBA Norm: —	EBA Gap: —	COVID-19 Adj.: –1.9	Other Adj.: —	Staff Gap: 4.2

Real Exchange Rate

Background. The REER depreciated by 2.6 percent in 2020, reflecting the depreciation of the NEER by 1.2 percent. This followed a depreciation of the REER by 0.3 percent and an appreciation of the NEER by 2.4 percent, both cumulative, between 2017 and 2019. As of May 2021, the REER had depreciated by 0.3 percent relative to the 2020 average.

Assessment. Consistent with the IMF staff CA gap, the IMF staff assesses the REER to be undervalued in the range of 2.5 to 14.5 percent, with a midpoint of 8.5 percent in 2020 (applying an estimated elasticity of 0.5).

Capital and Financial Accounts: Flows and Policy Measures

Background. Singapore has an open capital account. Because it is a trade and financial center in Asia, changes in market sentiment can affect Singapore significantly. Increased risk aversion in the region, for instance, may lead to inflows to Singapore given its status as a regional safe haven, whereas global stress may lead to outflows. The financial account balance reflects in part reinvestment abroad of income from official foreign assets, as well as sizable net inward FDI and smaller but more volatile net bank-related flows. In 2020 the capital and financial account switched to inflows of 4.2 percent of GDP from outflows of 16.5 percent in 2019 (outflows ranged from 10 to 18 percent in 2015–19). This reflects lower net outflows of portfolio investment led by resident banks switching from a net outflow position in 2019 to a net inflow position in 2020, as well as "other investment" turning from net outflows to net inflows among domestic nonbanks.

Assessment. The unusual capital inflows in 2020 are likely to be transitory, reflecting regional safe haven flows, and are likely to turn to outflows as the effect of the pandemic subsides in subsequent years.

FX Intervention and Reserves Level

Background. With the NEER as the intermediate monetary policy target, intervention is undertaken to achieve inflation and output objectives. Because Singapore is a financial center, prudential motives call for a larger NIIP buffer. Official reserves held by the Monetary Authority of Singapore (MAS) reached US$362 billion (106.6 percent of GDP) in 2020. Aggregate data on FX intervention operations have been published since April 2020.

Assessment. In addition to FX reserves held by the MAS, Singapore also has access to other official foreign assets managed by Temasek and GIC.[3] The current level of official external assets appears adequate, even after considering prudential motives, and there is no clear case for further accumulation for precautionary purposes.

Table 3.23. South Africa: Economy Assessment

Overall Assessment: *The external position in 2020 was moderately weaker than the level implied by medium-term fundamentals and desirable policies.* The CA turned into a surplus for the first time in nearly two decades on the back of depressed imports following weak domestic demand, a favorable income balance, and strong metal exports. As such, the CA surplus is deemed temporary. The pandemic led to nonresident capital outflows, partly offset by the IMF emergency financing, some asset repatriation and parent support.

Potential Policy Responses: Tackling external imbalances will require a combination of bold implementation of structural reforms to ameliorate competitiveness and gradual but substantial fiscal consolidation, once the pandemic is over, while providing space for infrastructure and social spending (to help reduce poverty and inequality). Reform efforts should focus on improving governance, the efficiency of key product markets (by encouraging private sector participation), and the functioning of labor markets. These reforms are expected to help attract less volatile and longer-term capital inflows, such as FDI. Seizing opportunities to accumulate international reserves, should they arise, would strengthen the country's ability to deal with shocks.

Foreign Asset and Liability Position and Trajectory

Background. With large gross external assets and liabilities (respectively, 164.5 and 132.1 percent of GDP at end-2020), South Africa is highly integrated into international capital markets. The NIIP improved markedly from 8.6 percent of GDP in 2019 to 32.4 percent in 2020 mainly due to nonresident capital outflows and valuation adjustments from rand depreciation. The NIIP is expected to moderate over the medium term as the CA balance is projected to return to a deficit. Gross external debt rose from 52.7 percent of GDP in 2019 to an estimated 55.9 percent of GDP in 2020 due mainly to accounting effects (a sharp GDP contraction during the pandemic). Short-term external debt (on a residual maturity basis) is estimated at about 15.2 percent of GDP in 2020.

Assessment. Risks from large gross external liabilities are mitigated by a sufficiently large external asset position, the liability structure (the bulk is in equities), and the currency composition of external debt (mostly in rand).

2020 (% GDP)	NIIP: 32.4	Gross Assets: 164.5	Debt Assets: 21.9	Gross Liabilities: 132.1	Debt Liabilities: 51.0

Current Account

Background. The CA deficit narrowed from 5.8 percent of GDP in 2013 to 2.5 percent in 2017 but widened to 3 percent in 2019 as the terms of trade deteriorated and the trade balance weakened. The CA turned into a surplus for the first time in nearly two decades in 2020, reaching 2.2 percent of GDP, due to sharp and mainly pandemic-related changes in the trade balance amid unusually depressed imports, strong commodity prices, some rand depreciation, and a favorable income balance. While highly uncertain, the CA surplus is projected to narrow to 1 percent of GDP in 2021, mainly due to higher imports as domestic demand recovers and a weakening income balance, despite the terms of trade remaining robust. Over the medium term, a CA deficit is projected to gradually widen to 2.5–3 percent of GDP as trade balance is expected to deteriorate.

Assessment. The IMF staff estimates a CA gap in the range of –2.1 to –0.1 percent of GDP in 2020. The staff cyclically adjusted CA is estimated at –0.1 percent of GDP, accounting for COVID-19–related adjustors of –1.8 percent of GDP to take account of the unique impact of the pandemic on gold exports, oil imports, travel services including tourism, medical spending imports, and lower dividend payments,[1] as well as the statistical treatment of transfers and income accounts.[2] The adjusted CA norm (0.6 percent of GDP) is obtained by subtracting 1 percentage point from the EBA CA norm (1.6 percent of GDP) to reflect lower life expectancy relative to other countries in the regression sample.[3]

2020 (% GDP)	CA: 2.2	Cycl. Adj. CA: –0.1	EBA Norm: 1.6	EBA gap: –1.7	COVID-19 Adj.: –1.8	Other Adj.: 2.4	Staff Gap: –1.1

Real Exchange Rate

Background. The CPI-REER depreciated during 2011–16, recouped some of the losses in 2017–18, and depreciated again during 2019–20. In particular, the REER in 2020 depreciated by about 9.2 percent in 2020 relative to 2019, mainly due to nominal depreciation during the pandemic. As of end-May 2021, the REER had appreciated by 6 percent compared to end-2020 and by 13.2 percent compared to the 2020 average.

Assessment. The IMF staff CA gap implies an overvalued REER with a midpoint of 4.0 percent (applying an estimated elasticity of 0.28). The two REER-based regressions point to undervaluation in a range of 10.5 percent (level approach) and 20.9 percent (index approach). Based on the CA approach, the IMF staff assesses the REER to be overvalued by 4.0 percent, with a range between 0.0 and 8.0 percent.

Capital and Financial Accounts: Flows and Policy Measures

Background. Net FDI slightly increased in 2020 (from 0.6 percent of GDP in 2019 to 1.7 percent). Net portfolio investment turned negative in 2020 (–2.3 percent of GDP) on account of nonresident capital outflows during the pandemic. Gross external financing needs stood at 13 percent of GDP in 2020.

Assessment. In 2021, COVID-19–related financial market volatility in emerging markets may persist, as yields in the US are increasing and despite overall favorable market sentiment and a search for yield. Following large capital outflows and asset sell-offs during the pandemic in spring 2020 and the corresponding significant rand depreciation, demand for South African assets has stabilized so far. As the CA is expected to return to a deficit in 2022, risks from large reliance on non-FDI inflows for external financing and sizable nonresident holdings of local financial assets are mitigated by a flexible exchange rate, relatively small currency mismatches, and a large domestic institutional investor base. The latter tends to reduce asset price volatility during periods of market stress. The South African authorities obtained financing under the IMF's Rapid Financing Instrument for $4.3 billion (100 percent of quota) in July 2020.

FX Intervention and Reserves Level

Background. South Africa's exchange rate regime is classified as floating. Central bank intervention in the foreign exchange market is rare. International reserves are estimated to have been about 18.2 percent of GDP, 140.2 percent of gross external financing needs, and 7.3 months of imports at the end of 2020. Reserves stand below the IMF's composite adequacy metric (74 percent of the metric without considering existing CFM measures and 82 percent of the metric after considering them).

Assessment. If conditions allow, reserve accumulation would be desirable over the medium term to strengthen the external liquidity buffer, subject to maintaining the primacy of the inflation objective.

Table 3.24. Spain: Economy Assessment

Overall Assessment: *The external position in 2020 was broadly in line with the level implied by medium-term fundamentals and desirable policies.* In 2020 the CA remained in surplus for the ninth consecutive year. Further strengthening the NIIP will require sustaining a relatively high CA surplus over the coming years.

Potential Policy Responses: To keep the CA balance in line with its norm, policies need to support investment and foster competitiveness to facilitate the recovery, while carefully managing the public debt load. Using financing from Next Generation EU funds to boost medium-term investments will be important to raise potential growth and support decarbonization and digitalization. Boosting competitiveness through productivity gains would entail continued wage flexibility, reforms to address labor market duality, implementation of product and service market reforms, and actions to enhance education outcomes and innovation.

Foreign Asset and Liability Position and Trajectory

Background. The NIIP dropped significantly during 2000–09, driven mostly by high CA deficits but also by valuation effects. Following a 15 percentage point increase in 2015–19 due to sustained CA surpluses, the NIIP declined again, reaching –84 percent of GDP in 2020, mainly due to the contraction in GDP. Gross liabilities stood at 290 percent of GDP in 2020, with slightly over two-thirds in the form of external debt. Whereas the private sector has deleveraged since the 2008–12 crisis, the NIIP accounted for by the general government and the central bank increased markedly, particularly in the context of the COVID-19 crisis, raising its share to 93 percent in 2020 (including TARGET2 liabilities, which reached 44 percent of GDP by the end of 2020).[1]

Assessment. The large negative NIIP comes with external vulnerabilities, including from large gross financing needs and potentially adverse valuation effects. Mitigating factors are a favorable maturity structure of outstanding sovereign debt (averaging almost eight years) and current ECB measures, such as quantitative easing, which lower the cost of debt.

2020 (% GDP)	NIIP: –84.5	Gross Assets: 205.9	Debt Assets: 94.8	Gross Liab.: 290.4	Debt Liab.: 179.7

Current Account

Background. After a peak CA deficit in 2007, corrected initially by a sharp contraction in imports, increased competitiveness from wage moderation and greater internationalization efforts contributed to strong export growth, leading to CA surpluses in 2012–20. As a result of historical data revisions, the average annual CA surplus during 2013–18 was revised from 1.5 to 2.3 percent of GDP. The COVID-19 crisis was associated with a stronger decline in exports than imports, largely due to the sharp decline in receipts from travel services, including tourism. As a result, the CA surplus declined significantly, from 2.1 percent in 2019 to an estimated 0.7 percent of GDP in 2020. With high uncertainty, in 2021 the CA surplus is projected to increase slightly as the pandemic recedes, supported by a gradual recovery in exports, notably tourism. Weaker-than-expected exports—particularly tourism receipts—are a key downside risk around this projection. Moderate CA surpluses are projected to continue in the medium term.

Assessment. The cyclically adjusted CA balance is –1.3 percent of GDP, yielding a CA gap of –1.6 percent of GDP. However, the weakening of the CA mainly reflects the pandemic's transitory impact due to shocks not captured by the EBA model, which amount to 2.6 percent for travel services, including tourism; –0.3 percent for oil; 0.3 percent for medical goods; and –0.3 percent for the global shift of household consumption from services to consumer goods. Adjusting for these effects, the 2020 cyclically adjusted CA balance is 1.1 percent of GDP. The EBA CA model suggests a norm of 0.3 percent of GDP for 2020. However, given external risks from a large and negative NIIP, the IMF staff views the appropriate CA norm to be 1.8 percent of GDP, with a range of 0.8 to 2.8 percent of GDP. This yields a CA gap of –1.7 to 0.3 percent of GDP. The IMF staff assessment puts more weight on external sustainability and is guided by the objective of raising the NIIP to below –50 percent over the medium to long term. With a sustained CA surplus of about 1.8 percent of GDP, the NIIP is projected to reach –50 percent of GDP over the medium term under current policies, though with high uncertainty, as zero valuation effects are assumed.[2]

2020 (% GDP)	CA: 0.7	Cycl. Adj. CA: –1.3	EBA Norm: 0.3	EBA Gap: –1.6	COVID-19 Adj.: 2.4	Other Adj.: –1.5	Staff Gap: –0.7

Real Exchange Rate

Background. In 2020 the CPI-based REER appreciated by 0.5 and the ULC-based REER depreciated by 4.6 percent from their average 2019 levels. The CPI-based REER is still moderately lower than its 2009 peak, partially reversing the significant appreciation from euro entry in 1999 until 2009. The ULC-based REER shows that the appreciation between 1999 and 2008 has been almost fully reversed, initially because of labor shedding, and thereafter due to wage moderation and strong output growth until 2019. After reaching its peak in 2008 the ULC-based REER depreciated by 24 percent. As of May 2021, the CPI-based REER had appreciated by 1.4 percent, and the ULC-based REER had depreciated by 0.2 percent relative to their 2020 averages.

Assessment. The IMF staff CA gap implies an overvaluation of 2.6 percent, using an elasticity of 0.28, while the EBA REER models estimate a small overvaluation of 4.0 (level) to 6.2 (index) percent for 2020. Therefore, based on the IMF staff CA gap, the IMF staff assesses the REER gap to be in the range of –1.4 to 6.6 percent, with a midpoint of 2.6 percent.[3]

Capital and Financial Accounts: Flows and Policy Measures

Background. Financing conditions have eased following some increase in sovereign bond yields in the early stages of the COVID-19 crisis. And by the third quarter of 2020 the private sector was continuing its deleveraging against the rest of the world. In 2020 the financial account balance was largely driven by the substantial increase in liquidity creation by the Eurosystem through the expansion of asset purchase programs and the refinancing of Spanish banks, as well as by net outflows of loans and other bank-related instruments from sectors other than the central bank. Consequently, the accumulation of TARGET2 liabilities, reflecting liquidity creation within the framework of the Eurosystem, was the highest since 2012 (13 percent of GDP in 2020), after having been negative in 2019 for the first time since 2015.

Assessment. As a result of the pandemic crisis, investor sentiment deteriorated in 2020, notably toward banks. Furthermore, large external financing needs leave Spain vulnerable to sustained market volatility, although the ECB's policies to maintain favorable liquidity conditions and monetary accommodation remain a mitigating factor.

FX Intervention and Reserves Level

Background. The euro has the status of a global reserve currency.

Assessment. Reserves held by the euro area are typically low relative to standard metrics, but the currency is free floating.

Table 3.25. Sweden: Economy Assessment

Overall Assessment: *The external position in 2020 was stronger than the level implied by medium-term fundamentals and desirable policies. The CA is expected to decline to its long-term average over the medium term as domestic and global fiscal policies normalize and structural reforms are undertaken.*

Potential Policy Responses: Given large fiscal buffers, Sweden is in a good position to provide further support to companies and households if the crisis is protracted. Over the medium term, policies that could support external rebalancing and bring the CA balance closer to its norm would require structural reforms. Also, there is scope for greener and growth-enhancing private and public investments to facilitate structural transformation and support domestic demand. The central bank has ensured ample liquidity, but further ability to increase aggregate demand may be limited. As the recovery resumes, past imbalances and policy distortions will need to be addressed through implementation of reforms that raise productive investment. Policies that raise potential output, decrease unemployment, and reduce household debt also remain important even as their aggregate impact on the CA is more ambiguous.

Foreign Asset and Liability Position and Trajectory

Background. The NIIP was 18 percent of GDP in 2020, with a small increase of 0.3 percentage points in 2020. It is expected to rise further in the medium term, reflecting the outlook for continued CA surpluses. However, these projections are subject to uncertainty as IIP data include significant errors and omissions, which have averaged –2.1 percent of GDP in the past five years.

Assessment. Gross liabilities are projected to increase to 275 percent of GDP in 2020, with about one-half being gross external debt (137 percent of GDP). Other financial institutions (87 percent of GDP) hold the bulk of net foreign assets, followed by social security funds (26 percent of GDP), households (20 percent of GDP), and the central bank (12 percent of GDP); nonfinancial corporations (60 percent of GDP), monetary financial institutions (51 percent of GDP), and the central government (11 percent of GDP) are net external debtors. Although rollovers of external debt (which includes banks' covered bonds) pose some vulnerability, risks are moderated by the banks' ample liquidity and large capital buffers.

2020 (% GDP)	NIIP: 18.0	Gross Assets: 292.7	Debt Assets: 88.0	Gross Liab.: 274.7	Debt Liab.: 129.4

Current Account

Background. Despite the global COVID-19 crisis, the CA increased to 5.2 percent of GDP in 2020, compared with 2019 (4.6 percent of GDP), supported by exports of goods (machinery and chemicals) in the first quarter and doubling of primary income from investments in the second quarter. Sweden is a net oil importer, with a negative oil balance. Lower domestic demand for external goods and travel services, including tourism, due to decreased economic activity and mobility has reduced imports in 2020 substantially compared with 2019. In addition, low oil prices have decreased the value of oil imports. The impact from the lower-than-usual imports of oil and tourism services is estimated to have improved the CA surplus by about 1.1 percentage points (see COVID-19 adjustor). The cyclically adjusted fiscal stance, which was not as expansionary as in the rest of the world, may have contributed to the mild increase in the CA as well. Over the medium term, the CA is projected to return to its long-term average of 3 percent of GDP.

Assessment. The cyclically adjusted CA is estimated at 6.4 percent of GDP in 2020, 5.1 percentage points above the cyclically adjusted EBA norm of 1.3 percent of GDP. However, the estimated EBA norm for Sweden has been below the actual CA balance for the past two decades, suggesting that factors not captured by the model, such as Sweden's mandatory contributions to fully funded pension programs and an older labor force, may also be driving Sweden's saving-investment balances. Overall, taking into account adjustments for oil (–0.4 percent of GDP), travel services including tourism (–0.5 percent of GDP), and medical (–0.2 percent of GDP) imports, which were affected by the COVID-19 crisis, the IMF staff assesses the CA gap at 3.8 percent of GDP in 2020, within a range of ±1.5 percent of GDP, reflecting uncertainty around the EBA estimated norm.

2020 (% GDP)	CA: 5.7	Cycl. Adj. CA: 6.4	EBA Norm: 1.3	EBA Gap: 5.1	COVID-19 Adj.: –1.2	Other Adj.: 0.0	Staff Gap: 3.8

Real Exchange Rate

Background. The krona appreciated by 5.3 percent in ULC-based real effective terms and by 2.4 percent in CPI-based REER terms in 2020 relative to its average level in 2019, partly reflecting the change in the repo rate from negative to zero since the beginning of 2020, financial inflows, and a milder recession than in peers. As of end-May 2021, the CPI-based REER had appreciated by 3.4 percent compared to the 2020 average.

Assessment. The IMF staff CA gap implies a REER gap of –10.9 percent in 2020 (applying an estimated elasticity of 0.35). The REER index and level models suggest a gap of –18.4 percent and –16.8 percent, respectively, for 2020. The ULC-based REER index was 5.5 percent below its 28-year average (since the krona was floated in 1993) in 2020. Because this indicator has fluctuated around a broadly stable level since the currency was floated, it provides a useful indication of valuation, which the IMF staff prefers. Overall, the IMF staff assesses the krona to be undervalued by 3 to 13 percent, with a midpoint of 8 percent, as guided by the ULC-based REER index. This REER gap may continue to decline once the situation, including monetary policy, normalizes.

Capital and Financial Accounts: Flows and Policy Measures

Background. Other investments (such as the provision of loans, insurance, pensions, trade credits, etc.) of about 2.5 percent of GDP constituted one-half of the financial account in 2020, with portfolio investment outflows (2.0 percent), direct investments (1.4 percent), and derivatives (–1 percent) being the remainder.

Assessment. Given their size, interconnectedness, and funding model, Sweden's large banks are vulnerable to liquidity risks stemming from global wholesale markets. However, banks have improved their structural liquidity positions in recent years. Also, the authorities have strengthened regulation by introducing liquidity coverage ratio requirements in foreign and domestic currency in addition to the overall liquidity coverage ratio. This created substantial buffers before the COVID-19 crisis and, together with the swift and strong policy response, eased liquidity and funding pressures for banks in 2020.

FX Intervention and Reserves Level

Background. The exchange rate is free floating. Foreign currency reserves increased by US$3 billion to stand at US$59 billion in December 2020, which is equivalent to 22 percent of the short-term external debt of monetary and financial institutions (primarily banks), about 11 percent of GDP, and 3.3 months of imports. There were no FX interventions in 2020.

Assessment. In view of the high dependence of Swedish banks on wholesale funding in foreign currency, and the disruptions in such funding that have occurred at times of international financial distress, Sweden should maintain adequate foreign reserves. A US$60 billion swap facility was agreed with the Federal Reserve to address risks to dollar funding related to the COVID-19 crisis; although it was not used, it provided an important backstop function.

Table 3.26. Switzerland: Economy Assessment

Overall Assessment: *Switzerland's external position in 2020 was broadly in line with the level implied by medium-term fundamentals and desirable policies.* However, this change from the previous assessment, in which the external position was judged to be moderately stronger, is subject to higher-than-usual uncertainty related to recent large downward statistical revisions to historical CA balances.[1] The 2019 CA balance is now nearly 5 percentage points of GDP lower than estimated at the time of the 2020 ESR. The revisions suggest a weakening in the external position and add to uncertainty. Data and time will be needed to assess the durability of this downward shift in the external accounts, distinguishing transitory and COVID-19–related effects from structural impacts. A number of pandemic-influenced developments, especially concerning the trade and income accounts, are expected to unwind in the coming years. More broadly, the continued strength of Switzerland's external balance sheet and macroeconomic policy mix would be at odds with an assessment of the overall external position as weaker. Net foreign assets increased in 2020, with reserves now exceeding 130 percent of GDP, reflecting FX operations conducted for monetary policy reasons in the context of FX inflow surges rather than reserve accumulation or exchange rate management purposes. Policy buffers also remain strong—in particular, fiscal buffers—despite the comprehensive response to the pandemic. Overall, these circumstances suggest caution in assessing the external position.

Potential Policy Responses: Fiscal policy should continue to play a key role in responding to the pandemic and ensuring a strong and sustained recovery. Monetary policy should remain accommodative and directed at price stability; macroprudential policies should focus on reducing financial sector risks. FX intervention may be used to partially mitigate strong appreciation pressures that would otherwise push the economy further into deflation. The Swiss National Bank (SNB) should continually review its framework and tools, especially in light of the experience during COVID-19, to consider whether adjusting or extending targets, instruments, and communications would enable it to continue to respond effectively to new challenges. Medium-term policies should be geared toward ensuring balanced domestic and external contributions to growth while improving the public-private mix in financial outflows and thereby easing pressures on the franc. In the post-pandemic environment, fiscal policy should remain supportive, continuing—and enhancing or accelerating, where possible—efforts to foster green, digital transformation and productivity gains and to address important challenges (for example, competitiveness, aging).

Foreign Asset and Liability Position and Trajectory

Background. Switzerland is a major financial center with a positive NIIP of 94.2 percent of GDP and gross foreign asset and liability positions of 758 and 664 percent of GDP, respectively, at the end of 2020. The NIIP reflects both a history of large CA surpluses and valuation changes.[2] Valuation changes reflect fluctuations of exchange rates and prices of securities and precious metals that interact with differences among assets and liabilities in terms of currencies and instruments.[3] Statistical revisions in 2020, to better account for foreign liabilities on FDI and portfolio equity investment, have involved large downward adjustments in NIIP estimates for 2008–19. On the basis of the revised series, the NIIP rose in 2020 by 11 percentage points of GDP, mainly driven by an increase in reserve assets. Projections of the NIIP in 2021 and beyond are complicated by heightened uncertainty; because of the large gross positions and compositional differences among assets and liabilities, even modest changes in exchange rates, asset prices, and returns may have a material effect on the NIIP.

Assessment. Switzerland's large gross liability position and the volatility of financial flows and investment returns present some risk, but this is mitigated by the large gross asset position and the Swiss franc denomination of about two-thirds of external liabilities.

2020 (% GDP)	NIIP: 94.2	Gross Assets: 758.0	Res. Assets: 135.9	Gross Liab.: 663.8	Debt Liab.: 205.2

Current Account

Background. Switzerland's CA surpluses averaged over 9 percent of GDP during 2010–19, although statistical revisions reflecting conclusion of the reporting calendar and improved coverage of domiciliary-company foreign liabilities led to downward revisions of surpluses for 2018–19. In 2020, the CA surplus decreased from 6.7 percent of GDP in 2019 to 3.8 percent. The decline likely reflected temporary shocks, especially related to COVID-19, such as weaker trade balances for gold and luxury watches and a larger drop in investment income receipts than expenses due to the relatively better performance of the Swiss economy during the pandemic. Other factors may persist. On balance, the CA position is likely to return toward 2018–19 levels in 2021 as the global economy recovers and the drag from temporary COVID-19–related shocks eases.

Assessment. The EBA CA norm of 5.6 percent of GDP is slightly lower than last year's norm. Based on a cyclically adjusted CA surplus of 3.9 percent and the norm, the overall EBA-estimated CA gap equaled –1.7 percent of GDP in 2020. Domestic policy gaps account for –1.1 percentage points of the gap and include excessive private sector credit (–0.7 percent of GDP) and fiscal overspending (–0.3 percent of GDP), while policy gaps in the rest of the world contribute 2.2 percentage points. Adjustments for (1) specific factors relevant for Switzerland that are not treated appropriately in the income account—namely, valuation losses on fixed-income securities arising from inflation (–2.8 percent of GDP) and retained earnings on portfolio equity investment (–0.6 percent of GDP); and (2) transitory impacts of the COVID-19 pandemic (1.9 percent of GDP) widened the gap to –3.2 percent of GDP (±2 percentage points).[4,5]

2020 (% GDP)	CA: 3.8	Cycl. Adj. CA: 3.9	EBA Norm: 5.6	EBA Gap: –1.7	COVID-19 Adj.: 1.9	Other Adj.: –3.4	Staff Gap: –3.2

Real Exchange Rate

Background. A narrower domestic-foreign interest rate differential and heightened risk aversion, especially at the outbreak of the pandemic, contributed to strong appreciation pressure in the first half of 2020; this pressure subsequently eased. Relative to 2019, the average NEER and CPI-based REER appreciated by 6.1 and 3.8 percent, respectively, notwithstanding sizable FX interventions. From a long-term perspective, the NEER has appreciated by 27 percent since the end of 2010, while the CPI-based REER has appreciated by 2.8 percent (reflecting lower domestic inflation).

Assessment. The IMF staff CA gap implies a REER overvaluation of 6.2 percent in 2020 (applying an estimated elasticity of 0.52). The EBA REER index and level models suggest that the average REER in 2020 was overvalued by 15.4 and 26.4 percent, respectively, with policy gaps accounting for a small amount of the total gap. This finding largely reflects a "reversion to trend" property of the empirical model in the context of prior rapid appreciation episodes. However, due to measurement issues, the results may not fully capture a secular improvement in productivity, especially in knowledge-based sectors. Consistent with the IMF staff CA gap, the IMF staff assesses the REER to be overvalued in the range of 2.2 to 10.2 percent, with a midpoint of 6.2 percent.[6]

Capital and Financial Accounts: Flows and Policy Measures

Background. Net financial outflows totaled 1.8 percent of GDP in 2020, with private inflows (14.8 percent of GDP) more than offset by SNB reserve increases (16.6 percent of GDP). This contrasts with 2019, when more moderate SNB reserve gains (2.2 percent of GDP) and private outflows (3.0 percent of GDP) jointly led to net financial outflows of 5.2 percent of GDP. During 2009–20, net private inflows averaged 3.6 percent of GDP, while the average annual increase in SNB reserves was 10.5 percent of GDP.

Assessment. Financial flows are large and volatile, reflecting Switzerland's status as a financial center and safe haven. From a long-term perspective, sizable net private financial outflows prior to the global financial crisis have declined and, on average, turned into net capital inflows, adding to appreciation pressures.

FX Intervention and Reserves Level

Background. Official reserve assets (including gold) amounted to US$1,083 billion (136 percent of GDP) at the end of 2020, up US$228 billion from the end of 2019 (including valuation changes). While FX interventions had been occasional and moderate since exiting the exchange rate floor in 2015, the SNB purchased CHF 110 billion in FX (net) in 2020, the highest amount since 2012.

Assessment. Reserves are large relative to GDP, but more moderate in comparison with short-term foreign liabilities. The high level of reserves also reflects monetary operations aimed at avoiding persistent undershooting of inflation as a result of FX inflow surges and given the limited scope for significant easing via other monetary pool tools. In particular, the supply of domestic assets for purchase is limited, and the marginal interest rate on bank deposits at the SNB of –0.75 percent is already the lowest in the world. The SNB's initiation of quarterly publication of (net) FX intervention information in 2020 was an important step to enhance transparency.

Table 3.27. Thailand: Economy Assessment

Overall Assessment: *The external position in 2020 was stronger than the level implied by medium-term fundamentals and desirable policies.* The CA surplus narrowed relative to 2019 due to the COVID-19 shock, reflecting a dramatic fall in the tourism-driven services balance partially offset by a strengthening trade balance as weak domestic demand drove a sharper contraction in imports than in exports.

Potential Policy Responses: In order to bring the CA more in line with medium-term fundamentals and desirable policies, the IMF staff recommends an accelerated, mutually reinforcing macro policy stimulus, led by a fiscal expansion, given available fiscal space, to revitalize domestic demand. This should be deployed toward targeted social transfers to mitigate the effects of the pandemic on the most vulnerable, as well as infrastructure investment to support the recovery and reorientation of affected sectors. In addition, the exchange rate should move flexibly as the key shock absorber, with intervention limited to disorderly market conditions. Further efforts to reform social safety nets should continue, and steps to address widespread informality should reduce precautionary saving and support consumption.

Foreign Asset and Liability Position and Trajectory

Background. Thailand's NIIP strengthened in 2020 to 11 percent of GDP from 0.3 percent in 2019. Gross assets rose to about 120 percent of GDP (driven by the increase in reserve assets to 51 percent of GDP), while gross liabilities increased slightly to 109 percent of GDP, comprising direct (about one-half) and portfolio (one-third) investment. Falling inward investment kept net FDI low; outward direct and portfolio investment recovered strongly by the end of the year, offsetting midyear outflows.

Assessment. The NIIP is projected to remain in a small creditor position over the medium term given CA surpluses. External debt rose to a still-contained 38 percent of GDP, of which short-term debt (on a remaining maturity basis) amounts to 15 percent of GDP; risks to external debt sustainability and liquidity are limited.

2020 (% GDP)	NIIP: 11	Gross Assets: 120	Res. Assets: 51	Gross Liab.: 109	Debt Liab.: 38

Current Account

Background. Thailand's CA surplus declined from 7.0 percent of GDP in 2019 to 3.3 percent of GDP in 2020, reflecting the impact of the pandemic. Containment measures weighed on domestic demand, which led to a larger contraction in imports than exports, which softened due to weak global demand and supply chain disruptions, notwithstanding a surge in net gold exports (gold is widely used as a store of wealth in Thailand, and many households without access to social safety nets had to rely on gold sales in 2020 to meet extraordinary liquidity needs). This led to a strengthening of the trade balance. However, the services account collapsed as international tourism arrivals fell to zero between April and October 2020. The CA in 2021 is expected to narrow to 0.5 percent of GDP as the recovery in domestic and external demand narrows the trade balance and tourism receipts are still slow to recover.

Assessment. The EBA CA model estimates a cyclically adjusted CA of 1.0 percent of GDP and a CA norm of 1.2 percent of GDP for 2020. The CA gap of –0.2 percent of GDP consists of an identified policy gap of 1.3 percent of GDP (mainly due to fiscal policy and FX intervention) and an unexplained residual of –1.5 percent of GDP, which partly reflects the unique nature of the COVID-19 shock as well as structural factors not fully captured by the EBA model. In this regard, adjustors to account for the large shocks to the travel services (including tourism) and oil sectors of 3.7 and –0.5 percent of GDP, respectively, are applied, as they are not accounted for by the standard EBA cyclical adjustment. Further adjustments regarding the global shift in household consumption composition from services toward consumer goods (–0.3 percent of GDP), net exports of medical supplies triggered by the health emergency (–0.2 percent of GDP), and the aforementioned surge in gold exports (–0.3 percent of GDP) are also applied. Overall, the IMF staff assesses the CA gap to be in the range of 0.7–3.7 percent of GDP, with a midpoint of 2.2 percent of GDP. This gap is expected to narrow over the medium term as policy stimulus is deployed, domestic demand recovers, and the social safety net is enhanced.

2020 (% GDP)	CA: 3.3	Cycl. Adj. CA: 1.0	EBA Norm: 1.2	EBA Gap: –0.2	COVID-19 Adj.: 2.4	Other Adj.: 0.0	Staff Gap: 2.2

Real Exchange Rate

Background. The baht has been on a gradual real appreciation trend since the mid-2000s, despite occasional bouts of volatility. In 2020 the REER depreciated 6.9 percent by April, relative to the end of December 2019, as emerging markets faced increased capital outflows due to the outbreak of the pandemic. The REER has since broadly resumed its appreciation, as the virus was controlled in Thailand through the year, and buttressed by positive sentiment about the vaccine, ending the year about 2.6 percent lower relative to its 2019 average. As of end-May 2021, the REER had depreciated by 3.7 percent compared to the 2020 average.

Assessment. Using an elasticity of 0.56 and based on the IMF staff CA gap, the IMF staff assesses the REER to be undervalued in the 1.5–6.5 percent range, with a midpoint of 4.0 percent. The EBA index REER gap in 2020 is estimated at 10.8 percent; the EBA level REER gap is estimated at –5.2 percent.

Capital and Financial Accounts: Flows and Policy Measures

Background. In 2020 the capital and financial account balance strengthened to –0.7 percent of GDP from –2.9 percent in 2019, driven by other investment flows. Nonresident holdings of Thai bonds and equities declined in March/April, but recovered by the end of the year, reflecting Thailand's strong external position relative to other emerging markets. Through the year, the authorities accelerated plans to liberalize FX outflows, including easing restrictions on resident holdings of foreign currency securities and deposits.

Assessment. Since 2013 Thailand has experienced episodes of volatility, reflecting external financial and political conditions. Nevertheless, Thailand has been able to weather such episodes well, given strong external buffers and fundamentals. The IMF staff encourages the prudent liberalization of the financial account and recommends a phaseout of the 2019 reduction in the limits on nonresident baht accounts. Instead, a comprehensive package of macroeconomic, financial, and structural policies should be pursued, complemented by continued efforts to liberalize capital outflows.

FX Intervention and Reserves Level

Background. The exchange rate regime is classified as (de jure and de facto) floating. International reserves (including net forward position) increased to 57.3 percent of GDP in 2020, which is more than three times short-term debt and 12 months of imports, and more than 200 percent of the IMF's standard reserve adequacy metric. In response to the COVID-19 shock, the exchange rate has been allowed to adjust, with some FX sales in outflow episodes.

Assessment. Gross international reserves (including net forward position) increased by more than US$28.7 billion in 2020. While official intervention data are not published, estimates suggest two-sided intervention for the year. Reserves are higher than the range of the IMF's adequacy metrics, and there is still no need to build up reserves for precautionary purposes. The exchange rate should move flexibly to act as a shock absorber, with intervention limited to avoiding disorderly market conditions.

Table 3.28. Turkey: Economy Assessment

Overall Assessment: *The external position in 2020 was moderately weaker than the level implied by medium-term fundamentals and desirable policies.* Expansionary monetary policy and rapid provision of credit by state-owned banks put pressure on the lira last year through dollarization, import, and financial account channels, which led in turn to sales of foreign exchange reserves to support the lira. Despite the marked real exchange rate depreciation, the CA deficit resurfaced because of lower exports (including tourism) and robust imports (including gold). The monetary tightening beginning in late 2020 saw a return of capital inflows and modest reserves buildup, but outflows and reserves losses resumed in March 2021, amid rising policy uncertainty and lira depreciation. Policy uncertainty, large gross external financing needs, and relatively low reserves increase Turkey's vulnerability to shocks. Only over time will the REER undervaluation, with its usual lags, help move the current account back toward its norm, aided by less expansionary policies.

Potential Policy Responses: Policies that could support Turkey's external rebalancing and bring the current account balance closer to its norm include (1) keeping credit growth at sustainable rates; (2) maintaining a firm monetary policy stance, with additional measured tightening if inflation expectations increase further, to, at a minimum, keep the ex ante real policy rate unchanged, which would also help ensure sustainable credit growth; (3) enhancing the fiscal anchor with a credible commitment to future consolidation to bring debt down over time—which would also create greater space for meeting pandemic-related needs in 2021 and minimize scarring; and (4) taking additional steps to build policy credibility, which would encourage capital inflows and support de-dollarization and a buildup of reserves.

Foreign Asset and Liability Position and Trajectory

Background. In 2020, Turkey's NIIP declined from –46 to –56.4 percent of GDP, driven entirely by foreign liabilities, which rose from 79 to 90 percent of GDP.[1] External debt increased from 57 to 63 percent of GDP, driven by lower US dollar GDP. Over 70 percent of external debt is held by the private sector, and about one-third is short term (on a remaining maturity basis). Debt is expected to remain sustainable over the medium term, but debt servicing remains vulnerable to global and domestic financial conditions.

Assessment. Turkey's NIIP has become more negative since the 2000s, with 2020 affected by one-off factors related to the pandemic. The size and composition of external liabilities, coupled with low reserves, increases Turkey's vulnerability to liquidity shocks, sudden shifts in investor sentiment, and a global upswing in interest rates. The FX exposure of nonfinancial companies, including short-term loans, is high, with the potential to affect bank asset quality. NIIP is projected to improve to about –45 percent of GDP in 2025, driven by a decline in liabilities, mainly loans.

2020 (% GDP)	NIIP: –56.4	Gross Assets: 33.6	Res. Assets: 13	Gross Liab.: 90.1	Debt Liab.: 62.8

Current Account

Background. After posting a surplus for the first time in nearly two decades in 2019, the CA registered a deficit of 5.1 percent of GDP in 2020, driven by weaker goods and services exports—including tourism—and robust imports. Credit-driven consumption and investment fueled imports, more than offsetting the lower oil import bill. Gold imports increased from 1½ percent 2019 to 3½ percent of GDP in 2020, driven by policy uncertainty, a weakening currency, and elevated inflation.

Assessment. The EBA CA model estimated norm is –1.5 percent of GDP (with a standard error of ±1.8 percent of GDP). The CA deficit of 5.1 percent of GDP narrows to 4.7 percent of GDP after cyclical adjustment. Adjusting for temporary pandemic-related shocks (1.6, –0.3, and –0.2 percent of GDP for travel services, including tourism, the global shift from services to tradable goods, and oil prices, respectively) and the surge in gold imports (1 percent of GDP) yields an IMF staff CA gap of –1.2 percent of GDP relative to the CA norm. One-off shocks and the range surrounding the norm increase the uncertainty around this assessment.

2020 (% GDP)	CA: –5.1	Cycl. Adj. CA: –4.7	EBA Norm: –1.5	EBA Gap: –3.3	COVID-19 Adj.: 1.1	Other Adj.: 1.0	Staff Gap: –1.2

Real Exchange Rate

Background. The average REER depreciated for a third consecutive year, with a depreciation of more than 10 percent in 2020. The nominal depreciation against the dollar in 2020 was 23.6 percent. As of end-May 2021, the REER had depreciated by 9.0 percent compared to the 2020 average.

Assessment. The IMF staff CA gap implies a REER gap of 4.9 percent in 2020 (applying an estimated elasticity of 0.24). The EBA REER level and index approaches suggest that the REER was undervalued in 2020 by about 31 to 35 percent. Considering the recent sharp depreciation of the REER, which is expected to support a rise in Turkey's CA balance toward its norm over the coming years, the IMF staff gives more weight to the EBA REER approaches as the CA continues to adjust. The IMF staff assesses the REER to have been undervalued by about 15–25 percent, with a midpoint of 20 percent and large uncertainties surrounding these estimates.

Capital and Financial Accounts: Flows and Policy Measures

Background. Net capital inflows increased only modestly in 2020, from US$5.5 to US$8.2 billion. Errors and omissions remained negative, likely reflecting unrecorded capital outflows. The modest increase in net inflows was driven by other investment (notably the increased bilateral currency swap agreement with Qatar), which more than offset larger net portfolio outflows and lower net FDI. Turkey introduced limits on bank swaps and other derivative transactions with foreign counterparties as well as export surrender/repatriation requirements (both CFMs) in August 2018. These were being unwound when new bouts of volatility resurfaced in late 2019. Limits on bank swaps and other derivative transactions with foreign counterparties were thus reintroduced and tightened in December 2019 and February–April 2020. These were relaxed in November 2020.

Assessment. The quality of financing continued to worsen in 2020, with increased reliance on short-term financing and reserve drawdown. With annual gross external financing needs projected at about 24 percent of GDP on average in 2021–26 (29.4 percent of GDP in 2020), Turkey remains vulnerable to adverse shifts in global investor sentiment. Remaining CFMs should be phased out as conditions improve to increase market liquidity and support dedollarization.

FX Intervention and Reserves Level

Background. The de jure exchange rate is classified as free floating. The central bank undertook significant FX sales in 2020 to contain pressure on the lira. Gross reserves declined from US$105.7 billion at the end of 2019 to US$93.3 billion by the end of December. Net international reserves dropped by US$26.2 billion to US$14.5 billion by the end of 2020.[2] The composition of reserves has also changed, with an increasing share of gold and non-SDR-basket currencies.

Assessment. Gross reserves decreased from 84 to 74 percent of the IMF's ARA metric during 2020, falling further below the floor of the recommended 100–150 percent ARA adequacy range and covering only 54 percent of short-term external debt (at remaining maturity). Steady reserve accumulation over the medium term is needed given Turkey's large external liabilities, dependence on short-term and portfolio funding, and large domestic FX deposits.

Table 3.29. United Kingdom: Economy Assessment

Overall Assessment: *The external position in 2020 was weaker than the level implied by medium-term fundamentals and desirable policies.* The CA deficit remained high in 2020, reflecting unprecedented high public borrowing to combat economic fallout from the COVID-19 crisis, only partially offset by private saving. The uncertainty around this assessment is significant, reflecting pandemic-related factors, measurement issues, the evolving impact on growth and trade and capital flows of the new EU-UK Trade and Cooperation Agreement, and continuing EU-UK discussions on financial services.

Potential Policy Responses: Following efforts aimed at sustaining the recovery in the near term, policies that could support the external rebalancing and bring the current account balance closer to its norm include structural reforms to boost the United Kingdom's productivity and international competitiveness. This would entail supporting reallocation to fast-growing sectors by upgrading the skill base and ensuring appropriate access to financing for firms, as well as encouraging firm digitalization and innovation. These efforts are particularly important as access to the EU market becomes more restricted.

Foreign Asset and Liability Position and Trajectory

Background. The NIIP declined to –30.3 percent of GDP in 2020 from –28.7 percent of GDP in 2019. Over the past five years, the NIIP has declined by 5 percentage points, reflecting a negative CA contribution (–19.5 percentage points), largely offset by the valuation effect.[1] The composition of assets roughly matches that of liabilities (about 87 percent of GDP in FDI, 137 percent of GDP in derivatives, and about 219 percent of GDP in other investment), although portfolio investment liabilities (177 percent of GDP) exceed assets in portfolio investments (139 percent of GDP). The United States, other European countries, and Japan account for about 75 percent of total UK external assets and liabilities, and external liabilities have a larger share denominated in pounds than assets.[2] The IMF staff projects the NIIP to decline over the medium term, although the large and volatile valuation effects make these estimates particularly uncertain.

Assessment. Despite some decline, the sustainability of the NIIP is not an immediate concern. Since 2000, valuation gains have offset about 40 percent of the effect of CA flows on the IIP, partially reflecting CA measurement issues and depreciation of the pound. However, fluctuations in the large gross stock positions are a potential source of vulnerability (including derivatives, gross assets and gross liabilities both exceed 500 percent of GDP).

2020 (% GDP)	NIIP: –30.3	Gross Assets: 587.6	Res. Assets: 6.6	Gross Liab.: 617.8	Debt Liab.: 345

Current Account

Background. The CA deficit widened to –3.5 percent of GDP in 2020 from –3.1 percent in 2019 and remained larger than its historical average. The wider CA deficits since the global financial crisis reflect mostly a weaker income balance, due in part to lower earnings on the United Kingdom's FDI abroad (especially in the euro area). A rise in the trade balance in 2020 reflects a larger decline in domestic demand than in trading partners. This was offset by a fall in the income balance. The worsening in the CA deficit in 2020 was due to a sharp fall in gross saving combined with a slightly smaller decline in investment (relative to GDP).

Assessment. The EBA CA model estimates a norm of –0.4 percent of GDP and a CA gap of –3.3 percent of GDP. However, the underlying CA is assessed to be understated due to measurement biases, including the impact of expected inflation differentials on the CA, estimated to be about 0.5 percent of GDP.[3] In addition, the decline in net imports of travel services including tourism during the pandemic (–0.3 percent of GDP), an increase in imports due to shifts in the composition of household consumption (0.3 percent of GDP), imports of medical goods (0.3 percent of GDP), and stockpiling before Brexit (0.1 percent of GDP) likely affected the CA temporarily but may not be adequately captured in the cyclical components of the CA.[4] Overall, the IMF staff assesses the CA gap in the range of –0.4 to –4.4 percent of GDP, with a midpoint of –2.4 percent of GDP. This range takes into account the uncertainty in the assessment related to the post-Brexit development in UK-EU trade flows and financial services and possible measurement issues.

2020 (% GDP)	CA: –3.5	Cycl. Adj. CA: –3.7	EBA Norm: –0.4	EBA Gap: –3.3	COVID-19 Adj.: 0.3	Other Adj.: 0.6	Staff Gap: –2.4

Real Exchange Rate

Background. The pound appreciated slightly in real effective terms in 2020 by about 0.2 percent relative to its average level in 2019 but has depreciated since mid-2016 by about 7 percent. This depreciation reflects an unwinding of past overvaluation as well as market expectations of more restricted access to the EU market under a post-Brexit trade arrangement. As of end-May 2021, the REER had appreciated by 4.1 percent compared to the 2020 average.

Assessment. The IMF staff CA gap implies a REER gap of 10.0 percent in 2020 (applying an estimated elasticity of 0.24). EBA REER level and index approaches suggest a gap of –3.8 and –12.2 percent, respectively, for 2020. Considering all estimates, the uncertainties around them, and broadly stable REER development in 2020, on average, the IMF staff assesses the REER to be overvalued between 0 and 15 percent, with a midpoint of 7.5 percent, similar to its value in last year's ESR.

Capital and Financial Accounts: Flows and Policy Measures

Background. Given the United Kingdom's role as an international financial center, portfolio investment and other investment are the key components of the financial account. In net terms, the CA was financed in 2020 by net other investments of 4.4 percent of GDP and net FDI inflows of 2 percent of GDP, while net financial derivatives and portfolio investments declined by 1.4 and 0.5 percent of GDP, respectively. Despite some turbulence in March, access to finance has remained favorable during the COVID-19 crisis, aided by the Bank of England's liquidity support and expanded quantitative easing.

Assessment. Large fluctuations in capital flows are inherent to countries with a large financial sector. This volatility is a potential source of vulnerability, although it is mitigated by sound financial regulation and supervision and a strong financial sector. An additional risk is that FDI and portfolio investment inflows may decelerate, driven by the change in the trade relationship with the European Union and shift of some financial services to the European Union.

FX Intervention and Reserves Level

Background. The pound has the status of a global reserve currency. The share of global reserves in sterling has not changed since 2015, at about 4.5 percent.

Assessment. Reserves held by the United Kingdom are typically low relative to standard metrics, and the currency is free floating.

Table 3.30. United States: Economy Assessment

Overall Assessment: *The external position in 2020 was moderately weaker than the level implied by medium-term fundamentals and desirable policies.* Larger private sector saving has largely offset the 2020 fiscal packages, resulting in a transitory modest deterioration of the CA balance. The deep economic contraction, and ongoing changes in fiscal, trade, and labor-market (including, for example, immigration) policies, add uncertainty to the assessment.

Potential Policy Responses: In the near term, given the unprecedented social and economic fallout from the pandemic, front-loaded fiscal support is needed to ease the burden on households and firms, and to support the economic recovery. Over the medium term, fiscal consolidation will be critical to place debt on a sustainable footing, support external rebalancing, and bring the current account balance closer to its norm. Consolidation should target a medium-term general government primary surplus of about 1 percent of GDP to put the debt-to-GDP ratio on a downward path. Structural policies to increase productivity, including of tradables sectors, such as upgrading infrastructure and enhancing schooling, training, and the mobility of workers, can further contribute to external rebalancing. Tariff barriers should be rolled back, and trade and investment disputes should be resolved in a manner that supports an open, stable, and transparent global trading system.

Foreign Asset and Liability Position and Trajectory

Background. The NIIP, which averaged about –42.6 percent during 2015–18, decreased further from –51.6 percent of GDP in 2019 to –67.3 percent of GDP in 2020. Under the IMF staff baseline scenario, the NIIP is projected to remain broadly unchanged through the medium term as the CA balance reverts to its pre-COVID average.

Assessment. Financial stability risks could surface in the form of an unexpected decline in foreign demand for US fixed-income securities, which are a main component of the country's external liabilities. This risk, which could materialize, for example, due to a failure to reestablish fiscal sustainability, remains moderate given the dominant status of the US dollar as a reserve currency. About 60 percent of US assets are in the form of FDI and portfolio equity claims.

2020 (% GDP)	NIIP: –67.3	Gross Assets: 153.6	Res. Assets: 3.0	Gross Liab.: 220.9	Debt Liab.: 102.6

Current Account

Background. The US CA deficit increased from 2.2 percent of GDP in 2019 to 2.9 percent in 2020 (from 2.0 to 2.7 in cyclically adjusted terms) compared with a deficit of 2.2 percent of GDP in 2015. The evolution since 2015 is explained mostly by deterioration in the non-oil and income balances. In 2020 the trade balance declined slightly from 2019 (from –2.7 to –3.2 percent of GDP) mostly due to changes in the non-oil balance, while the income account declined slightly due to a weaker primary account balance. The large increase in the fiscal deficit (relative to other countries), mostly due to COVID-19, led to only a small increase in the CA deficit in 2020 due to the large increase in private savings. The CA deficit is expected to remain above 2 percent of GDP over the medium term.

Assessment. The EBA model estimates a cyclically adjusted CA balance of –2.7 percent of GDP and a cyclically adjusted CA norm of –0.5 percent of GDP. The norm increased from –0.7 percent GDP in 2019 due to an increase of 1.3 percent of GDP in the medium-term desirable cyclically adjusted general government fiscal balance. The EBA model CA gap is –2.2 percent of GDP for 2020, reflecting policy gaps (–1.2 percent of GDP, all of which corresponds to fiscal policy) and an unidentified residual (about –1.0 percent of GDP) that may reflect structural factors not included in the model. On balance, the IMF staff assesses the 2020 cyclically adjusted CA to be 1.6 percent of GDP lower than the level implied by medium-term fundamentals and desirable policies. This assessment includes an IMF staff adjustor of 0.5 percent of GDP to account for the effects of the COVID-19 crisis on the oil and travel services (including tourism) balances (0.1 percent of GDP each) as well as the shift in household consumption from services to consumer goods and medical goods (0.2 percent of GDP each).

2020 (% GDP)	CA: –2.9	Cycl. Adj. CA: –2.7	EBA Norm: –0.5	EBA Gap: –2.2	COVID-19 Adj.: 0.5	Other Adj.: 0.0	Staff Gap: –1.6

Real Exchange Rate

Background. After appreciating by 2.8 percent in 2019, the REER appreciated by 1.4 percent in 2020. Through the second quarter of 2020, the REER appreciated 4.3 percent in relation to the end of 2019. Despite depreciating in the second half of 2020 by 5.4 percent, as of the end of 2020 the REER was still about 14 percent higher than the average for 2015. As of end-May 2021, the REER had depreciated by 3.9 percent compared to the 2020 average.

Assessment. Indirect estimates of the REER (based on the IMF staff CA assessment) imply that the exchange rate was overvalued by 8.2 percent in 2020 (applying the estimated elasticity of –0.2). The EBA REER index model suggests an overvaluation of 8.3 percent, and the EBA REER level model suggests an overvaluation of 12.4 percent. Considering all the estimates and their uncertainties, the IMF staff assesses the 2020 average REER to be somewhat overvalued, in the 5.2–11.2 percent range, with a midpoint of 8.2 percent.

Capital and Financial Accounts: Flows and Policy Measures

Background. The financial account balance was about –3.7 percent of GDP in 2020 compared with –1.8 percent of GDP in 2019. An increase in net direct investment (0.5 percent GDP) was offset by decreases in net portfolio investments (0.8 percent GDP) and other net investments.

Assessment. The United States has an open capital account. Vulnerabilities are limited by the dollar's status as a reserve currency, with foreign demand for US Treasury securities supported by the status of the dollar as a reserve currency and, possibly, by safe haven flows.

FX Intervention and Reserves Level

Assessment. The dollar has the status of a global reserve currency. Reserves held by the United States are typically low relative to standard metrics. The currency is free floating.

Technical Endnotes by Economy

Argentina

[1]To smooth the temporary effect of the sharp reductions in short-term debt and exports, and a collapse in the valuation of debt portfolio investments in the wake of the sovereign debt restructuring, the adjusted measure uses a four-year average.

Belgium

[1]Methodological and source data changes led to major revisions of the 2015–19 CA, distorting comparison with previous assessments.
[2]The error bands are based on the range for the CA gap (–2.8 to –0.8 percent), with a midpoint of –1.8 percent and an estimated semi-elasticity of the CA balance to the REER of 0.42.

Canada

[1]The statistical treatment of retained earnings on portfolio equity and inflation is estimated to generate a downward bias in the income balance of the CA on the order of 1.5 percent of GDP.
[2]EBA uses UN demographic projections. The COVID-19 decline in net immigration is considered transitory; immigration will continue to be one of the main sources of population growth in Canada. An EBA CA norm is lowered by 0.4 percentage point to account for this.
[3]The semi-elasticity of the CA with respect to the REER is set to 0.28.

Euro Area

[1]The export and import elasticities are taken as the average of estimates from Consultative Group on Exchange Rate Issues–inspired export and import equations using various types of REERs relevant for the euro area (with an autoregressive distributed lag (2,2,2) model on 2000–19 quarterly data). The trade balance elasticity is calculated using the share in GDP of exports and imports for extra-euro-area trade.

France

[1]The range of the REER gap (±4 percent) is based on the range of the CA gap (±0.5 percent of GDP) and an estimated semi-elasticity of the CA balance to the REER of 0.27.

Germany

[1]For Germany, the bulk of the EBA-estimated gap for 2020 reflects the regression's residual, rather than gaps in the policy variables included in the EBA model.
[2]The EBA REER index model has an unusually poor fit for Germany.

Hong Kong SAR

[1]Hong Kong SAR is not in the EBA sample as it is an outlier along many dimensions of EBA analysis, thus one possibility—though with obvious drawbacks—is the use of EBA-estimated coefficients and their application to Hong Kong SAR. Following this approach, the CA norm in 2020 is estimated at about 14.8 percent of GDP, implying a CA gap of –9.0 percent, which is almost entirely explained by the model residuals. The EBA CA gap is overstated as it does not properly reflect the measurement issues that are relevant for Hong Kong SAR, for which three adjustments are made. First, an adjustment of 3–5 percentage points, with a midpoint of 4 percentage points, is made to the EBA's implied contribution of the NIIP position. This is because the positive NIIP contribution in the EBA captures average income effects that are less relevant for Hong Kong SAR, given that the income balance relative to its NIIP is systematically lower than that of peer economies due to a persistently higher share of debt instruments on the asset side than on the liability side. Second, the opening of the Precious Metals Depository has resulted in a decline of 4–4½ percentage points, with a midpoint of 4¼ percentage points, in the gold trade balance that does not reflect changes in wealth but rather the increased physical settlement of gold futures contracts. Third, mainland China's increased onshoring has led to a decline in logistics and trading activities in Hong Kong SAR (1½ percentage points, with a midpoint of 1¼ percentage points), which did not result in lower consumption because it is viewed as temporary and to be replaced with increased provision of high-value-added services as Hong Kong SAR's own economy rebalances in response to mainland demand. See the 2017 Hong Kong SAR Article IV Selected Issues Paper for more details.
[2]The range is calculated by applying the average semi-elasticities of Hong Kong SAR and similar economies.
[3]The financial linkages with mainland China have deepened in recent years with the increase in cross-border bank lending, capital market financing, and the internationalization of the renminbi. As of the end of 2020, banking system claims on mainland nonbank entities amounted to HK$6.4 trillion, or about 237 percent of GDP, up by about 22 percentage points from the end of 2019.

Indonesia

[1]The 2020 assessment includes an adjustment for travel services (including tourism) and oil sectors, as well as the global shift in the composition of household consumption from services toward consumer goods. For Indonesia, these adjustors are 0.3, –0.2, and –0.1 percentage point of GDP, respectively, leading to an estimated effect of 0 percentage point of GDP. As Indonesia is among the few outlier countries regarding adult mortality rates, the demographic indicators are adjusted to account for the

younger average prime age and workforce exit age (this results in an adjustor of 0.9 percentage point).

[2]A range of ±1.5 percent is added to reflect the fact that the EBA regression estimates are subject to normal uncertainty (the standard error of the EBA norm is 1.4 percent).

[3]The semi-elasticity of the CA-to-GDP ratio with respect to the REER is estimated to be –0.17 for Indonesia.

[4]The midpoint of the REER range is calculated by taking the average of the estimated gap from the EBA index model (that is, 2.1 percent) and the REER gap implied by the IMF staff CA gap estimate of 0.7 percent of GDP (that is, –3.9 percent). To obtain the width of the range for the REER gap, the standard ±5 percent interval was applied to the midpoint of –1 percent, leading to a range of –6 to 4 percent.

Malaysia

[1]On December 2, 2016, the Financial Markets Committee announced a package of measures aimed at facilitating onshore FX risk management and enhancing the depth and liquidity of onshore financial markets. Two of these measures were classified as CFM measures under the IMF's institutional view on capital flows. In addition, the authorities' strengthened enforcement of regulations on resident banks' noninvolvement in offshore ringgit transactions was considered enhanced enforcement of an existing CFM measure. Over the course of 2017–19, additional measures were announced to help deepen the onshore financial market and facilitate currency risk management.

The Netherlands

[1]A sizable portion of the CA surplus reflects corporate saving of multinationals based in The Netherlands. Due to the volatility of such savings, the assessment of the EBA-estimated current account gap is particularly uncertain, justifying a wider-than-usual CA range.

Saudi Arabia

[1]At current oil exports, a US$1 change in the oil price results in a 0.5 percent of GDP first-round change in the CA balance. The average oil export price is assumed to be US$67.4 a barrel in 2021 (US$43.5 a barrel in 2020). Oil export volumes are expected to decrease by 1.9 percent in 2021.

[2]EBA models do not include Saudi Arabia. The IMF staff considered three approaches in the EBA-Lite methodology, including two that incorporate the special intertemporal considerations that are dominant in economies in which exports of nonrenewable resources are a very high share of output and exports. Using the CA regression approach, the cyclically adjusted CA norm is estimated at 6.5 percent of GDP (slightly higher than the CA norm of 6.3 percent of GDP in 2019). The Consumption Allocation Rules assume that the sustainability of the CA trajectory requires that the net present value of all future oil and financial/investment income (wealth) be equal to the net present value of imports of goods and services net of non-oil exports. Estimated CA norms from the Consumption Allocation Rules were –3.0 percent of GDP and 0.2 percent of GDP for the constant real annuity and constant real per capita annuity allocation rules, respectively. The Investment Needs Model takes into account the potential desirability of allocating part of the resource wealth to finance investment, which was not explicitly considered by the consumption-based model and produced a CA gap of –0.8 percent over the medium term. The CA gap in 2020 (–1.5 percent of GDP) represents the IMF staff's overall assessment, taking into account estimates from the three approaches.

Singapore

[1]Singapore has a negative income balance despite its large positive NIIP position, reflecting lower rates of return on its foreign assets relative to returns on its foreign liabilities, possibly due to the fact that the composition of Singapore's assets is tilted toward safer assets with lower returns.

[2]Nonstandard factors make a quantitative assessment of Singapore's external position difficult and subject to significant uncertainty. Singapore is not included in the EBA sample because it is an outlier along several dimensions. One possibility, though with drawbacks, is to use EBA-estimated coefficients and apply them to Singapore. Following that approach the CA norm is estimated to be about 14.8 percent of GDP in 2020 (including the multilateral consistency adjustment). However, the EBA gap is understated for two reasons, and adjustments are needed. First, a downward adjustment of 1.4 percentage points is made to the EBA's implied contribution of public health care expenditures to the norm to account for the fact that Singapore's health care expenditure is appropriate, given its high efficiency—even though its desirable, as well as current, public health care expenditure is significantly lower than that of other EBA countries. Second, a downward adjustment of 2.5 percentage points to the norm is made to better account for the effect of different net foreign asset components on the CA. Adjusting for these factors, the IMF staff–estimated CA gap is about 4.2 percent of GDP, to which the fiscal policy gap contributes about 0.5 percent of GDP and public health care spending and the credit gap both contribute about –0.2 percent of GDP.

[3]The reserves-to-GDP ratio is also larger than in most other financial centers, but this may reflect in part that most other financial centers are in reserve-currency countries or currency unions. External assets managed by the government's investment corporation and wealth fund (GIC and Temasek) amount to at least 70 percent of GDP.

South Africa

[1]The South Africa–specific COVID-19 adjustors of –1.8 percent of GDP in total comprise the adjustments for travel services (including tourism) exports (0.6 percent of GDP), medical spending imports (0.2), the shift in household consumption composition from services toward consumer goods (–0.4), oil imports (–0.4), gold exports (–0.9), and an improved income balance (–0.9).

[2]Net current transfers related to the Southern African Customs Union, assessed to have a net negative impact on the CA, are not accounted for in the regression model and warrant an adjustment to the cyclically adjusted CA by 0.7 percent of GDP. In addition, measurement issues pertaining to the income balance are likely to contribute to an underestimation of the CA by 0.7 percent of GDP.

[3]Because South Africa is among the few outlier countries regarding adult mortality rates, the demographic indicators are adjusted to account for the younger average prime age and workforce exit age. This results in an adjustor of –1 percent of GDP to the model-based CA norm.

Spain

[1]Based on data available through the fourth quarter of 2020.

[2]The EBA model suggests a CA norm of 0.3 percent of GDP, with a standard error of 0.8 percent of GDP. But the empirically based EBA norm does not fully account for the very negative NIIP, with about 60 percent of gross liabilities in the form of debt. Given external stability considerations, including potentially adverse NIIP valuation effects, a CA norm in the range of 0.8 to 2.8 percent of GDP is necessary to raise the NIIP by at least roughly 3 percent of GDP annually over the next 10 years. Over 2004–19, valuation effects were, on average, 1½ percent of GDP a year. CA surpluses during 2013–19 of about 2.2 percent of GDP, on average, suggest that maintaining CA balances aligned with the IMF staff–assessed norm of 0.8 to 2.8 percent of GDP would be feasible under current policies.

[3]The REER gap midpoint is obtained from the IMF staff–assessed CA gap and an estimated semi-elasticity of the CA to the REER of 0.28. The range of the REER gap is ±4 percent, which is obtained from Spain's estimated standard error of the CA norm (1 percent of GDP) and the aforementioned CA-to-REER semi-elasticity.

Switzerland

[1]In December 2020, the SNB published major revisions to the BOP/IIP data. There were two reasons for the revisions: (1) closing a data gap with regard to domiciliary companies; and (2) reflecting data newly available from reporting institutions. Changes under (2) included both information from a newly completed 2019 annual survey and corrections for previous reporting periods concerning companies with especially complex structures. The revisions due to (1) affected only the IIP data from 2008 to 2019; those due to (2) affected the entire BOP (current account, capital account, financial account) and the IIP for the period from 2014 to 2019. As a result, the net IIP showed an average decrease between 2008 and 2019 of CHF 128 billion (about 17 percent), and the current account surpluses for 2018 and 2019 decreased significantly, mostly due to adjustments in primary income expenses, while the 2014–17 balances changed less and in both directions.

[2]Other stock-flow adjustments include changes in statistical sources, such as changes in the number of entities surveyed and items covered, although their quantitative importance is not known.

[3]As a result, an appreciation (depreciation) of the Swiss franc has a negative (positive) effect on the NIIP, whereas a symmetric percentage increase in share prices in Switzerland and abroad would reduce the NIIP.

[4]The underlying CA is adjusted for Switzerland-specific factors in the income account: (1) retained earnings on portfolio equity investment that are not recorded in the income balance of the CA under the sixth edition of the IMF *Balance of Payments and International Investment Position Manual*; and (2) recording of nominal interest on fixed-income securities under the *Balance of Payments Manual* framework, which compensates for expected valuation losses (due to inflation and/or nominal exchange rate movements), even though this stream compensates for the (anticipated) erosion in the real value of debt assets and liabilities. In addition, the CA balance is also adjusted for transitory impacts of the COVID-19 pandemic on trade in goods and services, including adjustors for (1) tourism and travel services (an estimated 0.5 percentage point, including the impact on the decline in sales of luxury watches, reflecting the decline in international travel); (2) oil (–0.3 percentage point); (3) household consumption composition shift (–0.4 percentage point); (4) medical products (0.7 percentage point); and (5) precious metals (1.4 percentage points). Adjusting for these COVID-19–related effects, the underlying CA would need to be increased by about 1.9 percent of GDP (that is, resulting in a smaller negative gap).

[5]The CA gap range reflects the uncertainty inherent in the assessment.

[6]The country-specific CA-REER elasticity of 0.52 is relatively large due to the high openness of the Swiss economy.

Turkey

[1]A higher share of external assets relative to external liabilities is denominated in FX. Despite persistent CA deficits, the NIIP fluctuated with no clear trend during 2009–19, due to a mix of positive valuation effects and large net balance of payments errors and omissions.

[2]Net international reserves are defined as gross international reserves minus the central bank's FX liabilities to banks, including the Reserve Option Mechanism.

United Kingdom

[1]The official NIIP data may understate the true position—estimates of FDI stocks at market values imply a much higher NIIP. Estimates from the Bank of England suggested that the NIIP based on market values could have been close to 80 percent of GDP for mid-2017 (November 2017 inflation report). Market value estimates of FDI assets assume their valuations move in line with those of equity market indices in the United Kingdom and abroad. These estimates are highly uncertain, as actual FDI market values could evolve differently across different equity markets.

[2]Estimates in Bénétrix and others (2019) suggest that, in 2017, about 90 percent of external assets were denominated in foreign currency compared with 60 percent for external liabilities.

[3]Historically, unrecorded retained earnings on portfolio equity assets also contributed to the underestimation of the CA, but this was estimated at close to zero in 2020.

[4]The IMF staff assesses that part of such changes may be permanent and adjust the CA only partially. In addition, there is likely some overlap of various COVID-19–related adjustments.

References

Bénétrix, Agustin S., Deepali Gautam, Luciana Juvenal, and Martin Schmitz. 2019. "Cross-Border Currency Exposures." IMF Working Paper 19/299, International Monetary Fund, Washington, DC.

Cubeddu, Luis, Signe Krogstrup, Gustavo Adler, Pau Rabanal, Mai Chi Dao, Swarnali Ahmed Hannan, Luciana Juvenal, Nan Li, Carolina Osorio Buitron, Cyril Rebillard, Daniel Garcia-Macia, Callum Jones, Jair Rodriguez, Kyun Suk Chang, Deepali Gautam, and Zijiao Wang. 2019. "The External Balance Assessment Methodology: 2018 Update." IMF Working Paper 19/65, International Monetary Fund, Washington, DC.

IMF eLibrary Essential Reading Guides

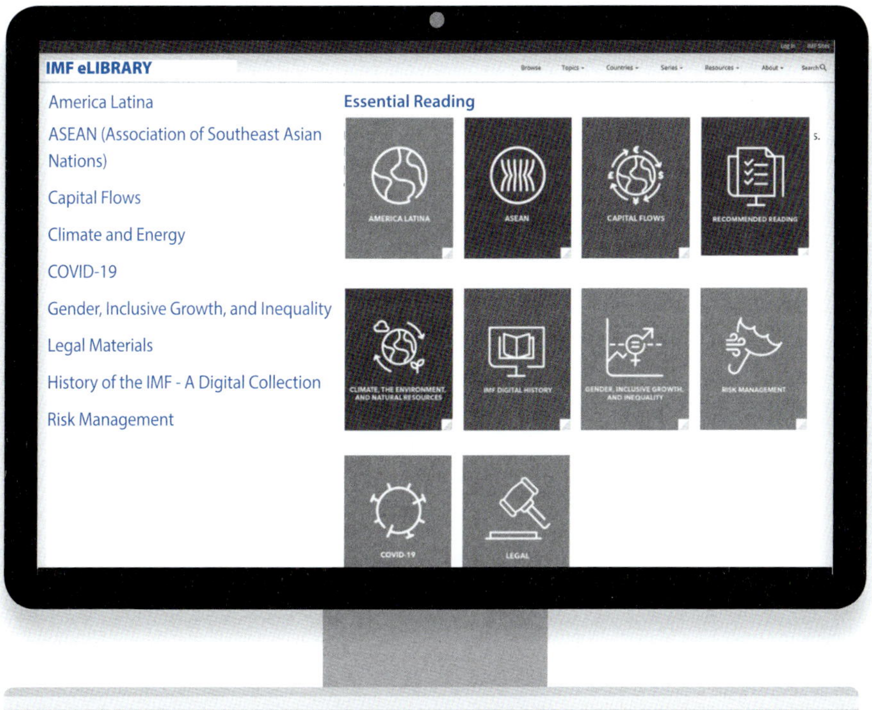

IMF eLibrary **Essential Reading Guides** are curated lists of the most relevant publications in subjects that are high interest. Links to full-text publications on the eLibrary and selected IMF materials help researchers get a jumpstart on research projects.

Scan QR code to access the Essential Reading Guides

eLibrary.IMF.org

INTERNATIONAL MONETARY FUND